Homiletical Theology in Action

The Promise of Homiletical Theology
Volume 2

Homiletical Theology in Action

———— The Unfinished Theological Task of Preaching ————

The Promise of Homiletical Theology
Volume 2

Contributing Editor
DAVID SCHNASA JACOBSEN

CASCADE *Books* • Eugene, Oregon

HOMILETICAL THEOLOGY IN ACTION
The Unfinished Theological Task of Preaching

The Promise of Homiletical Theology

Copyright © 2015 David Schnasa Jacobsen. All rights reserved. Except for brief quotations in critical publications or reviews, no part of this book may be reproduced in any manner without prior written permission from the publisher. Write: Permissions, Wipf and Stock Publishers, 199 W. 8th Ave., Suite 3, Eugene, OR 97401.

Cascade Books
An Imprint of Wipf and Stock Publishers
199 W. 8th Ave., Suite 3
Eugene, OR 97401

www.wipfandstock.com

ISBN 13: 978-1-4982-0783-6

Cataloging-in-Publication data:

Homiletical theology in action : the unfinished theological task of preaching / edited by David Schnasa Jacobsen.

x + 192 p.; 23 cm—Includes bibliographical references.

The Promise of Homiletical Theology

ISBN 13: 978-1-4982-0783-6

1. Preaching. 2. Bible Homiletical Use. 3. Hermeneutics. I. Jacobsen, David Schnasa. II. Title. III. Series.

BV4222 .H7 2015

Manufactured in the USA.

New Revised Standard Version Bible, copyright 1989, Division of Christian Education of the National Council of the Churches of Christ in the United States of America. Used by permission. All rights reserved.

Contents

Contributors vii
Acknowledgments ix

Introduction by David Schnasa Jacobsen 1

Section I: Homiletical Theology in the Descriptive Mode

1. Theological Attentiveness on the Path from Text to Sermon: A Descriptive Approach 17
  —*Sally A. Brown*

2. Wet Paint: Matthew 15, the Canaanite Woman, and Painted-Over Proclamation 43
  —*Adam Hearlson*

3. The How of Homiletic Theology 61
  —*Teresa Lockhart (Stricklen) Eisenlohr*

Section II: Homiletical Theology in the Confessional Mode

4. Nobody Knows the Trouble I See: A Spirit(ual) Approach to the Interpretive Task of Homiletical Theology 85
  —*Luke A. Powery*

5. Promise and Cross: Homiletical Theology, the Vocative Word *Extra Nos,* and the Task of a Revisionist Eschatology 108
  —*David Schnasa Jacobsen*

Section III: Homiletical Theology in the Analytical Mode

6. Doing Bible: When the Unfinished Task of Homiletical Theology Pushes the Envelope of Canonical Authority 131
  —*O. Wesley Allen, Jr.*

Contents

7 "Surely There is a God Who Judges on Earth": Divine Retribution in Homiletical Theology and the Practice of Preaching 147
—Rein Bos

Afterword by David Schnasa Jacobsen 173
Appendix A: Contextual Analysis 177
Appendix B: Exegetical Questions for Preaching 179
Bibliography 185

Contributors

O. Wesley Allen, Jr., Lois Craddock Perkins Professor of Homiletics at Perkins School of Theology, Southern Methodist University

Rein Bos, Senior Pastor of the Protestant Church in the Netherlands and Coordinator of the Curriculum and Professor of the Training Program for Ordained Pastoral Workers in the Protestant Church of the Netherlands

Sally A. Brown, Elizabeth M. Engle Associate Professor of Preaching and Worship, Princeton Theological Seminary

Teresa Lockhart (Stricklen) Eisenlohr, PhD, PreachingCoach.org

Adam Hearlson, Assistant Professor of Preaching and Worship and Director of Wilson Chapel, Andover Newton Theological School

Luke A. Powery, Dean of the Chapel and Associate Professor of Homiletics, Duke University

Acknowledgments

I wish to thank first of all the colleagues in the Academy of Homiletics who made this work possible by participating in the second Consultation on Homiletical Theology: Drs. O. Wesley Allen, Rein Bos, Sally Brown, Teresa Eisenlohr, Adam Hearlson, and Luke Powery. The collaboration among this group was itself a wonderful tribute to what homiletical theology can be, a more thoroughgoing way of doing the work of homiletics as a theological discipline. Special thanks go to John McClure and Ron Allen, who along with Sally Brown and Teresa Eisenlohr read drafts of my various contributions to this book. Of course, any enduring errors are peculiar to me. Nonetheless, I am convinced that all of them have at least made me a better homiletical theologian than I would have been without them. Another word of thanks goes to the Academy of Homiletics as a whole. This leading body of researchers and teachers in North American homiletics was kind enough to host last year's consultation at its annual meeting in 2014 in San Diego. The support from the leadership of the Academy's executive and the ongoing good vibes produced among the general membership has meant that this conversation has been a fruitful one for the field generally.

Funding for the consultation itself comes through the Homiletical Theology Project, which is my research program at the Boston University School of Theology (www.bu.edu/homiletical-theology-project). I remain grateful to my dean, Mary Elizabeth Moore, who has seen to it that this research project has been both well-funded and supported administratively through all its activities. BUSTH is a rich place to be a collaborative scholar and one of the few places in North America where one can pursue a PhD in homiletics. This means that the support for advanced work in preaching is both deep and wide. For this, and for many other reasons, I am grateful for my work with Dean Moore and the many fine scholars at the "School of the Prophets."

Acknowledgments

One of the great benefits of being at a place like BUSTH is the support of excellent emerging researchers. In the fall of 2014 I had the good fortune of having two dedicated research assistants, Reverends Yohan Go and Duse Lee. They are both PhD students in homiletics at BU and are developing fascinating research trajectories of their own. I am grateful for their help in organizing the 2014 consultation, editing the first drafts of the consultation papers, and just being brilliant conversation partners about homiletics and its theological tasks. Above all, I look forward to their own emerging contributions to the field.

One other crucial research assistant on this project was Tim Snyder, who is also pursuing a PhD at BUSTH in practical theology. Mr. Snyder was indispensable in preparing the volume for publication. Although he was busy preparing for qualifying exams and doing adjunct teaching, Mr. Snyder's keen eye helped to bring the book to completion. I am grateful for your help, Tim.

There is for me one last person to acknowledge here and I do so with both gratitude and a heavy heart. In many ways my interest in seeing preaching as a thoroughgoing theological task was inspired by Dr. Edward Farley, who along with Sallie McFague and Peter Hodgson helped me to fall in love with theology back when I was an MDiv student at Vanderbilt in the 1980s. As you peruse these pages, you will no doubt see Ed Farley's name and work cited with some frequency. In many ways, as my colleague O. Wesley Allen notes in his chapter to come, Ed Farley is the "grandfather" of this consultation on homiletical theology. While my gratitude remains after all these years, the news of Ed Farley's passing in December 2014 means that my heart is now also heavy as I write these words. Ed was my MDiv advisor in the days when Vanderbilt was launching its curricular emphasis on the "minister as theologian." I hope this book will help, in its own modest way, to carry that important vision forward.

Season of Easter, 2015
David Schnasa Jacobsen
Boston

Introduction

—David Schnasa Jacobsen

Karl Barth famously argued that all theology is sermon preparation. But what if all sermon preparation is actually theology?[1] This volume, and the series to which it belongs, is an invitation to rethink the discipline of homiletics as a thoroughgoing theological one. It seeks therefore to re-envision preaching itself as a theological activity and, through this, to trace the outlines of a full range of questions of importance to practitioners and theoreticians alike: a way of doing *homiletical* theology.

Although it may sound odd to our ears, the notion of a homiletical theology is not a new one. The first volume of this project, *Homiletical Theology: Preaching as Doing Theology*, sought to identify points in the Reformed and Lutheran traditions where theologians found the term serviceable and useful. Our goal in these pages is not to dust off or repristinate their ways of thinking about homiletical theology. Our goal is actually more modest: to demonstrate how various dimensions of homiletical theology, whether made explicit or operating more implicitly, shape the work that preachers do.

In his withering critique of late-twentieth-century theological education, Edward Farley argued that many practical theological fields had traded their fundamental theological interests for the kind of authority and legitimacy that other theoretical disciplines offered: religious education for pedagogy, pastoral care for psychology, and, yes, homiletics for rhetoric.[2] Because of the unique history of theology, Farley goes on to say, it is important to view theology in two senses: both as *habitus* and *scientia*.

---

1. Buttrick, Foreword, 8–10.
2. Farley, *Theologia*, 144–45.

Homiletical Theology in Action

Habitus refers to the basic disposition of theology. Theology in this sense is not something only for educated specialists, but a kind of practical wisdom shared by all believers in relation to the things of salvation. It is something believers do generally. Theology in the other sense, as *scientia* or discipline, is relatively new and seems in our day and age to be exemplified by a vision of the field roughly equivalent to what we might now call systematic or constructive theology.[3] Such theology requires critical thinking, eventually entails even the specialization of knowledge found in the Enlightenment university, and for that reason is now usually *limited* to what its specialists do. Farley's hope was not to see *habitus* overcome *scientia*, or the other way around, but to reunite them—and all of theology—as a unified task. In other words, Farley's hope was that theological education could be, well, theological in root and branch—even homiletics.[4]

The work within this volume on homiletical theology in action fulfills, I think, a piece of Farley's dream. It seeks to do theology in light of preaching's practices, theories, and contexts in a way that both reflects its *habitus* while not neglecting its task as *scientia*. On the one hand, it means that homiletics needs to re-envision itself as more than a merely technical discipline, that is, as just rhetoric in a clerical robes. More deeply, however, it requires helping the discipline to reimagine itself as theological in every respect. In the pages that follow, the assembled contributors to the 2014 Consultation on Homiletical Theology seek to do just that. By focusing on homiletical theology in action, they are not so much trying to establish a new division of labor in the Enlightenment university, or even a repristination of the premodern past. Instead, we begin to consider the possibilities and *limits* of seeing homiletics first and foremost as a theological discipline. It is modest in its wish to see homiletics as a place where Farley's unifying vision as both common *habitus* and critical, disciplined *scientia* are held together. If Farley is correct, the task of theology is not just one more specialization, but a subtly unified one, a disposition *and* a disciplined reflection common to practitioner and researcher, and part and parcel of the whole theological faculty.

The testing of the whole notion of homiletical theology in action was inspired by our colleague from Christian Theological Seminary, Dr. Ron

---

3. Farley, *Theologia*, 29–48. Here Farley traces the history of theology as *habitus* (disposition) and *scientia* (discipline) through various historical periods and social embodiments.

4. See Farley, *Practicing Gospel*, 71–92.

Introduction

Allen, who at the first year's consultation in 2013 wondered out loud what homiletical theology might look like "in action." As a new consultation in 2014, we therefore elected to develop chapters about what homiletical theology looks like by probing how homiletical theology "works" when confronted either by troublesome biblical texts or difficult aspects of the theological tradition (especially eschatology, divine judgment, pneumatology, Scriptural authority)—that is, in seeing how homiletical theology takes up the "unfinished task" of theology in our work as practitioners and researchers.[5] Particular scholars of preaching may not, of course, endorse some of the visions in the follow pages even as they are spawned by Dr. Allen's question. It is striking, however, that the visions of homiletical theology in these pages are as diverse as they are.

There is, however, a second sense in which the essays of this second stage differ from one another. Here, we discover that scholars are not only distinctive in their understanding of homiletical theology (the "what") but also in the methods they employ to clarify their distinct understandings (the "how"). So striking were these methodological differences that methodology itself emerged as a useful way to group the contributions to this volume. They coalesce under three headings: descriptive, confessional, and analytical approaches.[6]

The descriptive essays (Brown, Eisenlohr, Hearlson), to my mind, engage in theological method in the most self-conscious methodological and inductive way. They hold a theology of gospel "lightly" enough to let the theological reflection follow inductively through a series of moments that highlight both the sources and norms of a particular instance of homiletical theology as it unfolds before the reader. This is not to say that no confessional criteria are operative in the work of these authors; rather, these

---

5. The unfinished task of theology in preaching is a phrase I have used in two respects. First, any attempt to do theology in a different time and place is itself a new moment and a "taking up" of the unfinished task that is reinterpreting the tradition. There is, to my mind, no such thing as a *theologia perrenis*. Beyond that, however, I also wish to lift up something of the tragic, grief-filled, and traumatic conditions of the beginnings of Christian theology, even at the point of its earliest witnesses in the Scriptures. To my mind, elements of Christian anti-Judaism, the destruction of the temple, and the struggles to define early Christianity and Judaism in the wake of that event is intertwined with the theological attempts in the canon that seek to make sense of the gospel that is both Jesus Christ and the gospel-reign-of-God that Jesus himself proclaims. For more see my article "Preaching as the Unfinished Task of Theology."

6. I am grateful to my Princeton colleague, Dr. Sally Brown, for her help in discerning these three categories following our consultation meeting in December, 2014.

criteria are called into play as may be needed to shed light on the theological goings-on in a particular instance of homiletical theology in action. Some of these contributors to this volume, shaped deeply by contemporary conversations about practical theological method, sought to understand homiletical theology in a *descriptive* mode consistent with the descriptive moment in practical theology generally. Just as a descriptive or, in Eisenlohr's case, "portraiture" task launched the process of theological reflection in the work of say, Browning, Osmer, or even Farley himself, so also homiletical theology begins in an inductive fashion in the mode of descriptive work around the practices and contexts of preaching.[7]

Others of us were no less convicted of the need for an open-ended way of doing homiletical theology, but began nonetheless with some sort of confessional starting point. Here, one could argue, a more strongly held sense of "gospel" becomes itself the starting point of homiletical-theological reflection. Whereas in the descriptive mode, a sense of the gospel is more lightly held, here in homiletical theology's *confessional* mode some hunch or "working gospel" becomes the beginning of an open-ended dialogue with contexts, cultures, and situations. The confessional essays (Powery, Jacobsen), as I see them, are willing to pitch their tents with some basic commitment or understanding of the gospel that itself launches the theological reflection that ensues. The process is no less dialogical or contextual, but identifies as its point of departure an explicit theological commitment.

A final set of consultation participants wanted to query the doing of homiletical theology itself—which we have designated homiletical theology in the *analytical* mode. While the analytically oriented among us acknowledged the theological task of preaching generally, these contributors emphasized the need for some reflection on the ongoing impact of theological traditions as the means of pursuing homiletical theology. Homiletical theology could not simply be a theology that relied wholly on thick "descriptions" or the working hypotheses of starting points in "confessions," but needed to be cognizant of the pushback from a tradition that continues to shape homiletical theology even as homiletical theology seeks

---

7. The descriptive moment in practical theology is one of the distinctive markers of many practical-theological methods. See Browning, *A Fundamental Practical Theology*, 75–135, and Osmer, *Practical Theology*, 31–78. The term *portraiture*, although not identical with *description*, is a moment in Farley's theological method that has especially influenced the chapter by Teresa Eisenlohr. See Farley, *Ecclesial Reflection*, 193–216, for his notion of *theological* portraiture. For more on "working gospel" see Resner, *Living In-Between*, 67–68.

Introduction

to reshape the tradition. Tradition therefore sometimes "talks back," even in the midst of a vigorous conversation between some emerging sense of gospel and careful descriptions of contexts and situations. The two essays in this analytical mode (Allen, Bos) venture something of a "prolegomena" for doing homiletical theology in light of specific theological claims about scriptural authority and divine judgment in particular. These essays point to a larger theological task of providing a kind of theological prolegomena for homiletical theology, that is, analytically exploring its premises or the validity of its first theological judgments in the hope of refining and clarifying its processes of reflection.

These essays, then, invite you to join us at the ground floor of homiletical theology as a different way of doing theology. Difference, of course, is not *uniqueness*. Our hope is that practical theologians, constructive theologians, and others will find things here germane to their work. Yet because preaching has its own history, both as a practice and as a discipline called "homiletics," the difference is worth exploring further. For the Cappadocian fathers, the sermon was the chief place to *do* theology, as evidenced by their "theological orations" from the Byzantine period. For theologians like Origen, Luther, Calvin, and Wesley, sermons were indispensable to the theological work they envisioned for their own days. We hope that as homiletical theology is put "in action" in these pages, you will be encouraged to put your own oar into the water.

All of these distinctions also represent ways of inviting you, the reader, into the specific task that is homiletical theology. Whether you are in a pulpit or a researcher in homiletics, you are engaged in a theological task whenever you take up preaching's practices, theories, and contexts. Our attempt in these pages, prompted by troublesome biblical texts and difficult doctrinal traditions, is to provoke you to join in that struggle in a more open and vulnerable way. For us, preaching is not reducible to the application of prior theories, it is no mere *techne*. It is true that preaching includes technical and, of course, theoretical moments from other disciplines (rhetoric, performance, narrative, etc.). But all of these are moments within a wider theological ambit that both grounds and calls forth the work of the homiletical theologian, whether in its pedagogical, professional, or scholarly form.[8] Because we are focusing on those texts and doctrines that bear witness to the unfinished character of our theological traditions—every sermon is in essence a "handing over" of the tradition, now reinterpreted in

---

8. See Bartow, "Homiletical (Theological) Criticism," 154.

a new context or situation—there is no way to be a homiletical theologian apart from the task's intrinsic provisionality and struggle.[9] Our words are at best acts of theological naming seen "through a glass, darkly."[10] Our words are also fleeting, local, and ephemeral. And yet preachers stand up before God and everybody when they do their work as homiletical theologians. Unlike many other theologians, they engage in interpretation surrounded by signs and symbols of a living tradition: in embarrassingly close proximity to Scriptures read aloud in the assembled community, ritual actions performed in ways both local and universal, and creeds confessed in both ancient and modern forms. We preachers interpret, in other words, in the very *presence* of that which is interpreted: surrounded by pulpit, lectern, table, font, actions, traditions, and above all *people*. Nowhere else is theology more public. Nowhere else is theology so . . . homiletical.

In some of my courses with MDiv students I compare the work of the homiletical theologian to Jacob at the Jabbok in Genesis 32. It would be nice if the preacher's job were merely one of application: analyze the text, tweezer out a meaning, apply it faithfully to the church. In reality, however, preaching is only rarely anything like that. So much of what we do is born in struggle and in the midst of wounds. The sermons don't always fall off the shelf and sometimes texts even feel like a Kafka parable on steroids. They cause us, in other words, to *struggle* with what to say. For one thing, our biblical texts themselves represent not one theology, but several—we preachers must somewhere work in this theological breach. Sometimes the theologies that texts represent are only partially intelligible. On occasion, a biblical text's theology may even seem downright unworkable. It is this rough edge where the unfinished theological task of preaching takes place. It would be nice if everything in Scripture and tradition were round and smooth and diaphanous. However, because preaching involves ancient texts and modern people, both united and separated by countless contextual realities, the preacher has to struggle. At the river Jabbok, Jacob pauses to rest before returning to the land of his estranged brother Esau. The river is a kind of threshold and Jacob is, well, Jacob. He had been a schemer and trickster with his brother, but was returning to be reconciled with Esau. This need for reconciliation was no doubt *unsettling* enough to leave him at the river's edge and to send his family and flocks away. Jacob

9. Tilley makes a remarkable case for viewing traditioning as a kind of theological practice in his essay, "Practicing the Faith."

10. 1 Cor 13:12 (KJV).

Introduction

was unsure of his reception. What he perhaps did not reckon with was an intransigent, mysterious nighttime visitor with whom he would wrestle till dawn. I sometimes think of the homiletical-theological task in preaching as a little like Jacob that night at the Jabbok. The night is long, and the struggle with God, and by implication his own brother, is real. Jacob even presses his nightly divine visitor for a name and hopes to gain power that in the end he cannot have. But as morning breaks, there's enough for Jacob to continue. Jacob hobbles on to meet Esau . . . with a limp and a blessing.

As those who preach in the presence of tradition—within earshot of ambo, table, creed, and pew—we do our wrestling in an unusual place. We are fortunate to do so with some authority: an established (albeit blemished) office, recognizable *tradita* like the words of the Scriptures as well as the actions and words of the assembled community of faith. It is these authorities that help our theologizing to be recognizable. But such homiletical-theological work is not only authoritative in the recognizability of their presence; it is exceedingly *vulnerable* and remains evanescent. The words we speak and the contexts in which we speak them are sometimes juxtaposed in jarring ways. The names we name and situations in which we speak them sometimes leave us in paradox or even contradiction. Thank God, in those moments, that homiletical theology is never *finished*, but the beginning of a new conversation just now being set loose among the people of God. We preach as homiletical theologians, therefore, not because of an unblemished past brimming with authority and perfection, but because we participate in an unfolding conversation that holds enough promise both to lament and transform the situations and traditions in which we are enmeshed.

As strange as it may seem, you will see both this recognizability of the tradition and the vulnerability of the homiletical-theological task in the essays that follow. Each writer will be wrestling with the tensions that all homiletical theologians eventually face. We will consider each of them according to the mode in which the contributor does homiletical theology.

Homiletical Theology in the Descriptive Mode: Chapters 1–3

The process begins in the first chapter with Sally Brown's reading of the difficult and disputed Pauline theological claims of Galatians 5 in her article, "Theological Attentiveness on the Path from Text to Sermon: A Descriptive

Approach." Dr. Brown does two important things. First, she identifies five different levels at which theological interpretations of a difficult text like Galatians 5 are operating: (1) the working theology of the preacher, (2) the working *theologies* of the congregation, (3) the theological language embedded in the biblical text, (4) the "deeper theological semantic possibilities" that show up as a text is interpreted in relation to shared history and experience, and (5) the "theological horizon of understanding" of the preacher that is sermonically named by the preacher him/herself. Please note that this process is an activity of theological hermeneutics, a movement between these different horizons of understanding. Second, she commits herself to a practical-theological method that begins with description. Following the work of Richard Osmer, she begins with the task of describing thickly contexts and practices of the community before doing the interpretive, normative, and strategic work that properly comes later. In fact, Dr. Brown's unique contribution, to my mind, is to make a strong plea for beginning descriptively before running ahead to any normative or confessional claim. The result is a wonderful essay that helps the reader see the interpretive and theological task in its complexity and closeness to life lived in a diverse, multicultural community: New Community Presbyterian Church. In the process, Dr. Brown works through the troubling theological claims of a Pauline text that distinguishes between Spirit and flesh, old order and new creation, and how to understand the law, all in light of a church that struggles to live together in light of its many cultural differences. The result is a vision of homiletical theology that takes the descriptive moment seriously in light of its overall hermeneutical task.

In chapter 2 Dr. Adam Hearlson takes on the tricky story of the Canaanite woman and Jesus in his article, "Wet Paint: Matthew 15, the Canaanite Woman, and Painted-Over Proclamation." In the process of unpacking the sometimes deft and surprising theological exchange between Jesus and the Canaanite woman, Hearlson develops a powerful metaphor for the homiletical theologian: street artist. Just as a street artist "paints over" a surface or even another image on the street in order to "redeem" it, so also the homiletical theologian engages in a descriptive task, somewhere liminally between text and context, theology and homiletics, even heaven and earth. With Hearlson's contribution the troublesome text of Matthew 15 becomes the occasion for reflecting on homiletical theology. In fact, the exchange "between" Jesus and the Canaanite woman itself becomes a place of painted-over proclamation in the form of "redemption by addition."

Introduction

Jesus responds to her request for healing by describing Gentiles as "dogs" fighting for scraps when the children should rightly be fed. The Canaanite woman, in her textual riposte to Jesus, "paints over" his metaphor by adding to it and envisions dogs under the table catching the scraps *as* the children are being fed. It is in such in-between spaces where Hearlson sees the emerging field of homiletical theology as taking place. The result is a vision of theology that is, like street art, always provisional, constructive, and even creative. Hearlson writes, "Homiletical theology is a transient theology, subject and vulnerable to change with the public cries of every new Canaanite." It is important too, because here, in public spaces, the Spirit is operative in prying open closed worlds of order in the voices of those who publically claim God's "promise of abundance."

In chapter 3, "The How of Homiletic Theology," Dr. Teresa Lockhart (Stricklen) Eisenlohr engages in something analogous to a descriptive move, but rooted in Edward Farley's own theological method: portraiture. The notion of portraiture, which draws on Farley's work in *Ecclesial Reflection*, is of course only the first step in the fourfold method that Eisenlohr lays out. Moves toward "ecclesial universals" (the classic loci), "judgment" (a normative role for the gospel, even with respect to our own working theologies!), and "rhetorical shaping" are also needed points in the process of her more descriptive homiletic theology. Nonetheless, the fact that Eisenlohr *begins* with portraiture is itself consistent with the descriptive vision. In her case, Eisenlohr exemplifies her homiletic theology in action with respect to the same text as Hearlson: the Canaanite woman in Matthew 15. Of course, even such close attention to method does not come without focus on the *habitus* of the preacher. Eisenlohr sees homiletic theology as holding both together: theological reflection and discernment and the life of prayer. And yet by leading with the moment of portraiture, Eisenlohr invites us into deep reflection on the relationship of this text to a particular community, First Presbyterian in Collegeville. As she does the work of portraiture, Eisenlohr is careful to touch on several contextual elements: the makeup of the church itself, the liturgical context, communal/national/global contexts—but all in relation to this biblical text: Matthew 15:21-28. Throughout the whole process, however, even as the vision of the reign of God expands in the back and forth of Jesus and the Canaanite woman, Eisenlohr sees the entire sermon preparation task as a theological one—and one that refused to reify even the preacher's own theology.

Homiletical Theology in the Confessional Mode: Chapters 4–5

With this new section the accent of homiletical theology shifts from description to confession, from the inductivity of method to the working hypothesis of *habitus*.[11] Description is not absent in these pages—just as we saw confessional elements as moments in the approaches described above. Instead, here some sense of the gospel is more closely held as a starting point in the dialogue between gospel and culture that is homiletical theology. Because, however, the focus here is not so much on difficult texts, but problematic doctrines, theology comes to the fore in a different way. These two essays deal in particular with homiletical-theological struggles with pneumatology and eschatology respectively.

In chapter 4, Dr. Luke Powery develops his homiletical theology through his understanding of the Spirit. The title of his chapter is, "Nobody Knows the Trouble I See: A Spirit(ual) Approach to the Interpretive Task of Homiletical Theology." From the beginning Dr. Powery sees his contribution to homiletical theology as one of "discursive confession." What he pushes back on, in part, is the notion that Scripture is the starting point of any homiletical theological method. In contrast to that, Powery wishes to emphasize the Holy Spirit, who comes before all our texts. With this, Powery is also concerned to make room for bodies, bodies which have been marginalized by a homiletical-theological fascination with biblical texts. The result is a "spiritual turn" in homiletics that gives the Holy Spirit a central role in the theological work that is preaching, sees the Spirit in relation to texts and bodies and thus embraces the "spirituals" as a form of incipient homiletical theology. Such a notion does not ignore the Bible for the homiletical-theological method, but places it in its proper relationship, as the spirituals' interpretation of Jeremiah's word in the form of a question becomes reworked confession in "There is a Balm in Gilead." His vision of homiletical theology is closely tied to communities and the spiritual performance of texts in the present. Along the way, Powery inverts the Reformation's interest in a theology of Word and Spirit (which is usually text-centered and christocentric) into a theology of Spirit and Word that is properly pneumatological and connected to bodies and communities. Its goal is doxology, where it aims toward a surplus of love in the Spirit in the very presence of God. As such, Powery's vision for homiletical theology

---

11. The term *confessional* finds echoes in the important work of David Lose, *Confessing Jesus Christ*. Here we use the term as a way of thinking about the starting point of homiletical-theological method.

Introduction

in the confessional mode includes a more human vision of divine activity in preaching, its commitment to bodies as the locus of critical memory for interpretation, the provisionality of its biblical interpretations, and the importance of prayer as homiletical theology is itself the epicletic gift of God for blessing our messy interpretations.

With chapter 5 confessional homiletical theology considers its relationship to the problematic theological locus that is eschatology, and seeks to pursue the question in a more scholarly than professional mode.[12] David Schnasa Jacobsen treats in his essay, "Promise and Cross: Homiletical Theology, the Vocative Word *Extra Nos* and the Task of a Revisionist Eschatology," the problem that eschatology poses for the white mainline pulpit and seeks to identify both ways and guidelines for reconstructing eschatology not only in light of that context, but in conversation with other homiletical-theological cultural traditions and contexts. The result is a reconstruction and revisioning of Reformation theologies of promise, which are concerned with a strong sense of divine presence and/or grace in Word and Sacrament (Luther, Calvin) by bringing them into dialogue with other traditions of promise that see it as tied to an eschatological possibilizing of the present in connection with God's commitment to justice and human faith praxis. Here, building on and revising his earlier work in the article, "The Promise of Promise: Retrospect and Prospect of a Homiletical Theology," Jacobsen aims to decenter a theology of promise both by widening the ambit of its conversation partners beyond Eurocentric traditions and at the same time to locate it more deeply in relation to a theology of the cross, which "calls a thing what it really is." What results, claims Jacobsen, is "a more profound sense of gospel hope forged in suffering, but for the sake of opening a new praxis of faith."

Homiletical Theology in the Analytical Mode: Chapters 6–7

In this final section, two essayists consider homiletical theology in its analytical mode. As we are beginning to envision through these four volumes of *The Promise of Homiletical Theology* a more theological vision for the field of homiletics, it is important to consider the limits of the kind of practical and constructive work homiletical theology might entail. We return with this portion of the essays to Ron Allen's concern in volume I for

---

12. Bartow, "Homiletical (Theological) Criticism," 154.

recognizability.[13] Although homiletical theology may wish to claim for itself a more constructive vision for doing theology in preaching, the tradition, and especially the Scriptures, are its ground and condition. If homiletical theology is theology practiced in close proximity to the ambo and table and within earshot of Scriptures and creed, it necessarily reflects also on the *limits* of its activity. In the two essays here on homiletical theology in an analytical mode, two colleagues push back on homiletical theology to discern how it carries forward both its constructive and reconstructive tasks *and* its ongoing relation to the memorial tradition in all of its otherness. In this way, homiletical theology in the analytical mode begins to lay a groundwork for a kind of prolegomena to homiletical theology. They help to discern its ground and its limits especially with reference to its understanding and use of the Scriptures and the troublesome doctrine of divine judgment in particular.

In chapter 6, "Doing Bible: When the Unfinished Task of Homiletical Theology Pushes the Envelope of Canonical Authority," Dr. O. Wesley Allen asks what the limits of homiletical theology are in light of its unfinished theological task—especially with a view to its understanding of Scripture as a source and ground for its theological work. If the constructive task of homiletical theology begins with the unfinished theological task of Scripture itself, Allen asks, how *far* can we pursue this task and still honor both the otherness of Scripture and the hermeneutical task that it entrusts to preachers? In a daring exploration, Allen pushes the notion that the Scriptures themselves are "redacting" theology in their sources and asking to what degree a homiletical theology, which carries such a redactional task forward theologically, can do so and still be faithful to its founding tradition. By setting up the ultimate foil to his problem as a "redactional homiletic" engaged in "doing *Scripture*," and not merely "doing theology," Allen pushes homiletical theology to recognize the limits to its work and thus the true nature of its tasks. Allen writes, "The tension between *the already* of the fixed biblical text and the *not yet* of the consummation of 'the gospel' is where preaching and homiletical theology must reside." If homiletical theology wishes to see its theological role beyond simply "applying Scripture," it must also acknowledge the fixedness of the Scriptures as a *limit* to articulating the unfinished theological task of naming gospel anew.

In the final chapter, "'Surely There is a God Who Judges on Earth': Divine Retribution in Homiletical Theology and the Practice of Preaching,"

---

13. Allen, "Preaching as Spark for Discovery in Theology," 147.

Introduction

Rein Bos broaches the topic of the troublesome doctrine of divine judgment and retribution. If so much of homiletical theology seeks to work in the space where gospel and culture relate, Bos's essay seeks to push back on a homiletical theology that is tempted to explain or refute too glibly the wisdom of the Scriptures and tradition. Along the way Dr. Bos acknowledges both the difficulty and the promise of holding on to a notion of divine judgment. Its relationship to bad pulpit theology needs to be acknowledged, even though the reclaiming of this doctrinal locus entails probing difficulties for sensitive preachers today. By reminding preachers as well of the need to hold doctrines of judgment and forgiveness *together* in "canonical connection," Bos also succeeds in showing the potential problems of identifying any troublesome theological locus apart from its own theological interaction with other doctrines. Such complexity requires homiletical-theological *judgment*, and perhaps even in both senses of the word. In the end, Dr. Bos points out why this is so important for a developing homiletical theology—we live in moments where the irruption of new situations of terror, injustice, and crisis can make any breezy relationship with judgment or retribution untenable. Yet the persistence of such situations may also point to the value of doing ongoing analytical homiletical-theological work that does not shut the conversation down, but remains open to even Scripture's most troublesome texts and the theological traditions' most vexing doctrines.

Conclusion and Invitation

Clearly the complexity of this emerging theological work of homiletical theology makes for a difficult task, both in these pages and anywhere gospel is preached. If we take the story of Jacob seriously, we may just expect to emerge from this complex task of homiletical theology with a limp and a blessing. It is, however, an important work for the churches today. What we grope for in sermonic language is a way of discerning and naming God's presence and our vocations in the world that God still "so loves." It relies, of course, on the reality of our inadequacy to do the work. Theology, if Farley's notion of *habitus* is correct, is likely dispositional *gift* before disciplined task. But once we have rightly seen the limits of our speech and the vastness of the calling, perhaps we can engage in the unfinished theological task that is preaching—even if haltingly, as preachers humbly name God into the world again.¹⁴ And in this way, we also invite you to join in the conversation that is homiletical theology.

---

14. Discerning readers of my language in this paragraph will hear echoes of Buttrick's *Homiletic* and *A Captive Voice*, both of which bear witness to his own emerging theological vision for preaching. See also his festschrift, *Preaching as a Theological Task* (eds. Long and Farley).

Section I: Homiletical Theology in the Descriptive Mode

—1—

Theological Attentiveness on the Path from Text to Sermon

A Descriptive Approach

—Sally A. Brown

Introduction: Homiletical Theology in a Descriptive Mode

Contributors to the Homiletical Theology Project have related questions of theology to homiletical theory and practice in remarkably diverse ways. Contributions to the project have been shaped not only by our diverse interests, but also by different underlying assumptions about what "homiletical theology" is or does. Complicating any discussion of "homiletical *theology*," of course, is the range of meanings that the word "theology" itself has had, and continues to have, in contemporary academic discourse.

Theology can refer, for example, to a set of theological discourses that cohere in some particular way. Defined this way, theology includes sub-genres such as systematic, confessional, dogmatic, historical, philosophical, and constructive theology. From this perspective, "homiletical" theology could be thought of either as another sub-genre or as the homiletical appropriation or expression of any of these. On the other hand, theology can be thought of as an activity or mode of reasoning in response to a question or in response to the demands of a situation. In these cases, theology refers to something being *done*, *rather* than to a tradition (or several traditions) upon which one draws.

In this chapter, I want to consider homiletical theology as something a working preacher *does* on a weekly basis. My exploration of this "doing" of homiletical theology on the part of one preacher, in and for her particular preaching context, will take the form of specifically *descriptive* practical theology.

The Descriptive Task within Practical Theology

Practical theologians describe the distinctiveness of practical theology among the disciplines in various ways. In my view, what distinguishes practical theology from other modes of theological reasoning is its sustained attentiveness to *lived religious practices*. In other words, our first concern is with religious practices—and in their concreteness, not simply considered abstractly. Before beginning to talk about how any religious practice *could* or *should* be done, a practical theologian seeks to observe and describe it in specific settings.[1]

The specifically descriptive mode of practical theological inquiry is described by Richard R. Osmer as one of the four basic "tasks" of the practical theologian.[2] These four interrelated tasks are:

1. The *descriptive/empirical* task (describing what we see happening as a practice unfolds).

2. The *interpretive* task (using both theological categories and social-scientific constructs to express our understanding of why a practice is unfolding as it does).

3. The *norm-generative* task (proposing appropriate theological and social-scientific norms to test the fittingness, both theological and sociocultural, of the context-specific practice at hand).

---

1. For an example of practical-theological reflection that includes these tasks, see Fulkerson, *Places of Redemption*, 2007.

2. Osmer, *Practical Theology*, 1–15.

Theological Attentiveness on the Path from Text to Sermon

4. The *strategic/pragmatic* task (providing guidance to practitioners to improve ongoing practice in light of the norms we have developed).³

The *descriptive* mode of inquiry has often been suppressed in contemporary homiletics. It is tempting to assume we already know what is going on and how to fix it; the temptation is to rush straight to theory building. I have done it time and again myself (and may be caught doing it again). There is value in this kind of creative and constructive work; but ultimately, if we want to change what is actually going on in preaching practice today, there is no substitute for attending to lived practices.

This is my aim in this chapter. If we lament a lack of theological backbone in some of the preaching we are hearing today, maybe we need to look more closely at the process that produces it. In the pages to follow, I attend to dimensions of theological attentiveness in one preacher's sermon preparation process, slowing it down to see its working parts. The point is to foreground the role that theological attentiveness *may* play in sermon preparation, not to propose, commend, or defend this specific instance of homiletical practice in every detail. Inevitably, the descriptive mode of practical theology generates interpretive, criteriological, and strategic questions, but I leave systematic pursuit of those questions to others.

Theological Attentiveness in a Preaching Context: Five Horizons of Theological Understanding

That said, every effort at description needs a vocabulary suited to the task at hand. My sense is that all working preachers find themselves brokering a kind of buzzing conversation among multiple "horizons" of theological understanding as they interpret a biblical text and work toward the core theological affirmations of a sermon. By "horizon of theological understanding" I mean some set of convictions or claims about the nature of God and God's action, past and present, in and toward the world. Such horizons are social constructions and thus have a range of flexibility.⁴ Thus, I offer

---

3. Wood, *Vision and Discernment*, 39–40, 47. Wood suggests that the "fittingness" of Christian witness in relation to its purpose and context is the central inquiry proper to practical theology.

4. Gadamer, *Truth and Method*, 302. Gadamer tends to speak of each of the horizons brought to the interpretive situation, both on the part of the text and the reader who seeks to understand it, as univocal. Reconsidered in a socio-critical perspective, however, both of these horizons are likely to be pluriform and complex. This is particularly true

here a heuristic schema for identifying the five distinct "horizons" of theological understanding that appear to be in play in this preacher's process.

Briefly, the five horizons that I propose play into the sermon preparation process are:

1. The "working theology" of the preacher, both in terms of his or her overarching theological sense of what is "gospel," as well as more specific theological understandings pertinent to the text under study.
2. The "working theologies" of the congregation—a plurality of horizons, since no congregation represents a *single, univocal* horizon of theological understanding.
3. The overt theological language in a text, and the theological claims made there.
4. Deeper theological semantic possibilities that emerge as the text is read in relation to broader canonical and theo-cultural contexts, including both the historical past and the congregation's present experience.
5. The theological horizon of understanding that the preacher ultimately decides to articulate in the sermon itself.

None of these five horizons are original to me. All five are indicated, at least implicitly, in the theologically focused homiletics of Ronald Allen, as well as Burton Z. Cooper and John S. McClure.[5] The relationship between TH #1, the "working theology" of the preacher, and TH #2, the "working theology" of the congregation, receives detailed attention in the work of both John McClure and Leonora Tubbs Tisdale.[6] Tisdale and McClure both attend to TH #5, the theological claims of the sermon as it interacts with the congregation's theological imagination; so do James Nieman and Thomas Rogers.[7] Since grasping the distinctions among these five horizons

---

in the interpretive situation of the preacher. Not only is the textual tradition of Hebrew and Christian Scripture deeply redacted and therefore pluriform, but the preacher comes to the text on behalf of a congregation and larger social world whose horizons of understanding are richly complex.

5. Allen, *Preaching Is Believing*, 17–62; Cooper and McClure, *Claiming Theology in the Pulpit*.

6. McClure, *The Four Codes of Preaching*, 93–135; Tisdale, *Preaching as Local Theology and Folk Art*, 91–121.

7. Tisdale, *Preaching as Local Theology and Folk Art*, 110–21; McClure, *The Four Codes of Preaching*, 132–35; Nieman and Rogers, *Preaching to Every Pew*, 112–38.

of theological understanding is important to the rest of this chapter, they require elaboration.

Theological Horizon #1: *the "working theology" of the preacher—that is, the theological convictions and assumptions, conscious and unconscious, about God's nature and activity that frame the preacher's interpretation of congregational context, biblical text, and the wider world, and which shape the preacher's sermon crafting.* Today it is widely understood that any preacher brings to the preaching task a set of theological convictions as well as unconscious theological assumptions. I call this a preacher's "working theology." Some obvious sources for such "working theology" include a preacher's theological education, the impact of ongoing denominational debates and discussions (particularly as one takes an active role in these debates), reading both theological and non-theological material, online sources and conversations, interaction with other ministry practitioners, and everyday ministry experience. In other words, one's "working theology" is not fixed, but evolving. Being present to the suffering or dying, for example, surely shapes one's working theology, either subtly or dramatically.[8]

We can detect alertness to this horizon of theological understanding on the part of a preacher when he or she asks, for example, "What am I inclined to assume theologically about this particular biblical book before me, or specific texts within it?" or when he or she begins to compare a text's apparent theological claims with his or her working assumptions.

Theological Horizon #2: *the "working theologies" of the congregation. A congregation's working theologies are inevitably multiple; thus we need to think of this horizon as pluriform and complex, not univocal. It includes all those theological convictions and assumptions, conscious and unconscious, that shape church members' practice of faith, including the varied theological assumptions they bring to reading the Bible, listening to sermons, or debating issues.* Some of the working theologies present in a congregation may be similar to the preacher's in some respect; others will not. Naturally, these multiple theological understandings will vary in comprehensiveness and

---

8. Luke A. Powery foregrounds this dynamic in the opening sentences of his study of the manifestations of the Spirit in the language, content, and structure of sermons. Called upon to preside at the burial of his ten-year-old niece, but disturbed when a fellow pastor's sermon insisted on strident "celebration" with "no sign of lament," Powery reports that the lack of lament in that proclamation prompted him to "a discerning process about the signs of the Spirit in preaching." See *Spirit Speech*, xiii.

coherence. If asked, church members might sum up their theological perspective in phrases from a creed, hymn, or praise song. If pressed, they may cite sermons that impressed them, fragments gathered in Sunday school or camp settings, favorite religious pundits encountered in print or electronic media, or ideas picked up in a Bible study or fellowship group. Taken together, these sources may produce something considerably less than a comprehensive theological world view.

What makes such a horizon of theological understanding a "working" theology is that it has so far proven sufficient to the demands, great or minimal, that the believer places upon it. One's working theology only gets revised as it is tested by contrary views or the demands of experience, and its limitations come to light.

As will become clear in the congregational setting we are about to observe, tension or conflict in a congregation can bring into sharper relief the pluriform nature of congregational culture(s) and theological understanding(s). Mostly, these realities do not emerge because a preacher sets out deliberately to interrogate her congregation; in fact, that type of approach can intimidate and alienate some worshipers. Cultural and theological identities come to light as a pastor engages the congregation in ordinary ways—in a Bible study, at a potluck dinner, in pastoral situations, and in the give and take of committee work. Preachers who are alert to these complexities can find them frustrating; it is easier to aim sermons at a hypothetically "typical" church member than to take into account a welter of differences. Yet those who take complexity and difference seriously are probably more likely to preach in ways both sympathetic and challenging.

Theological Horizon #3: ***the overt or implicit theological claims a particular biblical text is making*** as understood in terms of its grammar, rhetorical structure, and sociohistorical context. Part of the preacher's work on the way to the sermon is to surface such claims in a text and the theological "world" it presupposes. As Ron Allen points out, getting at the theological proposal(s) of a text requires self-consciously noting our own intuitive or convictional theological assumptions about a text or its themes. It is crucial to let the text display *its own* assumptions and propose *its own* theological claims on its own terms. Clarity about this dimension of theology as it bears on preaching, Allen stresses, requires opening ourselves to the "otherness" of a text's claims and assumed world.[9]

9. Allen, *Preaching Is Believing*, 34.

Theological Attentiveness on the Path from Text to Sermon

Theological Horizon #4: ***the theological import of the text's deeper semantic possibilities.*** *These emerge when the text's claims, interpreted by means of historical, literary-rhetorical, and socio-critical lenses, are: a) set in dialogue with the questions and issues posed by the intended preaching context, and b) tested against a preacher's trusted sources within the breadth of Christian theological traditions.* Allen suggests that juxtaposing a text's symbol systems or rhetorical dynamics against contemporary realities can yield fresh insight.[10] For example, Allen observes that 1 Kings 17:8–17 sponsors certain theological claims he finds problematic (for example, the claim that God punishes by causing drought, thus deliberately producing innocent suffering). Yet, as Allen points out, the underlying narrative dynamics in the text—for example the fact that outsiders to Israel become the object of God's focused care through the prophet— can prove theologically helpful.[11] This type of theological "effect" of the text (as opposed to an explicit textual claim) belongs to TH #4.

Theological Horizon #5: ***the theological claims the preacher intends to express in the sermon itself.*** *The theological claims presented in a sermon emerge out of the interaction of the preceding four horizons of theological understanding (TH# 1–TH# 4). Over time, these theological claims contribute to the critically reflective theological vision and activity that the preacher hopes to foster in the congregation.* This fifth theological horizon emerges toward the end of the preaching preparation process. A theologically attentive preacher is likely to ask himself or herself what core theological claims the sermon will make, either explicitly (by way of overtly theological language) or more implicitly in the associations drawn and stories told. If the multiple horizons of theological understanding I describe here have been taken seriously, the claims of the sermon are likely to be anchored in the text, yet at the same time will be far more than a simple repetition of the text, since they will address what is most crucially at stake, theologically, in a given context at a particular time. Most texts yield a rich range of possible theological affirmations. What a preacher does, theologically, with Martha's conversation with Jesus and confession of faith in connection with Jesus' raising of Lazarus (John 11:20–27) will be nuanced one way in a sermon series on Christology and another if the preacher steps to the pulpit to face a distraught family suddenly bereaved of husband and father.

10. Ibid., 55–56.
11. Ibid., 56–57.

Observation, Description, and the Influence of Background Assumptions

In the pages to follow I invite readers to look over my shoulder and watch with me the unfolding process of sermon preparation. This descriptive journey focuses, in particular, on practices of theological attentiveness to the various horizons of theological understanding that interact as a preacher engages both biblical text and congregational life on the way to designing a sermon. I've chosen to describe the sermon preparation process of a preacher as she works through the week on Galatians 5:1, 13–25, her preaching text for Sunday's worship service in her multicultural congregation. I choose to focus on this process because of its deliberate theological attentiveness to the different "horizons" of theological understanding that interact in her setting, generally, and in the sermon preparation process in particular.

Several assumptions shape my descriptive process. Needless to say, every act of observation, to say nothing of description, is inevitably already interpretive. As Heidegger, Gadamer, and others in the now well-established hermeneutical tradition have cautioned us, there is no such thing as "non-interpretive" engagement with the phenomena of experience. Thus, for the sake of transparency, here are some pertinent background assumptions that inevitably influence what I see and how I see it.

First, text interpretation, sermon design, and preaching in the context of worship are all actions in which the outreaching God revealed in Jesus Christ makes a working partner out of a vulnerable preacher. The God who redeems and the preacher are mutually invested in bringing about an event of life-giving news for a waiting community of thirteen—or thirteen thousand. Preaching is a divine action; at the same time it is thoroughly human and therefore embedded neck-deep in historically and culturally mediated processes of semantic negotiation. Multiple horizons of semantic possibility interact, sometimes meshing and sometimes colliding. Yet because the Spirit of God is poured out on the church and its preachers, this process in all its human frailty becomes the crucible out of which emerges fresh and fitting meaning for a worshiping community.

Second, in the description to follow, I assume that Christian preaching emerges out of a conscientiously pastoral, context-responsive, and timely interpretation of Scripture. A preacher engages the text on behalf of her congregation.¹² The issue is not just what *she* makes of a text, but how it resonates with the realities of her congregation's life at present. She employs her best exegetical tools to help her hear the text speaking out of its distinctive cultural and theological horizon. At the same time, she brings to the text the questions arising from the multiple cultural and gendered horizons of her congregation, as well as specific pastoral situations.

Third, the horizons of theological understanding that interact in the preaching preparation process exert what can be termed "mutually critical" influence. That is, claims arising from the text and its semantic context may "reframe" some congregational understandings; on the other hand, the questions the preacher presses toward the text on behalf of her congregation can uncover previously unimagined layers of theological possibility.

Homiletical Theology in a Descriptive Mode

Observing Theological Attentiveness in the Preacher's Journey from Text to Sermon

The preaching context for this exploration is a small Presbyterian congregation located in a semi-urban neighborhood that has undergone fast demographic change in the last decade.¹³ Once solidly white working class, the neighborhood now includes an aging white population alongside hundreds of new residents primarily from India, Pakistan, South Asia, several Arabic-speaking countries, and West Africa. For many of these people, English is a second language, although many others are quite fluent in English. Many of the newer residents are professionals or small business owners, although some are unemployed or underemployed.

I. The Congregational Context

"New Community Presbyterian Church," as we will call it, was established five years ago when the dwindling and aging congregation of a once-vital

---

12. Long, *The Witness of Preaching*, 84, 86–87.

13. This situation is a composite portrait, with details altered to protect identities. It reflects the multicultural congregational and homiletical processes of three working pastors in the central New Jersey area who have shared both their preaching process in an elective course at Princeton Theological Seminary, "Preaching to Shape a Practicing Church" (Spring 2013).

Presbyterian church on this site made the decision to merge with the East Asian immigrant congregation that had been sharing their building for about four years. Today New Community Church is made up of a majority who were born in India, Pakistan, and South Asia, along with a substantial Caucasian minority, largely from the original congregation of the site. Scattered through the pews are a handful of West Africans, as well as two African American families. Single adults from all groups make up about 15 percent of the congregation. About 45 percent of the members are first-generation immigrants. Many have US citizenship. Their children, some of them born in the US, range in age from infancy to their early twenties.

The current pastor, Jodi, is not New Community's founding pastor, but his successor. She and her husband, both in their late thirties, live near the church with their middle-school-age children. Building a sense of common Christian identity has been a primary goal for Jodi and the church's Session (leadership board). Enthusiastic lay leaders have been doing their best to honor all the cultures that make up the congregation—but with mixed success. For example, at a recent potluck featuring the distinctive cuisine of the congregation's many cultures, serving tables were piled high with staples and delicacies from the congregation's heritage cultures. But when it came time to sit down for the meal, attendees sorted themselves into culturally homogeneous table groups. Organizers urged them to relocate for dessert, with mixed success.

Many congregants at New Community tend toward conservative theological views, a factor that has contributed to like-mindedness in some respects. But conflict has arisen over differing cultural values and norms. Recent controversy centers on appropriate behavior for young children in worship. Some cultures represented at NCPC are comfortable having preschool-age children stay near worship and move about the room, whispering with one another and playing (with occasional outbursts of debate or laughter) in the narthex. Some worship attendees find this distracting and have become vocal in their complaints, although these are typically directed to Jodi and to sympathetic church members rather than to the parents of these children.

This is the backdrop of congregational life as Jodi turns to the lectionary readings for Proper 6, Year C to work on next Sunday's sermon. For the past several weeks, she's been working with the second readings, a semicontinuous sequence from Galatians. This week's selection is Galatians 5:1, 13–25. Thanks to a seminary professor's interest in preaching as a practice of constructive theology, Jodi is alert to the way her own theology, those represented in the pews, and layers of theological meaning in the text impact her process of text interpretation and sermon design. As the narrative unfolds, I will indicate which of the several horizons of theological understanding are coming into play (TH# 1, TH# 2, etc.).

II. The Preacher's Working Theology Meets the Text's Overt Claims (TH #1 and TH# 3)

It is Tuesday morning, and Jodi lays out her commentaries and notes on Galatians. She reviews how her "working" theological assumptions about Galatians itself and theological topics it raises have been reshaped recently.

A first step was to overcome her inner resistance to preaching from Galatians. Paul's rhetoric seemed at times overwrought; at others, simply so strange or obscure that the gap between his world and that of NCPC seemed insurmountable. Unsurprisingly, other lectionary preachers posting on her favorite online preachers' blog advised steering clear of Galatians; with pejorative views of Judaism as "works religion" already too prevalent in their pews, they said, why risk letting Paul's rhetoric fan the flames of covert anti-Semitism?

This only made Jodi more determined to reexamine her own views of Galatians. Seminary had introduced her to the theology of the Apostle Paul, although Jodi recognized that her view of Paul was no doubt filtered through an education heavy on readings by leaders of the Reformation (TH #1). Thanks to some diligent work with commentaries, she had come to see that Paul does not regard Jewish law as pernicious; rather, he wants the Galatian churches, overwhelmingly Gentile, to maintain the Spirit-given freedom that formed the core of the good news as he'd preached it (TH #3).[14] Such freedom is the bedrock not only of their Christian identity but also of their congregational unity. If some succumb to the idea that circumcision is prerequisite to genuine Christianity, as certain itinerant teachers were insisting, the community could soon fragment and eventually disintegrate. Little wonder that rhetorically speaking, Paul stops at nothing to wean his Galatian converts away from their fascination with this teaching.

---

14. Witherington argues that "the majority, perhaps the vast majority, of Paul's Galatian converts are Gentiles not Jews, otherwise all these arguments about not submitting to circumcision would not be on target." See Witherington, *Grace in Galatia*, 7.

Homiletical Theology in Action

Jodi finds interesting the view of some scholars that the issue in Galatians is not what it takes to *get into* right relation with God, but what it takes for a community to *continue in* right relation with God and each other (TH #3).¹⁵ The issue, then, becomes not justification, but what *sustains* the unique identity and unshakable unity of the Spirit-born community: is it law observance or working out what Christ-won freedom looks like?

Rereading all of chapter 5 in the context of the entire book, Jodi recognizes that what one believes Paul is up to in Galatians as a whole shapes how one will make sense of chapter 5. If Galatians is about "faith alone" as the key to "getting into right relation with God" (a view Jodi remembers well from attending a friend's church camp years ago) the "ethical turn" of chapter 5 can be confusing. Works can contribute nothing to our justification, so why the ethical advice? Jodi finds intriguing the view of J. Louis Martyn and others that the "ethical turn" of Galatians 5 is actually not a set of moral injunctions but a *description* of the contrast between life in the "new creation" inaugurated in the death and rising of Jesus Christ versus the anxious, flesh- and law-bound self-aggrandizement characteristic of the old order (TH #3). If Martyn is right, chapter 5 isn't about which of two paths one will follow, but which reality one believes is truly "real"—which one "determines" the shape of our lives here and now: is it the old order of the flesh where law attempts to hold the flesh in check, or do we live in a "new age" of the Spirit in which freedom from the imperious claims of both "Flesh" and law is a gift and fact?¹⁶

> *Commentary*: Jodi's interaction with Galatians requires her to think carefully not only about the special challenges of preaching from this book, but about fundamental features of her own "working theology" (TH #1), especially her thinking about soteriology and eschatology. Martyn's view suggests that the new creation is already established in the resurrected Jesus, the firstborn and inaugurator of a changed reality in which Christians are already located. Other interpreters of Galatians see the choice confronting Paul's correspondents not as a matter of what they believe about the "really real," but how they will choose in a struggle between law/Flesh-based justification and justification by grace, through faith.

---

15. Ibid., 357.

16. Martyn, *Galatians*, 35–46, 96–105, and elsewhere. Witherington largely agrees with Martyn's framework, although he leaves room for a greater plurality of interpretations in some passages, including, for example, how best to make sense of the two covenants typology of chapter 4. See Witherington, *Grace in Galatia*, 334.

Is the conflict in Galatians between two paths, or two "worlds"? If the latter, then all frameworks by which we would "normally" define ourselves, understand our identity, and establish our identity with others are relativized—status, ethnic origin, cultural distinctives, and so on. Galatians 3:28 comports well with this view when it declares distinctions of ethnicity/culture, socioeconomic status, and gender nullified "in Christ" ("there is neither longer Jew nor Greek . . . slave nor free . . . male nor female" [NRSV]).

Encountering Martyn's proposal represents a challenge to some of Jodi's previous thinking. The interplay of theological perspectives—hers, the possibilities in the text, and the diverse theologies in her congregation—is going to be complex.

III. Surfacing the Congregation's Working Theologies (TH # 2 and TH #3)

Since the beginning of the Galatians sermon series, Jodi has been keeping alert to TH #2, the varied "working theologies" expressed by different members of her congregation. Fortunately, not long after she arrived at New Community Church she introduced a sermon text "feed-forward" group. Called "Leaning into Sunday," the group gathers for an hour and a half every Tuesday night to spend time with the upcoming preaching text. The nine or ten regulars, ranging in age from sixteen to eighty-six, are committed churchgoers. The gathering begins with a half hour of *lectio divina* and journaling on the text before shifting to more conventional Bible study and discussion.[17]

When they first began working with Galatians, most in the group thought of Galatians as "that book against works-righteousness religion." Some would add confidently, "Like Judaism, for example." Jodi has done her best, both in their meetings and in her sermons, to challenge *that* notion, although she's found that entrenched ideas die hard.

Satisfied that she's familiar enough with chapter 5 to be helpful to the "Leaning In" group, Jodi closes her commentaries and gathers up her Bible and notebook. If everyone is there tonight, every ethnic group found in New Community's pews will be represented.

---

17. *Lectio divina* refers to the classic Christian practice of slow reading of the text (usually aloud), followed by meditation, prayer, and contemplation (*meditatio, oratio,* and *contemplatio*).

Homiletical Theology in Action

Some of what Jodi learns Tuesday night about the range of her congregation's working theologies (TH #2) doesn't surprise her. Most seem untroubled by the turn to ethics ("Isn't that what religion is always about?" someone quipped). Only one person, the sixteen-year-old, wonders why Paul appears to be "laying down a bunch of rules" in chapter 5; hasn't he just said life in the Spirit isn't about rules? Jodi waits to see what others will do with this. An older gentleman announces, "Gotta have rules." He folds his arms firmly across his chest as if that is the end of the matter. Pressed, he expresses his belief that following Jesus means "doing the right thing." Someone else interjects that "the right thing" can look different, depending what you area "used to." This Jodi takes as a veiled reference to the current debate about worship.

Next, discussion develops over what phrases like "living according to the flesh" and "living according to the Spirit" mean. One couple whose church affiliation in their native country was Pentecostal, insist that those who are filled with the Holy Spirit do not need rules. If the congregation were truly "Spirit-filled," they argue, there would be no problems.

It is at that point that things take an uncomfortable turn. A mother of two young children, a member of the group with lenient parenting standards, declares, "I think 'the Spirit' means the spirit of tolerance, and freedom means everyone in the church gets to express their culture, whatever that is!" A grandmother whose young grandchildren are kept firmly in tow in worship retorts, "But letting children run wild isn't tolerance; it's making everyone live by *one* group's standard. Isn't that just what Paul was *against*?" The debate heats up. To Jodi's relief, someone switches the focus to verses 22 and 23, about fruits of the Spirit. "This seems to say we won't get anywhere without 'love' and 'longsuffering.' What does *that* look like?" The group cautiously discusses this, but the two debaters are silent. Each, still spewing, collects an ally on the way to the parking lot.

> *Commentary*: The pluriform nature of TH# 2, a congregation's working theologies, comes through clearly here. Clearly, the working theologies within a congregation are closely intertwined with personal histories as well as sociocultural assumptions and norms. It is worth noting that this would be no less true if Jodi's congregation, instead of being multicultural as it is, were made up entirely of white-privileged members. In both settings, it is all too easy to be blind to the constructed and self-interested nature of one's assumptions and how readily any of us co-opt theology

to legitimate and defend those assumptions and the privilege or power they confer.

Strikingly, Jodi has the wisdom not to go on the offensive in the Bible study, "trumping" others' contributions with her recent new insights thanks to her work with the text. Were this her habit she would know far less about her congregation's pluriform theological understandings.

To step aside into a more criteriological stance for a moment with respect to the theological task in preaching, baptism, and the sermons we preach in relation to it can become occasions when a congregation recognizes in a vivid way how God's claim upon us deconstructs our socially constructed assumptions and the scaffolding we have built to sustain them.

In baptism, all the sociocultural markers by which we have sought to distinguish ourselves, as well as whatever we take to be our failures or achievements—in other words, all that we have counted on to keep us afloat—is surrendered to a watery grave. We rise up with nothing left to us but the identity conferred upon us by God's promise. At our beginning, our identity is anchored in God's future. Our destiny becomes our new starting point; and it is a shared destiny. Still dripping grace, we come to a table where there is neither gluttony nor hunger and no special seating. We belong to God and one another, no matter what.

V. Text and Contemporary Context: Uncovering Deeper Theological Semantics (TH #4)

Back in her study Wednesday morning, Jodi reflects on what she has learned about TH #2. It was fascinating to see that some put cultural differences into the "freedom" category; while others protested that this amounts to setting up one culture's standard as community "law." At this stage, she experiences some hesitation: can a sermon on this text help her congregation work through the tension, or does its language only function to throw biblical fuel on the cultural fires? On the other hand, depending on the sense one makes of the informing theological framework of Galatians, a sermon on this text could radically reframe the way her congregation understands itself.

Homiletical Theology in Action

It has become apparent that in working out TH #5, the theological message of the sermon, Jodi will also have to think carefully about TH #3, the overt theological claims of Galatians. How the vocabulary of "Flesh" and "Spirit" works, of course, depends on one's view of the book as a whole; and one scholar after another that she's read insists that how we read chapter 5 depends enormously on how one interprets the difficult symbolism of chapter 4 with its "allegory" about two women, two mountains, and two covenants. Jodi flips hopefully through the lectionary commentary on her desk, and then remembers that the series of Galatians readings in Year C does not include this part. No surprise there. A well-meant mishandling of Paul's *midrash* could easily result in homiletical malpractice. Jodi pulls her commentaries down from the shelf.

She discovers that it is possible to treat the "two covenants" section as typology rather than allegory, so that the semantic key to its meaning is not a "this-*is*-that" relation, but rather "this *stands for/foreshadows* that." Read typologically, Hagar, Mount Sinai, the Sinai covenant of law, and "earthly Jerusalem" symbolically represent one kind of reality, while the "free woman" (Sarah isn't actually named), Mount Horeb, the Abrahamic covenant of promise, and "heavenly Jerusalem" symbolize a contrasting reality. But what are these two realities? Jodi is relieved to discover a cadre of interpreters who insist that Paul is not pitting Judaism and Christianity against one another, denigrating the former and celebrating the latter. This would be radically discontinuous with his theology in Romans. Truth be told, says one interpreter, the reference to "earthly Jerusalem" is less mysterious than it may seem. What if it is simply literal, an arrow laid on the ground in the Galatians' own world, pointing to the literal city of Jerusalem? That would be the likely home of the strongly Jewish, Torah-keeping Christian communities from which the circumcision-promoting extremists that are troubling the Galatian communities had most likely sprung.[18]

With this GPS clue to guide us, the two women, the two mountains, the covenants of law and promise, and the two Jerusalems signify *two contrasting versions of the gospel* on offer in the Gentile mission. One is Paul's, associated with the heavenly Jerusalem of the new age inaugurated by Jesus' resurrection. The other is the "gospel" of the circumcision party with its origins in earthly Jerusalem.

Jodi reflects on the difference this makes. It's a relief to know that disdain for Judaism itself is not at all what Paul is recommending—a nagging

---

18. Martyn, *Galatians*, 40, 457–66; Witherington, *Grace in Galatia*, 334.

anxiety she now realizes she has always had about Galatians. So what *is* the theological point? What if Paul's "heavenly Jerusalem" is an entirely new reality—a reality turned loose in the world by the one he had met on the Damascus road (Gal 1:11–17)? Could it be that Paul has been encountered by a light so bright that it makes what we've always taken for daylight look for all the world like darkness? In this new reality, Gentile outsiders to the original (and continuing) chosen community are now *included* in God's promised renewal of all things.

Jodi starts scribbling down thoughts as fast as they come to her, sensing a sea change in her own thinking: "The Galatian Gentiles' faith has been sealed by the outpouring of the Spirit on Gentile believers no less than Jewish ones (Gal 3:2–5). This is an eschatological sign that God is creating a new community that transcends religious and cultural divides. Debating which set of cultural norms for worship is 'more spiritual' will only blind us to who we really are at NCPC."

> *Commentary*: Jodi's gradual construction of a new framework of theological understanding leads her to something of a breakthrough here. If God has established a new creation that radically relativizes cultural norms, the relevance to her distinctly multicultural congregation is clear. It would be no less relevant, of course, to a congregation more ethnically uniform and more privileged. Paul's vision of a new commonwealth—a "new Jerusalem"—means we must regard with suspicion any and all explicit claims or implicit assumptions that one's culture- and class-bound prerogatives are sacrosanct—either of a piece with one's religious identity or somehow insulated from the claims of one's religious convictions. According to Martyn, Paul speaks of a new reality that renders us radically open to otherness, one that is making something new of us.

I would contend that TH #1, the horizon of theological understanding that comprises a preacher's "working theology," is never a finished work but a moving, evolving horizon. Three major contributors to its evolution are a) wrestling with the theological claims of biblical texts at both TH #3 and TH #4 levels; b) the ongoing work of brokering the interplay among these horizons and the (pluriform) horizon of congregation's working theologies (TH #2); and c) the preacher's conscious, and conscientious, critical reflection on the way his or her own theological understanding is being challenged or confirmed through theologically attentive homiletical work. I assume a mutually critical relationship among these various horizons.

There are, of course, other factors in the wider environment of ministry and life itself that impact a preacher's working theology. Theology is not a subject matter mastered but an open-ended dialogue that includes a preacher's prayer life as well as intellectual search and reflection. One's theology is shaped by interaction with colleagues and faith communities, ordinary experience as well as those confrontations with profound loss, suffering, and injustice that test the limits of faith and can leave us stripped of words. We read, we test, and reread in light of new experiences even the confessional traditions we most prize. Theological understanding is never absolute or complete.

VI. Moving Toward the Sermon (TH #5)

Jodi recognizes that New Community Church is teetering on the edge of serious fragmentation over what may seem to outsiders a petty conflict. Because the vast majority of NCPC members are relatively recent newcomers from other parts of the world, their protectiveness of their cultural identities is understandable, but their anxieties around this may be blinding the congregation to the possibilities that being "in Christ" opens up.

If a vote were taken today about handling the presence of young children in worship, Jodi muses, it is not clear which side would win. It hardly matters; the damage would be done. She pictures either an exodus or long-term bitterness on the part of whichever side felt it had "lost." Jodi taps out a sentence on her computer: "Without a source of identity and unity that *transcends* cultural differences, chances are good that this congregation will be fractured, quite possibly along cultural lines. It could eventually fall apart." She doubts lines like these belong in the sermon, but they clarify what's at stake.

Can her sermon on Galatians 5 reframe her congregation's understanding of themselves, not as wary strangers to one another, but as a sign to the world of the reconciling power of God? Can she invite them to embrace as Spirit-established fact and Spirit-given gift a unity that transcends cultural divides, one that makes them servants, each of the other—the radically other? One thing is certain: this sermon can't scold. It will need to do what the text does—namely, to launch a powerful vision of the truly *new* community that God's Spirit alone can create, one that radically relativizes cultural divides and makes of us something new.

Before leaving her office to make her Wednesday afternoon hospital calls, Jodi makes five columns representing TH#1, 2, 3, 4, and 5 and jots down key theological insights she wants to hold onto under each heading. That finished, she heads for the hospital.

> *Commentary*: Note that Jodi has not reached closure at this point; she is still testing her theological hunches. She is also testing the best ways to handle the confrontation of theological horizons of understanding (TH#3, TH#4 and TH #5 with TH#2) that she must negotiate in the sermon. One possibility strategy may be to lead the congregation along the very same path of discovery she herself has been experiencing in past weeks, and particularly these past few days.

It is after 5 PM when Jodi gets back from the hospital. Her afternoon there was far from routine. She had barely reached the hospital when her cell phone buzzed; she was needed in the maternity wing. An NCPC member, a young woman carrying her first child, had gone into labor nearly eight weeks early. When tests showed the placenta beginning to break down, a hasty Caesarean followed, bringing a tiny but tenacious baby boy into the world. Standing beside the baby's anxious father, Jodi wiped away tears of relief as nurses in Newborn Intensive Care tethered the infant to a half-dozen machines. Jodi had barely finished praying with the new parents when she was called to the cardiac care unit. A church member who had had bypass surgery the previous day had taken a turn for the worse about an hour earlier. Now efforts to support her faltering heart were failing. An agonizing hour after Jodi arrived at the room, the woman passed away, her husband, two of her four grown children, and Jodi by her bedside.

One thing Jodi knows about NCPC is that this congregations pulls together around such births and deaths. Joys and tragedies that touch one touch all. Jodi suspects that this coming together on the holy ground of birth and death, joy and sorrow, will "proclaim" New Community Church's true "new creation" unity in a way that words cannot.

It takes a half hour of centering and meditative prayer to bring herself back to the sermon preparation task. She needs to decide what will be the core theological affirmation of Sunday's sermon on Galatians 5:1, 13–25. She narrows the options to two distinct theological frameworks that make sense of her preaching text in different ways. These two frameworks suggest different understandings of the import of God's saving work for present life. They present different understandings of the implications of God's new creation for the here and now. Jodi summarizes them:

> *Option 1*: Righteousness before God is established by faith in God's promise, not law observance. Yet our ultimate freedom and fulfillment lies in the not-yet of God's eschatological future. Although Christ made our freedom possible, it is reality only as Christians choose it. For the present, we must strive for God's reign through obedience (relying on the Spirit's power) instead of yielding to the impulses of our sinful flesh. Experiencing our Christian freedom requires continuous moral effort on the part of believers. Within this theological framework, chapter 5 says: "You must stop falling back into bondage to the flesh. This means resisting the idea that law can justify you. At the same time, freedom doesn't mean indulging yourself in sins of the body or fleshly competition for power. Say no to these things and bear the fruits of the Spirit in order to inherit God's future for you."[19]

> *Option 2*: Galatians 5 is not moral advice, nor is it an injunction to bring the new creation into being through moral effort. Rather, Galatians 5 contrasts the "old order" of the flesh's struggle with sin under law with the new reality already brought about by God's free act of "apocalypse" in Jesus Christ (in Martyn's terms, the "invasion" of new-creation reality into the territory of the old order). Freed from the futile striving that law forces upon sinful flesh, a striving that produces competition and envy, believers live out of the new identity and unity granted by their Christ-won, Spirit-established freedom. While the vice list of chapter 5 (vv. 17–21) describes the deeds characteristic of the "old-age" reign of the flesh, the virtue list (vv. 23–24) describes the values of God's new creation. These flourish amid believers' "other"-embracing practice of service, one to another.

---

19. In support of this interpretation, Ronald Fung writes: "Making the reality of the indicative conditional upon the execution of the imperative in this way is not putting the imperative cart before the indicative horse; it simply emphasizes that the new life (with the Spirit as its source) must become evident in the new conduct (under the Spirit's direction) and cannot exist without it." See Fung, *The Epistle to the Galatians*, 282–83. The sense here seems to be that the new life *cannot exist* without human beings, under the Spirit's direction, making it evident. Martyn and others would disagree; the new creation is a fact, whether or not human beings embrace its practices.

Jodi recognizes that although option two has challenged some of her former theological assumptions about the flesh/Spirit dichotomy in Galatians, in several ways she finds it persuasive. In fact, she finds it more persuasive. Option two lines up fittingly with other writings of Paul—for example, 2 Corinthians 5:17 with its almost breathless announcement: "If anyone is in Christ, behold—new creation!" It also aligns with one of her core theological convictions—namely, that God's saving work has to do with communities, and not just individuals.

If Martyn is right about Paul's apocalyptic theology, believers *themselves* are not the battleground between flesh/law and Spirit; rather, the battleground is daily life where two realities compete to shape our life together, especially amid cultural difference and conflict. "Old-order" reality is not flawed simply because of its bondage to flesh; it is also in bondage to law, attempting to establish both personal righteousness and the boundaries of community by means of rules. But the new order—the new creation inaugurated in Jesus Christ—establishes us in a new order whose unity is a given, and which thrives by means of love and mutual service, calling radically into question whatever we have counted on either as the basis of our self-confidence or the ground of our unity (TH #4, challenging TH#2).

Guided by option two's theological framework, Jodi can envision with New Community Church what it means to be an entirely new kind of human community—one already inaugurated by the Spirit (TH #5). Gathered by the Spirit as a community belonging to God's new creation, the cultural differences with NCPC are secondary. Their mutual obligation to love, to serve, and to make room for one another is a given in this new reality. The cultural norms of a majority cannot be allowed to function as NCPC's "terms of union."

Jodi also notes that the option two reading can include the idea that individuals, as well as communities, can fall prey to the self-promoting, self-justifying preoccupation with rules characteristic of the "old order" defeated at the cross.

Next she ponders how to interpret verse 25 ("if we live in the Spirit, let us walk in the Spirit"). Is the force of "if" conditional here, as some commentators argue, so that whether or not they live "in the Spirit" is up to believers themselves? Or could it carry the sense of "since" (as in—consulting one's train schedule—"if this is the train we've chosen, we're not going to Chicago")? This reading suggests that living in the Spirit is not a choice for believers but a fact—the fact that determines everything else. Jodi tries out a paraphrase: "Since we live in [have our existence because of] the Spirit, [then] let us walk [move through the contested territory of this world] in the Spirit."

The core affirmation of the sermon Jodi will preach Sunday is becoming clear: she wants to help her community glimpse a vision of their *God-given* unity as their starting point, rather than regarding unity as something that can only be achieved through a series of cultural battles, each with its winners, losers, and casualties. Instead, made one by the Spirit, NCPC can refuse to let even cherished cultural habits drive them apart. The sermon will need to include a clear invitation to risk practicing an "other"-serving love that suffers long and practices kindness, humility, and forbearance. Surely their future will require yielding, giving, and forgiving on everyone's part—not for the sake of working out who they *could* be, but as the natural consequence of being *who they already are* as citizens of God's new creation in the risen Christ.

Clearly, a vision like this will take time and repetition to take root in the imagination of congregation members, and it will need to be worked out in concrete practices. Could a multicultural group of members, including parents and grandparents of young children, brainstorm ways to do worship differently? Could they create within their worship space a comfortable area for parents with young children, yet also create space for others where they could sit close to the front and feel fully involved in worship without undue distraction?

Jodi recognizes these details are not hers to work out, but theirs. Her part is to offer them the theological vision she believes can radically reframe the congregation's present challenges. She enters several more sentences under TH #5: "As an outpost of God's new creation in Jesus Christ, New Community Church is unified by common birth in the Spirit. The Spirit leads us as we discover what freedom in the Spirit looks like in our time and place, in our situation, amid our differences and our conflicts. We acknowledge we are diverse, but our starting point is a Spirit-given unity. We belong to each other in a way that transcends 'old-order' affinities like being in the same generation, speaking the same language, or living by the same cultural norms. Living in the Spirit means discovering our new, God-given identity as a truly 'new' community. It means imagining new ways of being together that nourish those that are 'other,' culturally and in many other ways."

Sunday's sermon has begun to take shape. It will be heard within the context of yesterday's events—a remarkable birth and a tragic death, both of which affect her small congregation profoundly. She knows without asking that church members are already turning toward one another, celebrating with the joyful and weeping with the sorrowing—across cultural lines. Birth and death, celebration and lament—these run deeper than cultural divides. The songs and sighs of the Spirit transcend all cultural difference.[20]

Implications for the Development of Homiletical Theology

My aim in this essay has been to describe one preacher's attentiveness to five distinct horizons of theological understanding that bear upon her sermon preparation process. Needless to say, there are other types of homiletical theology as important to preachers' work as the descriptive approach demonstrated here. Ronald J. Allen commends bringing systematic theology to the pulpit.[21] Burton Z. Cooper and John S. McClure help preachers identify their own theological world view, while the work of empirical practical theologians suggest that we need more scientific study of the cumulative theological effects upon congregations of the sermons we preach.[22] Yet, focusing on homiletical theology in the descriptive mode is necessary, not only because it is sound practical-theological procedure, but because it is essential to a fully developed homiletical theology.

As a component of sound practical-theological method, descriptive attentiveness to lived practice takes seriously the concreteness, diversity, and complexity of religious practices. When practical theology begins instead with theological norms and "applies" these to practice, practices are typically treated in an abstract way and norms tend to be universalized without

---

20. For a rich discussion of lament and celebration as marks of the presence of the Spirit, see Powery, *Spirit Speech*, chapter 2.

21. Allen has been a major advocate for the recovery of theology in contemporary preaching. A primary difference between Allen's work on theology in preaching and what I undertake here is that Allen focuses on building systematic theology into the content of sermons, while my concern here is with practices embedded in the homiletical method of the preacher, regardless what purpose, content, and form finally shapes the sermon. See Allen, *Preaching Is Believing*, 202.

22. On identifying theological world view, see Cooper and McClure, *Claiming Theology in the Pulpit*, 1–69. On empirical approaches to preaching and its effects, see Pieterse, *Communicative Preaching*, 39–73.

regard to contextual realities. Preaching practices today are extremely diverse, both within and beyond the North American context. Sound theory construction and pedagogy in homiletical theology will need to take these diversities seriously, not by merely nodding in their direction, but by observing and describing the context-specific, theologically mindful practices of working preachers and examining their effects. Practical theology in the descriptive mode needs to be central to this ongoing project.

Second, observing pastoral practice in a descriptive mode keeps us alert to the fact that the work of pastors and congregational leaders themselves is strongest when it includes the same four reasoning processes, or tasks, that comprise practical-theological reflection. Working pastors and lay leaders, like academic practical theologians, undertake descriptive, interpretive, norm-generative, and strategic tasks in guiding congregation life and public witness. Congregational leaders no less than academics can tend to skip the time-consuming work of close observation and in their impatience to "fix" areas of congregational life that are sources of congregational dissatisfaction, running the risk of oversimplifying complex situations and suppressing important diversities of all kinds with a congregation.

Third, descriptive homiletical theology is essential to sound pedagogy that addresses the theological dimensions of preaching, both for beginners and seasoned preachers. Effective teachers of preaching are patient observers. They watch what learners are *already doing* as a first step toward coaching them toward better practice.

Even beginners in preaching bring to the task certain "working" theological and rhetorical assumptions. What we see going on in a preacher's efforts, theologically, reveals something about what he or she has been taught to value as "good preaching." These theological and rhetorical assumptions are powerfully shaped by the contexts that have identified their promise for ministry. Simply overlaying abstract prescriptions over this deep structure of reinforcement is likely to result in little change. Before rushing in to modify a preacher's practice, we do well to observe as sympathetically as possible what he or she is doing and discern the factors that have shaped that practice. Sound homiletical pedagogy begins with attentiveness to what *is being done* before moving on to interpret its dynamics, develop useful criteria both theological and rhetorical, and guide the preacher toward better practice.

This chapter's exploration of theological attentiveness in one preacher's process of preparing to preach opens up important questions. Some readers may be asking, for example, "What about the horizon of divine presence—even guidance—in sermon preparation?" As I indicated in laying out my informing assumptions about preaching, it is my conviction that God is the active coagent of preaching throughout all its phases. God, whose Spirit has been poured out on the *whole* church and not just its preachers, chooses to work through the sometimes messy, thoroughly human processes we have observed in this chapter to bring the saving Word to church and world. God works in the back and forth between horizons of partial and culturally embedded theological understandings.

Prayer and the study of Scripture both had a place in the process we have just described. At the study desk, pondering the challenges of both a plurality of text interpretations and congregation life, our preacher prays. Standing shoulder to shoulder with parishioners in a hospital room where the life-support machines have gone silent and the form on the bed is utterly still, she prays. In her study of the text, Jodi displays a clear interest in the explicit and implicit claims of Galatians about what God is doing in the world and how God is present and active within her congregation's life together.

Although Jodi's process in this case did not include consulting classic confessions or other time-honored repositories of what the church has believed, she might well choose to do that on other occasions. Such sources can serve as channel markers for testing the validity of possible theological claims of a text or sermon; but these sources, too, need to be read critically. They offer a preacher time-tested guidance; yet they are time-bound and partial horizons of theological understanding, subject to revision.

A preacher myself, I stumble my way toward Sunday, more often than not, through hectic days of trying to be too many things to too many people in too many places. And yet even when ministry and teaching are most hectic, and study time scarce and interrupted, I trust that God is at work through many means, shaping the Word of saving hope that needs to be spoken in Christian worship. When at last I step to the pulpit, sometimes short on sleep and shorter still on eloquence, I look out at the upturned, hopeful faces of worshipers who refuse, against all odds, to give up on Christian preaching. I lift my voice to preach, confident that amid the confused clutter of both my life and theirs, amid the ragged incompleteness of my theological understandings and theirs, God has been speaking and will speak again.

My colleague William Stacy Johnson declares that "God has . . . determined not to be God without us."[23] God also refuses to preach without us. Out of the crucible of our Spirit-infused life together, despite our blind spots and our limitations, God determines to bring forth the Word that saves and heals not only us but all creation—the object of God's fierce love.

---

23. "What happens in the drama of salvation is God determining to be God for us in a definite way. God is so much the God who is 'for' us as to be also irreversibly 'with' us. What happens in Jesus Christ, in other words, is constitutive for who God is. So committed is God to being with us that *God has also determined not to be God without us*" (emphasis mine). See Johnson, "Making Grace Real," 20.

—2—

Wet Paint

Matthew 15, the Canaanite Woman, and Painted-Over Proclamation

—Adam Hearlson

Introduction

When reflecting on questions surrounding the terms, actions, and boundaries of homiletical theology, I cannot not help but feel like I am sinking to the bottom of a vast semiotic sea. I cannot wrap my head around the term "homiletical theology,"—let alone the field of homiletical theology—without also finding some corresponding analogy to serve as my life preserver. I suppose this is natural when discussing a new phenomenon that no one is quite sure exists but is excited to discuss. The creation of new definitions, new boundaries, and new fields cannot be done *ex nihilo*. The discussion of something that may or may not exist requires a commitment to abstraction, a dedication to observation, and a confidence in analogy. That homiletics and theology exist is no proof that homiletical theology exists. And yet, without the aid of these two other fields and their practices, our search for the definition and boundaries of homiletical theology would be impossible.

As one ill-suited for the hard abstract work to discern the shape of this task and also unprepared for the necessary empirical observation, I find myself gravitating to the analogy as a tool for discussing homiletical theology. "What does homiletical theology resemble?" is an important question for discerning what homiletical theology is. Thus, my discussion of homiletical theology is intentionally inductive and provisionally descriptive. As a descriptive task, this work is a bit like groping in the dark. I don't have a clear vision of the field and so I must resort to descriptions that borrow from other more fully formed fields. In a recent online forum, John McClure described homiletical theology as "theology performed redemptively between (God, church, world, etc.)."[1] Similarly, I see the study of homiletical theology as a descriptive process done in the between places. Between theology and homiletics, between Scripture and context, and between heaven and earth. The task of description from this liminal place requires using metaphor and analogy to aid in the descriptive act. What "is," is described from territory of "is not." Thus this descriptive account of homiletical theology is not a way to trace the outlines of a new field but to begin to notice the field emerging from between what is and what is not. So as I begin this description of homiletical theology I admit that I am not yet ready to tell you what homiletical theology is; instead, I am ready to tell you what it is like. Homiletical theology is like the Canaanite woman in Matthew's Gospel and street art.

The Canaanite Woman, Street Art, and Homiletical Theology

When the Canaanite woman in Matthew 15 comes and kneels at the feet of Jesus beseeching him to heal her afflicted daughter, he brushes her off saying, "It is not right to take the children's food and throw it to the dogs."

As a child, I frequently invited myself to dinner at the homes of my friends. One family hosted me too many times to count and they had a rule at dinner: guests ate last. I was free to eat at their house and they were gracious enough to feed me, but the family had priority when it came to the food. I can still remember the father of the family, a big probation officer chiseled from granite, saying, "Adam, blood is thicker than mud." I didn't quite understand his meaning so he explained further, "Family eats first."

When food is scarce, questions of priority become important. For a family on a tight budget trying to feed the kids, the addition of another

---

1. John McClure, post, Homiletical Theology Project Facebook Group Page.

hungry stomach can upset the finely tuned equilibrium of need and provision. When there is not enough food to go around, then hard decisions need to be made. Scarcity demands planning; shortages require clear ideas of priority.

Blood is thicker than mud. Family eats first.

So when Jesus rebuffs the Canaanite woman it is not only the obvious impertinence of the statement that stings, it is the corresponding world view that seems so problematic, especially in light of the Jesus' decision a chapter earlier to feed thousands of people with a few loaves of bread and some fish. Jesus is supposed to be above the parochial priorities that govern our lives. And mostly he is; just a few verses before Jesus' encounter with the woman in need, Jesus seems to revel in the opportunity to provide an abundant feast for hungry people. Among his own people scarcity was no impediment for Jesus. Matthew's gospel notes that after everyone had eaten, the disciples collected another twelve baskets full of food (14:20). Food that was thought to be scarcer than hen's teeth was actually abundant. A meager meal could feed a multitude. Priority was given to all who were hungry. By the end of the meal the message is clear: God's mission involves feeding hungry people.

As Jesus enters into a Gentile region of Tyre and Sidon he encounters another hungry soul. Considering the miracle of abundance in chapter 14, it is surprising to hear Jesus make reference to food and scarcity when rebuffing the Canaanite woman's pleas. This rebuke takes on special significance in light of the socioeconomic climate of the Ancient Near East. Scholars note that the meeting of the Canaanite woman and Jesus is a collision of two socioeconomic worlds.[2] Tyre and Sidon were wealthy coastal cities that had little arable land and relied upon the surrounding rural areas to grow their food.[3] Gerd Theissen notes, "The economically stronger Tyrians probably often took bread out of the mouths of the Jewish rural population, when they used their superior financial means to buy up the grain supply in the countryside."[4] Thus, when Jesus meets this hungry woman from rich suburbs he cannot forget the exploitation and hunger that he saw among the 5,000 hungry souls. The feeding of the 5,000 anticipates God's promise of abundance in a world free of scarcity, but when faced with a

---

2. This argument is famously forwarded by Gerd Theissen. See Theissen, *The Gospels in Context*. See also Gench, *Back to the Well*.

3. In Acts 12:20 Tyre and Sidon do their best to appease an angry King Herod because they relied so heavily upon the Galilean region for their food.

4. Theissen, *The Gospels in Context*, 79.

person whose lifestyle is built upon the backs of so many hungry people, Jesus becomes positively miserly.

Jesus insults the Canaanite woman and emphatically states that his mission is closed to outsiders and reserved only for Israel. Blood is thicker than mud. Family eats first. In a world of scarce resources, the priority has been set. Yet, standing in the tradition of Abraham, Job, and Ruth, the Canaanite woman refuses to receive the vision of scarcity. The Canaanite woman's retort is at once a brilliant act of subversive speech and a daring example of faithful boldness. She says, "Yes, Lord, yet even the dogs eat the crumbs that fall from their masters' table." In effect she says, "That's not what I hear. I hear wherever you go, everyone gets fed." The Canaanite woman repaints Jesus' insulting picture to include the hungry beneath the table. Her retort transforms the image from an empty table to a table overflowing with food. At the master's house, food is so abundant that scraps are falling off the table. Turns out there is enough for everyone to be fed—even the dogs. With her witty and astute rejoinder, the Canaanite woman reshapes Jesus' theology by providing a broader picture of abundance and need. The woman becomes Jesus' teacher by helping him imagine a world, a ministry, and a faith that does not abide by assumptions of scarcity but lives up to the promises of God's abundance. In sum, Jesus couldn't see the breadth of his own mission without the aid of the Canaanite woman.

The story of the Canaanite woman might not seem like the most natural place to begin a discussion about homiletical theology, but as the only extant text in the Gospels where Jesus changes his mind and learns something, it can serve as a helpful entry point for thinking about the ways in which homiletical theology is a provisional creative art. The story of the Canaanite woman is a reminder that theology that funds practice, vision, and mission (that is, all theology worth wearing) is always subject to change when it encounters the Canaanite women among us. The Canaanite woman is not a systematic theologian, but her theological imagination broadens the theology of Jesus. To use another analogy, she has the courage and boldness to add to what seemed to be a finished painting. The goals were set. The priority was decided. The picture was hung in the museum. Along comes the Canaanite woman who spray-paints herself into the finished picture of Jesus. This theological vandalism is a central practice of homiletical theology. Eschewing authority and privilege, homiletical theology comes bold and brimming with creative imagination. For the purposes of this essay, I want to talk about how homiletical theology might use this Canaanite vandal as an example. Guided by a courageous imagination and little respect for the sanctity of tradition, the Canaanite woman is more like a street artist than a theologian. She is more vandal than preacher.

To describe the Canaanite woman as a street artist, and by extension to describe homiletical theology as street art, is to embrace a theological vision that is by nature public, impermanent, and provisional. Homiletical theology is a transient theology, subject and vulnerable to change with the public cries of every new Canaanite.

Homiletical Theology as Public Disruption

Street art operates within a different environment than most fine art. Whereas fine art assumes a gallery, that is a space set apart for reception, street art assumes a public context where art intrudes on daily life. Moreover, street art assumes a different life-span than most fine art. Once the spray paint is applied, or the poster is wheat-pasted to the building, it cannot come off without destroying the work itself. To remove the art from the immediate context—the public building, sidewalk, or billboard—is to destroy its function as an intermediary between the immediate context and lived existence. Street artist and designer Shepherd Fairey speaks of his own work as "an experiment in phenomenology" where novel phenomena disrupt our expectations about our world.[5] Fairey wants his public art to awaken the wonder about the surrounding environment. Street art disrupts expectations by placing an act of creative imagination into a place where an audience would least expect it. Where public order is expected, Fairey creates small acts of disorder. Where a common decorum is expected, Fairey sows insubordination by pasting posters depicting the wrestler Andre the Giant on random billboards across the US. Underneath the portrait of Andre is the word "OBEY."

Distressed at the way in which people have become inoculated to the propaganda and advertising that pervades public places, Fairey creates posters that playfully subvert the culture of surveillance and advertising. Fairey's posters are nonsense, providing no authority to obey and no means of obedience. Without an obvious motive or product, the posters are designed to awaken questions about public behavior. Obey whom? Obey what? The poster without a meaning is designed to provoke questions of meaning. For the more paranoid among us, the poster also creates an element of danger, piercing the cultural constructions of priority and order.

5. Fairey, "Manifesto."

The posters seem to signal the possibility of an unknown cabal trying to sow revolution, but one cannot be sure. Not knowing the motives of public art can be distressing. That these posters seemingly appear out of nowhere, put up illegally in the middle of the night, only adds to their disruptive force. The posters have little effect when placed in a museum. Without the immediate public context to play off of, the posters lose their power. By hanging the posters in private, they are denatured of their disruptive power. The posters cannot pierce our expectations when we expect to see them hanging on the wall. The setting of the posters matters because the public is where we are most vulnerable, where we are least in control, and where the screams of the world might confront us.

In Matthew's gospel, the Canaanite woman accosts Jesus in public, screaming to him for help. In the parallel story in Mark, the Syro-Phoenician woman meets Jesus in private. Matthew's gospel changes the setting of Mark's original version and places the story of the Canaanite woman in a place where the actions of the Canaanite woman are especially disruptive. As scholars note, the conflict of the story is not simply over Jesus' mission to the Gentiles, but is also a conflict over women's role in culture.[6] The Canaanite woman breaks free of the cultural norms that relegated women's activity to the domestic sphere and makes a public scene by screaming (*ekrazen*) at Jesus for help. "Have mercy on me, Son of David; my daughter is tormented by a demon" (v. 22). The cries of the woman parallel the cries of the two blind Jewish men who pleaded for sight earlier in Matthew's gospel (9:27).[7] The Canaanite woman, calling on "the son of David," uses the theological moniker used by the blind men to make her own plea. Yet, whereas the blind men follow Jesus into a private home, the Canaanite woman's cries remain public. Ignored, the woman persists and the disciples ask Jesus to send her away. Apparently she is too disruptive for the disciples. Finally, she catches up to the group of men and she falls to her knees and pleads for a miracle for her daughter. What a scene. Of course, it is likely no one crowd witnessed this scene. The text describes Jesus withdrawing (15:21) from the crowds and implies that Jesus is seeking a secluded place away from the throng of followers.[8] Still, the secluded place ought not tarnish the courage necessary to speak publically. The fact remains that social norms

---

6. Wainwright, "The Gospel of Matthew," 650–51.

7. Ibid., 651–52.

8. Special thanks to O. Wesley Allen for his conversation about whether categorizing the Canaanite woman's actions as public is as cut and dried as I would like.

are violated by the cries of the woman. Moreover, these cries are magnified by the fact that any passerby might notice the screams. The public spaces of our world are unpredictable and even secluded spaces are dangerous for the street artist intent on disruption.

The fact that Matthew sets this scene in public heightens the desperation and faith of the Canaanite woman who is willing to cross so many boundaries on behalf of her daughter. Moreover, the public scene magnifies the joy that comes when the woman succeeds in crossing the barriers that had been erected to keep her from God's abundant table. This is no secret encounter with plausible deniability for all involved. Instead, a woman appears out of nowhere and accosts Jesus in public. To reset the story in a private setting tempers the risk and the joy that comes from such bold speech. The public cries of the woman add an element of danger to the story while also reaffirming Friedrich Hölderlin's famous line: "But where danger threatens, that which saves from it also grows."[9] The dangerous speech of the Canaanite woman could have resulted in further rebuke and shaming. Word might have traveled back to her suburban home that she sought help from an itinerant rabbi from Galilee. Yet her bold speech results in a healthy child and a new mission. Due to his encounter with this bold woman, Jesus sees his well-ordered public ministry disrupted by the creative vision of an outsider. So influential is the Canaanite woman's vision, that Jesus not only heals the daughter, but immediately after Jesus' interaction with the Canaanite woman, he decides to produce another dramatic public meal for the gathered masses, who are, lo and behold, all Canaanites.[10] Notice that the one who changes Jesus' mind is not one who had access to private conversations with Jesus. The Canaanite woman has to demand access in public because that is the only way to gain an audience. She abandons protocol and decorum because her daughter would be long dead if she waited.

In his constructive chapter in *Homiletical Theology*, David Schnasa Jacobsen wrote that homiletical theology is the task of naming the gospel from a position between Scripture/tradition and experience/culture.[11] Jacobsen goes on to say that homiletical theology is aptly situated to name something new because it is positioned between the stasis of tradition and

---

9. "Wo aber Gefahr ist, Wächst/ Das Rettende auch." Hölderlin, *Poems and Fragments*, 550–51.

10. Gench, *Back to the Well*, 12.

11. Jacobsen, "The Unfinished Task of Homiletical Theology," 46.

the transitory nature of culture.¹² Yet, homiletical theology is not simply situated or positioned between tradition/Scripture and culture/experience; it *speaks* from its mediating position. Homiletical theology is a generative theology that rethinks the tradition in light of the Holy Spirit's in-breaking activity in the present. Homiletical theology is thus the task of locating the *public* presence of the Spirit and publicly proclaiming that presence. Put another way, homiletical theology is the Spirit-inspired imagination that finds creative expression in the preached word. Like the creative proclamation of the Canaanite woman, homiletical theology follows the example of the Spirit whose in-breaking work is likely to disrupt the public order and break apart calcified visions of priority. The Spirit-inspired imagination is therefore not reserved for a select few; it is publicly available to any who would look. The creative expression is not reserved for the one with a PhD or a pulpit but for anyone with the courage to publicly pronounce God's promise of abundance. You don't need a gallery to be an artist; after all, the world is full of blank walls.

Homiletical Theology as Impermanent Creation

In December of 2005, the Los Angeles County Art Museum destroyed its parking garage to make way for a new $60 million contemporary art museum. Such an inauspicious event would have gone unnoticed if it were not for the decision made five years prior by the museum to commission street artists Barry McGee and Margaret Kilgallen to paint the interior walls of the garage. As McGee tells it, the husband and wife tandem painted without premeditation or guidance for about a week before they needed to return north to their home in San Francisco. Not long after that week in the garage, Kilgallen died of cancer at the age of thirty-three. Neither McGee nor Kilgallen imagined that the work would stay up for very long, after all, that's the nature of a medium that uses public spaces as its canvas. While some in the burgeoning street art community raised objections to the demolition of these art pieces, their cries did little to dissuade the LACMA from making space to raise up a new temple of contemporary art.¹³ The walls came down and the paintings were lost. Pictures of these pieces remain

12. Ibid.

13. See Mike Boehm, "There's nowhere else to park this art exhibit," *The Los Angeles Times*, November 12, 2005; and Tyler Green, "LACMA's Choice," *Los Angeles Times*, November 25, 2008.

and a single painting of Kilgallen that was painted on plywood was salvaged before the demolition. In all, the paintings had a life of nearly six years in a poorly lit garage on Wilshire Boulevard. And yet, even in those six years, the paintings inspired unexpected creativity. When McGee was interviewed about the demolition of the garage, he said that when he had occasion to visit these garage pieces, he was pleased to see that someone had stuck a piece of chewed bubblegum on one of his paintings. "It made it that much better," he said.[14]

Street artists renounce their claims of ownership when they choose to make public space their canvas. Any person can add, subtract, or erase. No guard stands watch over their work. McGee recognizes this fact when he says, "I always thought [the LACMA murals were] a temporary thing … that's the nature of the beast," when painting on public spaces.[15] Street artists recognize that the created work has a shelf life. It is created for a particular moment and then released by the artist. The artists absolve their ownership of the work as soon as it is painted on private property that is not their own. When your artistic medium might land you in jail, it is unlikely that you will take responsibility for the art. Like the Canaanite woman who comes and goes without a name, street artists often go by pseudonyms—Banksy, Space Invader, Blek Le Rat. Much of the street art displayed in public places will not live to see the new year. It will be painted over or erased, or in the case of the LACMA, torn down.

The story of a museum destroying the art it commissioned is intriguing because it undermines the notions we bring to museums and the art they house. Museums are called upon to collect, sort, guard, preserve, recondition, and display objects and artifacts, not destroy them. And yet, this has not always been the case. In ancient Rome, the temples of the muses, from which our word "museum" derives, regularly destroyed objects in their collection. The value of temple artifacts was measured by their ability to render visible the invisible world of the gods.[16] Objects were given by artists as offerings to the gods and with a change of possession came a change of relationship to the object. As the gods received the object into worship, the object was imbued with new sacred status. Preventing this object from

---

14. Boehm, "There's nowhere else to park this exhibit," *The Los Angeles Times*, November 12, 2005.

15. Ibid.

16. Pomian, "The Collection," 164.

fulfilling its sacred role was considered an act of sacrilege.[17] Moreover, removing this object from its place within the temple would render the object useless. Its value only made sense within the context of the temple. When the art or object ceased to function as an intermediary it was ritually destroyed. Precious metals were melted down and recast, and less valuable objects were buried. In some cases, to prevent their use in secular environs, objects were intentionally broken.[18] The artists or the viewing public had little proprietary claim to save these objects, because as offerings, the objects formally belonged to the gods.

Noting the provisional nature of liturgical objects, what do we do with the picture painted by the Canaanite woman? When Jesus finally speaks to the Canaanite woman he says something that we wished he hadn't: "It is not fair to take the children's food and throw it to the dogs" (Matt 15:26). The Canaanite woman replies, "Yes, Lord, even the dogs eat the crumbs that fall from the master's table." The Canaanite woman is bold and courageous with her reply. She remains persistent as the only advocate for her afflicted daughter. She absorbs the insult and presses on. With a Spirit-led imagination, she repaints Jesus' exclusive picture to include her and her daughter. The text provides no indication that she sought to expand Jesus' own mission; she seems singularly focused on the welfare of her daughter. That she expanded Jesus' mission is due to the fact that she cared so deeply for her own daughter. Yet, the immediate goal ultimately had far-reaching consequences. As Elizabeth Schüssler Fiorenza notes, "The Syro-Phoenician woman whose adroit argument opened up the future of freedom and wholeness for her daughter has also become the historically still visible advocate of such a future for the Gentiles. She has become the apostolic 'foremother' of all Gentile Christians."[19] While the legacy of the Canaanite woman is rich, it is important to ask whether her repainted picture of the world is worth keeping.

The story of the Canaanite woman is a contentious one among feminist interpreters. While it is true that Canaanite woman bests Jesus in a theological argument and expands Jesus' mission to include Gentiles, she does so at considerable cost. In reflecting upon classroom discussions about the actions of the Canaanite woman, Schüssler Fiorenza notes that

---

17. Ibid.
18. Pliny The Elder, as quoted in Pomian, "The Collection," 165.
19. Fiorenza, *In Memory of Her*, 138.

feminist students disagree about whether this story advocates patriarchal values. Students argue that,

> The woman does not challenge ethnic-religious prejudice of Jesus but confirms it with, "Yes, Lord." She does not argue for equal access; she begs for crumbs. Thus she accepts second-class citizenship which she herself has internalized. She acts like a dog who is grateful even when kicked. Hence it is not surprising that commentators praise her for her humble submission. This is indeed a sacred text that advocates and reinscribes patriarchal power-relations, anti-Jewish prejudices, and women's feminine identity and submissive behavior.[20]

From a post4colonial perspective, Musa Dube expands the critique of the story by discussing the way the story foreshadows future imperial power in the guise of mission. Dube argues that the depiction of the woman as Canaanite is an allusion to those who must be conquered and dispossessed and that the common reading that the woman changes Jesus' mind does not resolve the power dynamics at the end of the story.[21] Dube continues, "That the Canaanite woman is portrayed as accepting the 'dog' social category assigned to her and that her request is granted on these conditions, however, has frightening implications for a narrative that foreshadows the mission."[22] The story seems to imply that future non-Christian followers are not immediately received as equals, but as dogs waiting on the falling crumbs of the master's table. Outsiders are tolerated so long as they know their place and they don't take more than allotted to them. For all of her cleverness and creative imagination, Dube asserts that the Canaanite woman is caught in a narrative that is thoroughly imperialistic and patriarchal. Dube's critiques alert us to the ways in which Matthew's vision of mission, obedience, and healing may be saturated with imperial values and reified structures of priority.

Given these critiques of the story it is natural to ask, does the picture that the Canaanite woman paints hold the same power now that it did when employed in the presence of Jesus? Do the roles present in the picture accurately depict the coming reign of God being initiated by the Holy Spirit right now? Does God's *basilea* include masters, children, and dogs? For centuries, scholars have commended the Canaanite for her humility

20. Fiorenza, *But She Said*, 162.
21. Dube, *Postcolonial Feminist Interpretation of the Bible*, 148.
22. Ibid., 151.

and willingness to assume her role as a dog living on crumbs. "Might we all be so humble to be like the dogs that live off the crumbs," they say. And yet, the power of the story is not the picture that is painted and repainted with masters, children, and dogs, but the willingness to paint over what came before. That she was courageous enough to repaint the master's picture is her gift to us. And, like a street artist, she releases all claim to preservation when she decides to paint over Jesus' picture. When the artistic offering no longer completes the task for which it was created, it is free to be painted over. Like the offerings made to Roman temples, when the object ceased to be make visible the invisible God, then it was free to be melted down and refashioned for new usage.

As homiletical theology seeks to be inspired by the public working of the Holy Spirit, it must hold lightly its foundational theologies. What the Canaanite woman makes clear is that our theologies—even the theology of Jesus—are made up of symbols that are by nature historically conditioned. These symbols attempt to make visible the invisible God and provide order amid the unpredictable in-breaking of the Spirit. As these symbols create identity and fund faith, they begin to cloak themselves in self-evidence and display an air of timelessness. Yet, the fact that these symbols and pictures are historically constructed is proof that they are neither self-evident nor timeless. Moreover, when homiletical theologians are exposed to the new work of the Spirit in history, they are confronted with the possibility that the picture that they have been painting is incomplete and in need of change. The creative inspiration of the Spirit encourages homiletical theologies that remain open and impermanent. To engage in homiletical theology is to expect that our homiletical theologies will eventually be painted over, erased, or torn down. Indeed, to engage in homiletical theology is to also encourage people to add to our theologies. Homiletical theology is an invitation to extend the canvas, to add chewing gum to the street art, to melt down and refashion. Homiletical theology is an invitation to pursue redemption by addition.

Homiletical Theology as Redemption by Addition

In 1993, Nazi graffiti[23] started appearing across Washington, DC. Swastikas and SS lightning bolts were spray-painted in black paint on public build-

23. I make only technical distinction between the words *graffiti* and *street art*, and do not intend to provide some moral distinction between these two terms. I use the

ings. Troubled by the spreading Nazi graffiti and the inaction of authorities to remove it, street artist Josh MacPhee decided to take matters into his own hands. Rather than just painting over the graffiti and creating a brand-new, fresh canvas for more Nazi graffiti, Josh decided to add to the graffiti. As he and his friend Brad looked closer at the SS lightning bolts, they realized that they looked a lot like the "SS" in the band KISS's logo. Armed with this bit of wit, Josh began adding a "KI" to the bolts and then stenciling a picture of the band over the swastika. As Josh tells it, "This way we could cover the Nazi garbage and at the same time create something so absurd that the Nazi vandals wouldn't know what to do! After a couple of nights of work the town was covered with KISS and soon after the Nazi graffiti stopped altogether."[24]

In order to destroy the message of the symbol, Josh MacPhee added to the symbol. Rather than erase the violent power of the SS bolts, MacPhee was able to use them toward new ends. McPhee destroys the symbolic power of the bolts by addition rather than subtraction. It is not in the nature of street artists to erase. Street artists don't carry turpentine in their bags—they carry more paint. Their art is not simply impermanent but also an invitation to addition. When the canvas is as big as the public world, there is no limit to the ways in which other artists might add to a piece. Of course, this new image is now vulnerable to those who disagree with his image. The new redemptive image could easily be changed back to something violent and hateful. This is the risk of pursuing strategies of addition.

When the Canaanite woman confronts Jesus, she comes not with turpentine but with more paint. She claims no power to erase Jesus' picture but attempts to expand the picture. She shows Jesus that the canvas is actually bigger than he originally thought. The picture of a master feeding children is stretched to portray the hungry dogs beneath the table. This addition in turn calls into question the original vision of Jesus. The woman's expanded vision is a bold attempt to redeem the picture of Jesus by adding to it. Jesus' own narrow vision is exposed by the insertion of a few dogs beneath the table. Their presence in the picture seems to jar Jesus into a realization of his own skewed visions of priority and his miserly conception of abundance. The Canaanite provides new perspective by adding to the picture.

---

term *street art* as an inexact umbrella term for all manner of terminal, public art created illegally and sometimes, in the special circumstances, legally. Graffiti is a type of street art that uses spray paint to create an image without the aid of a stencil. In the end, these definitions are bound to break down as the street art world shifts and changes.

24. MacPhee, *Stencil Pirates*, 9.

Homiletical Theology in Action

In *Historical Metaphors and Mythic Realities*, anthropologist Marshall Sahlins argues that while history tends to reproduce itself, seemingly static cultural categories can be functionally redefined with the insertion into culture of new novel phenomena. The presence of new symbols, ideas, and practices requires a reevaluation of previous symbols, actions, and practices.[25] The reproductive forces of culture are brought up short in the face of new experiences, new symbols, and new practices. These novel phenomena disrupt the reproductive forces of culture and force the culture to rearrange its social system to account for something new. The novel phenomena force the social system to make room and change—if only a little—to make room for a new idea, symbol, or practice. Over time and with enough new phenomena, the reproductive force of the system loses its efficiency and become conspicuous in its weakness. Slowly, the reproductive forces of the system lose their determining power and are forced to change. Change, when it comes, comes as a result of addition.

In *The Power to Speak*, theologian Rebecca Chopp encourages those who proclaim God's emancipatory Word to destroy the oppressive discourses of our cultures by adding new signs and symbols to those discourses. Chopp's work makes clear that the discourses of our world are not fixed, but can be altered and changed with the insertion of a new sign. Chopp writes, "Words themselves are fixed neither by their essences nor by their self-referentiality, but by their context, the cultural practices in which they are used, by the interest of the persons using them, and by one sign's relation to another sign."[26] For Chopp, the presence of a new emancipatory sign dislodges the structure from its fixed vantage and promotes greater openness to the current working of God. Christian proclamation resists the tendency of words and discourse to remain static and calls for an openness that allows signs to shift their reference and their effect depending on the situation.

The Canaanite woman adds new signs to a situation in order to dislodge Jesus from his cultural and religious assumptions. To question and resist the hegemonic picture that Jesus has painted would be to take a stance as the "other" and therefore entrench the binary logic that funds Jesus' original picture.[27] Instead, the woman takes the picture Jesus has already painted and uses it toward new ends. Where Jesus claims to care

---

25. Sahlins, *Historical Metaphors and Mythical Realities*.
26. Chopp, *The Power to Speak*, 31.
27. See McClure, *Other-Wise Preaching*, 140.

only about the needy who sit at the table, the Canaanite woman shows the needy underneath the table. While Jesus uses the word *dog* as an insult, the Canaanite woman reframes it as a metaphor for all those in need of mercy. Interestingly, in the end, it is not only the woman who receives redemption. She receives the mercy she sought, but her new picture allows Jesus to redeem his own vision of ministry and mission.

The Canaanite woman is not a social activist, her creative word is not designed to expand Jesus' mission to encompass the Gentiles. She is concerned with the well-being of her daughter, and yet her concern inspires within her a poetic imagination. In this way she stands in the tradition of the prophets who, as Walter Brueggemann puts it, "are not political scientists [or] ethical teachers. They are speakers (not writers) who commit linguistic acts that assault the presumed world of the king, who expose the pretensions of the royal system, and who invite listening Israel to entertain new dimensions of social possibility which they had never before considered."[28] The Canaanite woman imagines a new world that contrasts starkly with the world over which it is laid. This world requires a creative imagination to see that which is not yet, but could be. Moreover, the Canaanite woman doesn't require the world to be wiped clean in order for it to be redeemed. The world can be redeemed from its current place and while in its current configuration.

Homiletical theology is at its heart concerned with the ways in which the creative Spirit-inspired imagination might pursue redemption by addition. Homiletical theology is certainly critical of the signs, symbols, and pictures that aid oppression and subjugation, but its task is not primarily critical, its task is creative. Homiletical theology is the discipline that can help us choose the right addition that might create redemptive and emancipatory moments in the world. It is the discipline that stokes our imagination to see how the oppressive picture in front of us might be altered to create a more emancipatory vision. Of course, our vision of emancipation is buttressed by a theological and moral vision of redemption, freedom, and love. Our visions of what counts as "redemptive" must be subject to critique by those who bear witness to our additions and the Word of God that we hope to proclaim. What we thought was redemptive might need its own covering. In this way, our own redemptive pictures are not simply re-visioning—often times they are repentance. They are another opportunity to make things right. In this way they are like cover-up art.

28. Brueggemann, *The Creative Word*, 52.

In a story I heard recently, an ex-skinhead needed to cover up his offensive tattoos. The white power symbols were a disturbing reminder of his former life and attracted enough violent attention that he feared for his own safety. He went to a cover-up tattoo artist and asked him to turn the symbols into something else. One by one the tattoo artist transformed each symbol into something new. Swastikas became birds. Iron crosses became sailing ships. The tattoo artist couldn't erase anything, he could only add to what was already there, but the addition was enough to transform the symbols and save a life. Homiletical theology is the task of envisioning how to make something new amid the old. It is a Spirit-led imagination that sees the possibility of good news where most only see bad news.

In traditional visual mediums, cover-up art is called *pintemento*. Traditionally, *pintemento* is an instance when an artist painted a new composition over a previous composition. Sometimes, the alteration is minor—a hand or head is slightly moved. Other times whole swaths of the canvas are repainted. Translated literally, *pintemento* means repentance. The *pintemento* is the indication of another chance to make something right. Likewise, homiletical theology encourages painted-over proclamation. This painted-over proclamation is a creative repentance where past wrongs are not totally erased or destroyed, but are transformed by the addition of new redemptive visions. The former picture is still public. The initial picture is never fully erased (if you look closely you can still see its outline) but if you stand back you see a second (third? fourth?) chance to make right what once was wrong. Like the Canaanite woman, homiletical theology produces bold public pictures of God's abundant mercy, and like Jesus, homiletical theology is willing to be changed by the presence of each new Canaanite that dares to paint over its beautifully wrought pictures.

Habeas Corpus: Implications for the Development of Homiletical Theology

The purpose of this chapter is to provide some guiding analogies for thinking about homiletical theory as an action. As I end this chapter, I admit that I have not produced an example (historical or current) of a practicing homiletical theologian in the wild, just analogies for envisioning the preconditions of the field. As I see it, the growing edge of homiletical theology will be the careful observation of those who do homiletical theology as a practice in a particular place. In this essay I am concerned with homiletical theology in action, but I am also concerned with what homiletical theology looks like as a practice. The primary difference being that an action can be observed synchronically and abstractly through the use of analogy, while a practice is situated in a real place and time. Practices are always shifting and changing and thus a diachronic mode of observation is necessary. Discussing homiletical theology as an action can help us define the necessary boundaries of the field. Discussing homiletical theology as a practice will require us to observe how the action of homiletical theology makes meaning in a particular place and time and how that meaning might challenge our initial suspicions about the definitions, terms, and boundaries of the field. Both street art and the retort of the Canaanite woman are responses to a very local context by those who use their bodies in the creation of their response. The creative words and pictures are not born into an abstracted world and neither do they travel well from one context to the next. These creative acts are responses to the surrounding world. Similarly, theology is also a response to the surrounding world. For homiletical theology to avoid definitions untethered from reality it needs to contend with the places in which it is practiced. As Mary McClintock Fulkerson suggests, "Place is a structure of lived corporate, bodied experience and, as such, contests the view from nowhere."[29] It is our places that structure our knowledge and join people with shared experience. Our abstract theological visions are always refracted through the shared experience of the place. This refraction is then focused in our bodies.[30]

In my discussion of homiletical theology above, I have taken cues from the creative imaginations of the Canaanite woman and street artists to describe the central tenets of what I would like to see in the burgeoning field of homiletical theology. These tenets are built largely from my own theological convictions that are, in turn, born from my white, middle-class, cis-gendered, straight body. Conspicuously absent from my description is another person's body, that is, I have not found another practicing homiletical theologian to inform and challenge my vision of the field. I have used the Canaanite woman and street artists to help envision what a practicing homiletical theologian will look like, but that theologian has had no opportunity to answer my description. The time is coming where the field will need to bring forward someone actually doing homiletical theology. The great writ of *Habeus Corpus* applies to our research as much as to our

29. Fulkerson, *Places of Redemption*, 26.
30. Ibid., 31.

laws. As homiletical theology emerges as a field of study it will need to be influenced by practicing bodies. It will not suffice to provide analogies of practice, but the careful examination of actual practices in all of their temporal and spatial messiness will be critical.

Until this point, the discussions surrounding the field of homiletical theology have focused on the conceptual categories that aid in defining the boundaries of the field. These discussions have been largely conducted without a sense of place or body. This is to be expected as the field develops from its nascent forms. Defining the conceptual boundaries of the field and providing guiding definitions will aid in the eventual observation of homiletical theological practices. Moreover, visions of homiletical theological practice can be prescribed (and indeed they should), but they do not exist until they find a body to practice them and redefine them to suit the place. The future of this field will call for sustained observation of homiletical theological practice that critique and redefine our preliminary definitions and categories. I sincerely hope the ideas, definitions, and descriptions of homiletical theology that we envision in this book will eventually be hopelessly obsolete. This book will be a success when the field of homiletical theology regards this modest beginning as an important record of history and a humorous testimony of what we thought way back when. I would like nothing less than to see this work become just a faint outline peeking out beneath a new homiletical theology masterpiece.

—3—

The How of Homiletic Theology

—Teresa Lockhart (Stricklen) Eisenlohr

Homiletics has been in flux for a few decades now. As Western Christendom has been effaced and a new cultural communicative sensorium is emerging with ever-changing technologies,[1] preachers wonder what it is that they're doing as they stand and deliver sermons week in and week out. What we are doing with this discussion of homiletical theology is nothing short of a historical examination of homiletics itself. It may well be the first collective self-conscious attempt to shape the theological discipline called homiletics. The elements of homiletics—theology of preaching, rhetoric, philosophy of language, communication theory, hermeneutics, semiotics, theology, spirituality, psychology, sociology, worship, ritual theory, liturgical theology, performance theory, etc.—are all still present. But the kaleidoscope containing these various pieces is shifting with the times. New patterns within homiletics are emerging, and *homiletical theology* is a term that helps us name homiletics as theology.

My work here has been deemed descriptive[2] homiletical theology because it depicts homiletic theology in action. I define homiletic theol-

---

1. See Ong, *Orality and Literacy*; McLuhan, *Understanding Media*.

2. We need to be careful of the categories we form for any new work, keeping in mind that any category is a heuristic designated to help us see certain things. See Heidegger, *Being and Time*. Heidegger shows how such categories can become concretized architectures that obscure the living quality that all our heuristics are designed to help us see.

ogy, most simply, as the theological discernments that take place during the preparation of any given sermon.[3] It is a *way* of thinking theologically through sermon preparation. As such, homiletic theology is a constructive theological method for preaching. Though thoroughly theological, it differs from academic theologies in that its rhetorical context, audience, and situations are different. Nonetheless, preachers are doing theology when they prepare a sermon. The present essay is a description of homiletic theology in action, drawing upon the phenomenological theological method of Edward Farley[4] because his philosophical assumptions regarding language, revelation, and God are more in keeping with the preachers' calling and the needs of our current culture.

Most simply, this method consists of four movements:

1. *Portraiture.* This is like a brainstorming session where the theologian puts into play the many elements of what may be of God in a kind of collage. This includes what's going on in the church; the liturgy that Sunday; the community; national and global news; Scripture and all its meanings of past and present for the communion of saints; theologies; individual's lives that may be pertinent; stories and analogies; etc.

2. *Ecclesial Universals.* In theology, these are the classical loci (Christology, soteriology, eschatology, pneumatology, revelation, etc.). For preachers, these are the things that "keep coming up" as we look at all of the things that go into the mix of a sermon. The universals that keep emerging can also include those things that may be contrary to what church tradition knows to be of God, since this is called sin, which our proclamations are to counter (see 2 Cor 10:3–5a). This may also consist of similar things being clumped together under a more general category, as well as various theological loci.

3. *Judgment.* Judgment is that moment in the process of sermon preparation where we hold our discoveries up to the light of God's sovereign activity in the world, i.e. God's reign through Christ and the Holy Spirit at work to redeem and bless the world. This touchstone is the eschatological vision of the world and God being in right relationship, as originally intended. This is the gospel that is used as a theological

---

3. Stricklen, "The Way and The Way of Homiletic Theology."

4. Farley, *Ecclesial Man* and *Ecclesial Reflection*. See also Harrington, "The Way to God or God's Way to Us."

The How of Homiletic Theology

norm for the validity of a preacher's findings to test whether or not that which has emerged in earlier steps are of God and worthy of being preached. This is also where preachers need to be aware of their own theologies that shapes their perceptions, as Ron Allen and John McClure recommend,[5] for we are often looking at the portraiture of our notes and reflections through the lens of our own theologies' understandings of traditional theological themes (God, creation, sin, salvation, Christ, Holy Spirit, eschatology, etc.), and these may be too narrow to be useful. Holding our sermons up to the touchstone of God's gospel is also important each time we preach, for, out of a love for our parishioners, it is easy to want to meet people's perceived needs and thereby fail to provide what it is that they really need—God's rule, not theirs.

4. *Rhetorical Shaping*. Sunday comes the same time every week, often with the work of sermon preparation not where we'd like it to be. Once these steps of theological thinking are somewhat finished[6] (or when Sunday morning arrives!), one can begin crafting a sermon in accord with the rhetorical needs of the situation, thinking about how words can help the gospel come alive for this particular people, addressing the things that keep us from hearing and receiving the gospel as good news. (Our sinful proclivities are ever insidiously present even when we long to hear a word from the Lord.) Sometimes this work is being done within the pulpit itself as the preacher departs from the prepared sermon text to follow the Spirit, whose promptings are known by the discipline of attending to the Word day in and day out.

These steps in theological thinking, while progressive, are not as cut-and-dried as one might like. Classical German essay structure notwithstanding, theological thinking is messy; this is not rocket science. Preaching deals with perceptions in complex situations that are not knowable except in fragmentary ways. Moreover, God calls each preacher with her or his own unique ways of perceiving reality. While this method is helpful, it is not a preset form that dictates exactly how sermon preparation will occur. It is a way of doing theology during sermon preparation that can help us discern what it is that God is longing to say through us at this time and this place.

5. Allen, "Preaching as Spark for Discovery in Theology"; McClure and Cooper, *Claiming Theology in the Pulpit*.
6. Moltmann, "Session Two."

Homiletical Theology in Action

Having reviewed the basic process of homiletic theology, let us now picture it in action with one further note. This process depends upon a theology of preaching that explores why we preach at all.[7] I also assume that preachers are people of prayer. All sermon preparation, and thus homiletic theology itself, begins with the preacher's perennial plea: "Lord, help me!" or "Speak! Your servant is listening" or some such cry that continues throughout this process. Homiletic theology is about spiritual discernment, and this requires attention to where the Spirit is at work in all and through all and with all in the world and in our perceptions and interpretations of the Holy One.[8] That being said, homiletic theology proceeds to probe the elements involved in preparing any given sermon.

1. Portraiture

This is the step where the preacher considers everything from a variety of viewpoints, including Scripture, context, parishioners' lives, church life, what's going on in the world, what's happening liturgically that Sunday, and anything else at play in the delivery of that Sunday's sermon. We will look at how Pastor John, who has been the pastor at First Presbyterian Church in Collegeville, USA, for seven years, does homiletic theology. He walks around with this knowledge, sensing its minute changes as a living reality. Although he could easily provide detailed answers to the questions of Appendix A, we do not have the luxury of space to describe all of his embodied knowledge. We will have to content ourselves with certain pertinent details instead.

---

7. Childers, *Purposes of Preaching*.

8. Too many preachers have a spurious pneumatology that is laziness dressed up in theological language: "I just let the Spirit speak when I preach." This is a heretical notion of the Spirit possessing people in ecstatic moments instead of working through the natural forces of the world, as Elijah's showdown with the priests of Baal indicates (1 Kgs 17:21–39). Of course the Holy Spirit is at work (sometimes, yes, in extraordinary inspiration), but it is usually working in all, through all, and with all (Eph 4:4–6). During the Montanist controversy, the church decided that the true spirit of wisdom and knowledge could not deprive us of our intellectual capacities (Basil, *Commentary on Isaiah*, cited in Heschel, *The Prophets*). For further discussion about the difference between the ecstatic communion with the gods and the biblical notions of God's Spirit that gripped the prophets, see ibid.

The How of Homiletic Theology

The Church in Collegeville

First Presbyterian Church of Collegeville is a small-town church in the heart of the Midwest. Corn and soybean fields surround the small town, which is an hour away from a major city. There is a top private liberal arts college there that is the town's primary employer. Consequently, education is highly treasured. Although there is a growing group of working poor in the community, First Presbyterian is predominately white and middle class. The diverse people from across the planet in the town are mostly associated with the college. Recent immigrants to the area do not find First Presbyterian to be a viable church home due to the implicit norms of white privilege. The 7 percent of those who are not white at First Presbyterian are professors and their families. The Presbyterians in Collegeville value family, friends, various entertainments (especially high school and college arts and sports, as well as movies), doing good things for others, and having all the comforts that a media culture tells them that they need.

Those who attend First Presbyterian are, for the most part, highly educated and politically liberal. There is a longtime group of folks associated with local agriculture who regularly get their information about current events from Fox News. This is one of the power-wielding groups in the church, the other being liberal professors from the college, who are staunch supporters of National Public Radio. Both groups are comprised of decent, hardworking people who are genuinely nice. When they see someone in need, they take care of the need efficiently, kindly, and quietly, which is partly why they are currently suffering from compassion fatigue.

Liturgical Context

First Presbyterian likes liturgy with a traditional shape in contemporary language woven around the Scriptures of the day. They value the good old prayers and want some repetition of these, but not too much. The worship service is interlaced with high-quality music of different genres, accompanied by a variety of instruments. They have the new Presbyterian hymnal and enjoy singing. They never applaud in worship, though if the choir leads them, they might clap to music—but not too much. They prize good preaching. The congregation expects a connection between their worship on Sunday and an extension of that worship in how they live their lives to the glory of God at work in the world.

Homiletical Theology in Action

Most of the members at First Presbyterian understand the Bible to be God's Word written by fallible humans. They follow the Revised Common Lectionary because of their commitment to live under the Word of God, but the preacher is free to choose other texts when issues need to be addressed. The congregation has been focusing on the lectionary's texts from the Gospel According to Matthew because three years ago, the congregation did the Old Testament readings.

Homegrown vegetables sit out on the tables in the narthex to the neo-Gothic sanctuary for anyone who'd like them. A huge food basket collects items for the local food bank. On any given summer Sunday around 100 to 125 gather. The preacher looks out mostly on a sea of silver hair with occasional flashes of children's movements. Frazzled parents fight to pay attention, and teens text in the back row, asking where they're supposed to stand during their presentation about the recent mission trip to Honduras during the prayer requests. A good number of college students filter in and out throughout the year.

They enjoy what they have at First Presbyterian—a safe place to explore tough questions, a sense of true fellowship with one another despite some differences, opportunities to worship the Lord and serve in the world. Pastor John loves them, and they love him. For the most part, it is a happy, though perhaps too contented, church.

Communal, National, Global Contexts

National events during the week have no doubt triggered painful communal memories. Robin Williams shocked everyone when he committed suicide. Ferguson, Missouri, erupted in violence when an unarmed African American was shot several times and killed by police. This will trigger the memory of their own case of questionable police action two years ago when an unarmed Latino named Raul Estevez was killed late one night. In his frustration over not being able to be understood due to his broken English, Estevez suddenly flung himself across the counter of a convenience store and grabbed the cigarettes he'd been requesting. As a reflex, the frightened store clerk tripped the alarm to the local police station. Estevez apologized, laughed with the clerk over the misunderstanding, paid for the cigarettes, and walked out. But police had been summoned, and when Estevez failed to halt upon command because he couldn't comprehend that the command could possibly be for him, he was shot in the back. The official autopsy report indicated that the shot literally scared him to death, causing a fatal heart attack. The police officer involved, the brother of one of First Presbyterian's members, devastated by what happened, committed suicide ten weeks later. People still quietly debate whether or not Estevez's autopsy was correct. As a result of this event, First Presbyterian is now a center for intense ecumenical gatherings to talk about race relations.

Gaza's tentative peace agreement smolders in the Middle East. The Islamic State (ISIS) has the world scared with its sudden advance. Russia is poised with convoys on the borders of Ukraine, supposedly with humanitarian aid, but who knows? Ebola outbreaks in Africa loom large on the horizon. In short, life's stability feels a bit tentative right now.

The Biblical Text

Pastor John explores the biblical text read during worship for its literal meanings and what it probably meant to those living at the time of their oral and written compositions (which are often not the same). He examines the original language. At the same time, he makes connections with our world today. He questions the text thoroughly. He prays it, pictures it, enacts it, lives with it, and watches for its unfolding in the world today.

Despite recent events that could call for a departure from the lectionary, Pastor John decides to stick with preaching the lectionary's Gospel text for the day, Matthew 15:21–28, the healing of the Canaanite woman's daughter. Although a troublesome text, it has something that speaks to the situations weighing on everyone's minds. The other lectionary texts (Gen 45:1–15, Ps 133:1–3, Rom 11:1–2a, 29–32) for the day will be read as part of worship, but Pastor John doubts that they will be part of the sermon.

Focusing on Matthew, Pastor John thoroughly explores standard exegetical avenues[9] using good critical commentaries from a variety of perspectives. Because he understands that no one can comprehend a part apart from its whole, he has studied all of Matthew and knows its major themes and movements. Along with other scholars, he thinks Matthew was written about 80–85 CE from a Jewish perspective as Christians struggled with their identity and how they were to deal with Gentiles who wanted to join the way of Christ. In Matthew, Jesus' pre-resurrection ministry was generally constrained to the Israelites, with some notable exceptions,[10] including this one. Only after his resurrection does Jesus commission his church to

---

9. See Appendix B.
10. See also Matt 8:10, 11:20–23, 12:38–42, 14:22–23 but contrasted with 14:34–46.

preach the gospel to all peoples, though Gentile faith bookends the beginning and end of Jesus' life with the magi and professing centurion at the cross.

This passage occurs in a section where people are responding to Jesus' great teaching on the mount and its concomitant deeds of power and mercy. Those in need respond to Jesus' ministry by seeking him out. Those in religious power and authority respond by sending out people to question Jesus. As he continues his healing and teaching ministry, the criticism of the Pharisees increases, as do requests for healing. After the religious authorities again question him, Jesus goes to Tyre and Sidon, ancient Canaanite territory.

The Canaanite woman is praised for her faith, equivalent to that of the friends who lower their paralyzed friend through the roof, the woman with the issue of blood, and the two blind men (9:29). To Matthew, faith is both (1) an acknowledgment of God as Lord and the agent of healing and (2) a humble willingness to do whatever it takes to seek the Lord's favor.

Paying close attention to the actual pericope, the preacher sketches out his exegetical findings on a chart that helps him think along with the text in ways that will be helpful for preaching. He divides the structure of the text into units of meaning down the page. Then across the page, he charts the following for each unit of meaning:[11]

Literal Meanings/ Translation	Theological Affirmation Here	Image	Sin's Roadblocks/ Hearers' Disposition to Theology Here.	Contemporary Analogues—Personal, Ecclesial, Social
	What is being said about life with God in this particular unit of meaning?	What images are in the original language which may lead you to think of other imagery as well?	How do we resist hearing the theological affirmation being made here? And where are folks with regard to this?	What is all of this like in our experience today? These may be images, illustrations, analogies. Cover all the dimensions—don't just go personalist or ecclesial or social. Don't fail to consider using allusions to other Scriptures, too, if they can be highlighted for people.

---

11. See Buttrick, *Homiletic*.

Because of the difficulty in publishing this entire chart, we must content ourselves with a peek at these notes from each section.

Matthew 15:21

Leaving Gennesaret, Jesus *anachōreō* (withdraws, retreats) to Tyre and Sidon, traditionally the land of Canaanites, Israel's enemies.[12] Retreating to recharge, and escape possible danger, is a necessary thing sometimes. But who in their right mind retreats into enemy territory? Does the territory of Israel's ancient enemies seem like a retreat compared to those of his own kind who question Jesus' every move? There are contemporary analogues: there's an upcoming church retreat; should we go to Afghanistan? (Yeah, right!) We're tired of being harassed by life's current conflicts in world, denomination, community, and our homes. Our compassion fatigue leads us to want to withdraw, perhaps permanently, but retreats, while necessary, are temporary.

Matthew 15:22

A Canaanite woman comes out to meet him, shouting: "Lord, Son of David, have mercy! My daughter is being demonized evilly." She seeks Jesus out, not to test him like the good religious authorities, but to receive mercy for her daughter. Like the centurion earlier, she respects his Jewishness and goes out to him so that he need not enter her home and be defiled (cf. Mark 7:24). Her action is shameful: no good woman sought out a man in public. She is assertive, body stretched forward (running?), voice high-pitched, yelling in desperation. She risks all in seeking healing for her daughter from Jesus, whom she, a Gentile, addresses as Lord and "Son of David!" This is better than what he's been called by most Israelites. She recognizes him as the Davidic Messiah. This may just be a rhetorical move on her part—probably a redaction to suit the Gospel writer's intent. We can understand, though, because we've been there in the desperate prayer in the hospital: "Lord, have mercy! Please! You're our only hope, God—for our child on drugs, our friend with cancer, our world rife with violence." She reminds us of the "inappropriate" pushiness of the person who broke into worship one Sunday asking for help for her hungry children, persons who protest

---

12. Davies and Allison, *A Critical and Exegetical Commentary*, 547.

without concern for what others think, or even protestors in Ferguson who are willing to risk jail for their just cause. Presbyterian folks don't know what to do with demons, which are destructive forces that bedevil us—e.g., prejudiced police brutality. Clamoring for divine help with these forces is often done by outsiders who see the destruction up close.

Matthew 15:23a

Jesus is silent. There's no response whatsoever. He passes on by, ignoring her. This is like when our prayers are met with silence. We're like a child clamoring for parent's attention, only to be met with nothing, leading some to just walk away from God saying there is no God or he doesn't care because he should answer us if he does. Look at the Holocaust, all the innocents' suffering. There is a story from a parishioner going through a hard time who said, "I feel like a two-year-old clinging to God's leg, but he's just shaking me off." We think of Jesus' own desperate prayer in the garden and his cry of dereliction from the cross that seems to fall on deaf ears. Utterly alone—it feels like that sometimes in our work as a church for others. Why doesn't God help us in our healing work? Is this what it feels like to the African American community when crying for justice?

Matthew 15:23b

The woman must continue to follow Jesus and cry out. Evidently her persistent clamoring annoys the disciples, leading to their petitioning of Jesus: "Send her away! She's too noisy." Is this an allusion to Shimei clamoring after David (2 Sam 16:5–13, 19:16, 18–23)? Isn't she as valorous as the woman with the judge in Luke 18:1–8? Think of a clamoring ruckus, like protestors in Ferguson some would like to send away because they're bothering the peace. It's unclear whether the disciples want her just sent away or whether they want Jesus to heal her already (as indicated by a form of *apolyō*, which is the word used for unbinding/freeing someone). Either way, Jesus has both groups clamoring after him. All are caught up in the noise of a desire for healing. Isn't this yearning for others' healing God's yearning, too? Faith is a persistent pursuit of God's good will, even when the heavens are silent. If the disciples want the daughter healed/loosed, they are interceding with God on her behalf. More than likely, though, they, like us, want God to take care of such folks who interrupt our lives with their noisy needs so we can proceed unaffected. Our helplessness against such need makes us uncomfortable, as with a pastoral colleague who's been depressed for years and is now mixing booze and depression meds and posting suicidal thoughts on social media. Such persistent clamoring for help leaves us tired although we want them healed, too. We set up whole systems to deal with people whose need we don't want to deal with—social services shell games that keep people away from us yet "healed." But still the cries persist: "God, do something!"

Matthew 15:24

Jesus replies, to the disciples (and the woman?): My mission is clear—"I was sent only to lost sheep of Israel" like the good shepherd of Ezekiel. But this is a cold response, unlike any other. Why? Did Jesus really understand that his mission was only to Israel? A preferential option for Jews. Election. The Matthean community dealing with Jews/Gentile issue at the time of the writing. The Israel/Palestine conflict today. Yahweh is not a tribal god, though—although this would please conservative America, who thinks we need to take care of our own kind: "We've got enough problems in America. We don't need to be traipsing all over the world helping others. We might get Ebola." Ecumenical liberals think God saves all people of all faiths. But Jesus is quite particular here, not universalistic.

Matthew 15:25

The woman hyper-specifies Jesus' particularity: "Lord, help me!" The one right here in front of you is a person, not a category. The clamoring gives way to silence as she kneels before him, calls him "Lord," and places herself in a supplicant and worshiping position (*proskuneō*). This is the power of humility before God. Like Selma marchers kneeling in prayer on the bridge. Even the most jaded among us will strain forward to see what happens next. There's a naked vulnerability in this request that commands respect. It's the most basic prayer there is. Do we, as a church, ever pray this prayer of desperation? Though the woman asks, "Help *me*," it's really a cry for her daughter. Connectedness of all. Like the woman from Bosnia who'd been repeatedly raped during the civil war there crying out with a primal "Kyrie Eleison" at presbytery meeting's worship service, helping us hear the depth of the cry, not just for us as individuals, but for all the suffering of the world. Isn't this God's cry too?

Matthew 15:26

Jesus' response to woman is: "It's not fair to take the children's food and throw it to the dogs." Although possibly the repetition of a traditional prejudiced saying, this is a huge stumbling block for us—Jesus calling this woman a dog when she wants healing for another? Our response: "Oh, Jesus, no you didn't!" What's with this Jesus? Feminists say, "Told you this was a patriarchal religion." Even if it was a play on words (canines, Canaanites), it's harsh, like kicking a puppy. Where's our nice Sunday school, stained-glass Jesus with the sheep on his shoulder? This Jesus is embarrassing, so our tendency is to look the other way when we get to this part of Scripture. The image is of a floor where children eat, which usually has plenty of stuff on it for any dogs to scarf up. These were not our well-groomed puppies, but scruffy, disease-ridden packs of stray dogs. Responses to the images: "I like dogs!" "I'm afraid of dogs." "Eeeww. Dogs are dirty." "What? Doesn't Jesus like cats?" All this clamoring of other voices arises. Is Jesus demonstrating an awareness of human finitude here? We can't feed everyone. Doctors Without Borders and Red Cross workers do have to send some people away, which seems cruel. Many feeding programs deny those who are high or drunk out of a concern to conserve resources for those more deserving. But isn't Jesus the one who just made enough bread for everyone? And will again? This doesn't seem like a test, as some commentators say, just wrong.

Matthew 15:27

The woman works with what Jesus gave her, persisting in her cause with a witty retort: "Yes, Lord, but even the dogs eat crumbs that fall from their master's table." The man has just called her a dog, yet the woman persists! Is her need so great that, like a good mother, she'll do anything to help her daughter? Again, like civil rights protesters of all kinds, including those deemed "feminist bitches." She again calls him Lord and implies that he is her master and that even if she is a dog, she should get some crumbs. This recalls Jacob's *chutzpah*, Moses's and Abraham's pleading. Her God is so large that crumbs are enough for healing. She's willing to accept whatever status he wants to confer on her but unwilling to accept anything less than wholeness for her daughter, like God-for-us. Does she prompt Jesus' divinity out of his being stuck in human finitude? He re-engages in ministry after this encounter instead of continuing his withdrawal. The image is of dogs and children eating together. Today's mamas are happy with this arrangement—no cleaning up to do, but scruffy dogs? No. There's still something disturbing here. We have a hard time with idea that some people are second class. Many would have given up and left, concluding that there couldn't be any help from "those people who think they're better than us." She works with existing reality yet continues to ask God for what's good, which is why we persist in working for shalom for all—healing for baby Paul in our congregation, for example, help for a loved one's mental illness, racial reconciliation though folks call us "do-gooders." Her response is like Ferguson protestors working with the presuppositions of their situation to create protest with hands up, die-ins, and lying in the street the same number of hours Michael Brown's body lay dead in the street. These symbols of abject humility (surrender, death) before the powers that be are enough to start a witty/wise movement for healing. Liturgically: *Dayyenu* liturgy with the response "it would have been enough." Communion liturgy: "we are not worthy so much as to gather the crumbs that fall from your table." Is her acceptance of her position before the Lord more apt than that of Jesus, the disciples, us? She shows us that this is where all humans are—beneath God's table—thus calling Jesus out on Israel's presumed superiority. She calls Jesus' understanding of God up short with her witty reply. Yahweh is Lord of *all*.

Matthew 15:28

Jesus praises her faith and her daughter is healed. Faith is persistence in following the divine desire for wholeness. Does she show the method of how faith works, too—accepting the terms of what is and turning them toward God's aims? In the process, corrective revelation happens. Healing happens. Except for those for whom it doesn't (roadblock). What about those who persist in prayer whose children aren't healed? After all the struggle with God, when you accept the reality and God's sovereignty and your place in it all, when you're willing to accept any crumbs that may fall from God's table, then you're close to the kingdom. As close and as happy as dogs under the Thanksgiving table, even when our prayers are not answered. Analogies: praising the faith of the saints down through the ages—a roll call of faith

Homiletical Theology in Action

(Hebrews), including that of the Ferguson protestors who are praised while those who just want the clamoring commotion to stop are not.

Things are kept open at this point with more insights added over time. The portraiture moment of homiletic theology is important. Most preachers make the mistake of moving too quickly from this stage and just going with "whatever grabs them." However, to lead a congregation faithfully, the preacher needs to be savvy about many things, which is, admittedly, difficult. Under the oppression of time constraints, many don't do this. Many preachers are doing this kind of assessment all the time in their work; they just may not deliberately mark it as a conscious process. Doing homiletic theology well, though, requires such prayerful considerations.

2. Ecclesial Universals

Pastor John turns from the stack of notes he has and begins to note what keeps appearing as important for consideration. Some universals become clear as the exegetical chart is filled in. He takes out a blank piece of paper and jots words or phrases down that keep reappearing. He doesn't think about ordering *these* in any way; he just writes down:

> dogs—not pets but scruffy scrappers, ethnic slur
> Children
> Children's bread—communion? Who's admitted into God's reign
> Enemies/enemy territory
> *****"Lord, help me!"*****
> "Do something, Jesus!" "You're our genie, God, so hop to it!"
> "Get rid of her—nuisance"
> ***Ferguson—civil rights***
> Noise/controversy/commotion
> Voices clamoring
> Tired, compassion fatigue
> Retreat/withdrawal
> Estevez/Michael Brown
> Suicide?
> Jesus' responses: nothing then nasty
> *****Faith persistence, humble submission to God*****
> Don't like/know what to do with this Jesus
> Word play/twist on reality to open up larger horizon

Does she expand Jesus' understanding of kingdom mission with her witty faith?

Pastor John keeps playing with this, making connections and associations. He starts clumping like things together by drawing connections, literally, on his paper, then orders them according to some thread of logic so that he ends up with these clusters:

Compassion fatigue—need so great, can't do everything, "it's all too much"

Retreat/withdrawal

Enemy territory

"Those people," Ferguson protesters, feminists, immigrants, mentally ill

Noise/controversy/commotion—like this week's protests in Ferguson, MO, clamoring for justice for Michael Brown and all who are profiled to death

No response, like prayers that can't get through

"Do something, Jesus! You're the genie God. Get rid of her!"

"Mission doesn't include her kind" Only have so much, have to take care of our own

Lord, help me, the connected me, responsible for others. Not a category, but *me*.

Don't like non-responsive Jesus, yet when this Jesus responds, we'd just as soon he didn't—nasty! "Bitch." Seriously, Jesus? Where's our nice, stained-glass good shepherd Jesus who holds the little lambs?

"Even dogs get scraps under master's table." Her reply surprisingly accepts his terms, working what is, twisting the symbolic world like a kaleidoscope where the same fragments open up to the pattern of another world—the largesse of God's world.

Shows us a picture of faith that persists, wrestling with the Lord with chutzpah.

Other things have slid in, as more will; other things have dropped, and more yet may. Things are deliberately kept loose, arranged and rearranged later in the week after further reflection. However, theological method requires that the things that keep coming up are somehow *ecclesial* universals, part of the pattern of Christian life, not just anything that clamors for our attention. This is why we need judgment.

3. Judgment

Judgment is not about condemning people in our preaching, but about subjecting our thoughts and words to the scrutiny of God's sovereign way. It is important to hold our findings to the light of the "world of the gospel"[13] to see how and whether they are true to God. This requires a conscious theology of preaching and a sense of what the gospel is that we're called to preach, two subjects that each deserve their own books, beyond the scope of this paper.

Judgment is that moment in homiletic theology when Pastor John steps back to ask the big question about what it is that God wants to say through his preaching at this time in this place. This means that he sees this particular sermon as part of his overall calling as a preacher to (1) paint a vision of what God's realm is like and (2) encourage people to live more in accord with this reality than sin's illusions.

When he looks back over his most recently derived list, he notes that ten of the twelve items are quite negative. This does not bode well and may have more to do with his own need for a vacation than anything else. Yet the Scripture itself is rather dark. Jesus' prejudice is seen in a harsh light. The disciples and Jesus react negatively to the woman. The woman's need is certainly not happy. What receives the focus in the story is that one popularly thought of as a dog is commended for her faith. At this point, Pastor John thinks Jesus' harsh words are sarcastic to highlight the prejudices his ministry challenges. This is when Pastor John perceives a Word from the Lord for his people as he thinks about their prejudices that keep those in need at bay. Because of his belief that Christ meets us where we are in order to take us to where he is, Pastor John wants to honor where the church is at the moment by articulating the world's needs that feel so overwhelming that they want to scale back, while also helping them grow into a larger view of God's grace, as the Canaanite woman does with Jesus.

4. Rhetorical Shaping

Even as we shape sermons using the best communicative techniques at our disposal, we do so thinking theologically as the spiritual guides of our flock. Keeping in mind that preaching aims toward the promised land of God's reign (the omega point and reason why we preach at all) while only being

---

13. Farley, *Practicing Gospel*, 71–92.

able to get people to take one step further into that sovereignty (point B) with each sermon, it has to start where people are (point A) in order to gain a hearing and walk with them through the challenging spiritual landscape. It's not easy to give up our death-dealing ways in a death-dealing culture. We need help from a guide who understands the territory and can tell us that the losses and arduous journey is worth its hardships. This is where the preacher is like a wagon train leader or spiritual Sherpa. The preacher executes this task by blazing a rhetorical pathway of words so that her hearers can get from where they are at point A in any given time and place to point B, one step deeper into the territory of divine rule.

Point A: Where People Are at the Moment. Pastor John sees that his people are struggling with compassion fatigue and discouragement. They've been working on racial reconciliation for two years, and the news from Ferguson has left them sad. Robin Williams's suicide on top of that has triggered tragic memories of the death of Estevez and the suicide of the policeman who shot him. This is a tender spot that needs acknowledged. At the same time, Pastor John feels called to slyly uncover latent prejudices that keep others from the table of God's grace. This is his sermon's Point A.

Point B: Where This Sermon Is Going. In this particular sermon, the pastor knows that his Point B is showing the obdurate persistence of faith for the Lord's more expansive healing of others. Getting there will entail turning the tables on our prejudices through wily wit, similar to how the meaning of the Scriptures unfolds.

Highlights along the Way from Point A to Point B. Pastor John marks some items on his ecclesial universals list that he needs to note during his sermon. He circles the word *clamoring* and wonders how he can make the sermon clamor with cries of the world's needs. He also considers how he can uncover latent prejudices that keep "those people" at bay only to find that they teach us about God in a way that exceeds our "superior" presuppositions. He realizes that Jesus' response to the woman is such a huge roadblock that he has to address it. And he has to do all this in fifteen minutes in a sanctuary that may be hot, depending upon the weather, because the air conditioner doesn't work well when it gets over eighty-five degrees on Friday and Saturday. Knowing that it takes at least two-and-a-half to three-and-a-half minutes to form just one concept in people's minds, he realizes that he has to do all of this in four moves, perhaps five if the language is tight and well-focused.

Sketching Options. At this point, Pastor John starts sketching some move options, using just one focused idea for each move to get the logical flow of the sermon possibilities in order to discern how best to proceed.

Option 1:

1. The sermon begins with a clamoring of all the world's desperate needs—people like the distant woman who beg for our prayers on Facebook, West Africans watching their loved ones dying of Ebola, brothers and sisters clamoring for justice in the Ukraine, in Ferguson, here in Collegeville as we still struggle with our own Ferguson with Raul Estevez and the suicide of Officer Scott Jessup. "With all the world's needs vying for our attention, no wonder we're tired. We're all compassioned out."

2. Jesus understands. He's retreating from all the clamor of controversy. Perhaps he's withdrawing because he's sick of all the taken-for-granted prejudices he's encountered: Israel's exclusivity with regard to God's grace and their presumed superior status over lesser people like Canaanites—prejudices he satirizes by repeating in this particular situation to highlight how awful they are.

3. Still, let's be honest. There are times when the Lord doesn't respond or when he seems downright nasty. Story of woman in bad time: "Feel like holding onto God like a two-year-old clinging to her mother's legs, but it feels like God's just trying to kick me off." Not everyone petitioning the Lord gets healed.

4. Regardless, faith persists. Like the Canaanite woman who uses the logical and metaphorical power of what is given to turn and extrapolate it to reveal new truth, Ferguson protestors around the US stage die-ins. Illustration of Sudanese visitor to a church who'd initially been snubbed only to persist in attending even when he overheard someone talk about the "ignorant heathen murderer." He became an elder, and showed Sudanese hospitality at a fellowship dinner, choosing the one he'd overheard malign him to demonstrate how Sudanese Christians welcome one another with honor.

5. Conclusion: Now hear the sarcasm drain from Jesus' voice to commend faith's persistence around the world, extending to even us in our compassion fatigue.

Option 2:

1. The introduction of the sermon charges the elephant in the room by addressing the congregation's compassion fatigue, dismay over national and international events, and the fear that events in Ferguson will cause old wounds to bleed.
2. Jesus understands, for he was in retreat mode, wearied from religious controversy and the press of human need.
3. Then a Canaanite woman explodes onto the scene, hounding us with cries for healing. Can you hear her crying in West Africa, the Ukraine, Nigeria, Ferguson, here in this sanctuary?
4. No wonder the disciples just want the clamoring to stop. It's all too much, isn't it? They just want Jesus to stay on task—with Israel.
5. But the pleas for help quiet as the woman kneels before Jesus, "Lord, help me." Not a category, but me. Three little vignettes of personal stories about discrimination each ending with the refrain, "Help me."
6. But Jesus does the unthinkable. He calls the woman a dog, which outrages us. If this is Jesus, no wonder people are leaving the church. He's only a savior for his own kind, an elitist savior. He's racist, and misogynist. Had we been the woman there, we'd have huffed off, outraged.
7. But the Canaanite woman persists, for she knows her cause is God's will, and she's not going to give up. She takes what the Lord says and twists the metaphor to reveal the largesse of a God whose grace is so large than even a spare morsel can heal like the medical personnel fighting Ebola, like protestors of what happened to Michael Brown staging die-ins, and like those who persist in tedious committee meetings for racial reconciliation in our own fellowship hall.
8. What's Jesus' response? Here's faith, disciples. Not the prejudices of what our people think—i.e., that faith comes only through Israel, that Canaanites are dogs. No, God doesn't profile anyone. As this woman knows, God's grace is so much bigger than that of just one people.

That's why we're called to welcome all people as children of God, including immigrants who come here seeking a place at the table just like us.

Option 3

1. Listen to the cries of the Canaanite woman in all the needs around the world clamoring for our attention.
2. No wonder we're tired and want to retreat.
3. Jesus understands, for he was in retreat mode, wearied from religious controversy and the press of human need.
4. But still the pleas come: "Lord, help *me*." Not a category, but me.
5. Then comes Jesus' startling response. It's hard to imagine that Jesus could possibly tell a desperate mother that his mission doesn't include her, a dog. Who is this Jesus and what's he doing? Dealing with the prejudices of his people.
6. Here's what real faith looks like—a humble Canaanite woman, not Israel's presumed privilege.

Pastor John sketched out another option that begins by addressing the troublesome picture of Jesus, but he abandoned this approach because it would only end up being a sermon that talks about Christology. Instead of proclaiming the gospel and encouraging faithful living, it would be more like a lecture, which is not in accord with what God is longing to do with this sermon on this day. It may be appropriate to preach such a sermon at certain times, but this isn't one of them. He also had some other aborted possibilities unworthy of mention.

Option two is too long for a hot August day—not a theological criterion, but a crucial rhetorical one. Options one and three are similar, though option one draws focus to us a bit too much. Option three seems more in keeping with kingdom norms, so he proceeds with Option three, adjusting and filling in the outline by stealing from other optional approaches, then composing the sermon with his best linguistic skills in oral language.

Of course, the sermon could take many shapes. This is the beauty of the incarnation: God meets us where we are here and now to help us take one step further into deeper kingdom living. Thus our preaching seeks to do the same. With a prayer on his lips, then, Pastor John goes to worship to preach, continuing to engage in homiletic theology as he responds to the Spirit's movements by making necessary last-minute adjustments, even as he preaches, letting the offering of his words go to work as the Word sees fit.

Homiletic theology, or thinking theologically through the task of sermon preparation, helps a preacher wrestle with the living Word of God on behalf of her people. It is an awesome responsibility to dare to preach what we think God is longing to say to the world, and it is one we dare not shirk, for whether they know it or not, people are asking us if there is any Word from the Lord. If all they get is some nice person's reflections about life, they can often find better ones elsewhere. But if, in all our honest human frailty, we dare to plumb the depths of human existence before God in Christ, and, in the power of the Holy Spirit, stand to say in trembling voice, "Hear the Word of the Lord!" we may find that people will indeed do just that. And bit by bit, week by week, God's rule will emerge more clearly from out of the chaotic fog of our human endeavors with glimmers of transformative grace. And that, we believe, will be enough—no, more than enough—to help the Lord do the work of redeeming and repairing this broken world.

A Final Word: Homiletic and/or Homiletical Theology

Here endeth my sparse (yes, sparse!) description of homiletic theology in action. Where does this leave our struggle to define homiletical theology? At this point, I see two basic understandings of the term emerging—one that is a broader theological reflection on some aspect of homiletics and another that is more specific to designate the act of thinking theologically through the act of preparing a sermon. This is why I continue to use the term *homiletic theology* to designate the more specific theology done during sermon preparation. Though distinct, homiletic and homiletical theology are correlative. The specific task of sermon preparation gives rise to broader theological questions that homiletical theology tackles, which, in turn, feeds into how we do sermon preparation. These broader theologies are important, for each homiletic theologian works out of certain theological assumptions which affect the decisions we make when we preach. There is thus a dynamic flow between homiletical theology and homiletic theology, like cake batter in a mixing bowl is brought down into its central task then sent back out to the broader reaches only to be drawn back in again. Homiletic theology, while constructive in nature, is not just constructive theology. It partakes of all different types of theologies in order to use what is best in any given context to preach the gospel. In this way, the preacher is not just preaching her own theology (an idol if ever there were one!), but drawing from various theological configurations throughout the church's history to do what it is that all our theologies attempt to do—talk about God in such a way that others might come to know the ineffable mystery of God's grace in Jesus Christ through the Holy Spirit.

Section II: Homiletical Theology in the Confessional Mode

—4—

Nobody Knows the Trouble I See

A Spirit(ual) Approach to the Interpretive Task of Homiletical Theology

—Luke A. Powery

Introduction: Toward Homiletical Theology in a Confessional Mode

There is no such thing as disinterested or unbiased theology. This essay is no different in that Christian theological discourse, including what is to follow, is a matter of "faithful persuasion."[1] As such, whether made explicit or not, theology, and more specifically homiletical theology, is discursive confession. I, therefore, must confess that this essay approaches homiletical theology in a confessional mode.

There are various types of homiletical theological methods, but the following essay will reveal a confessional approach in that it pushes back on the notion of Scripture as a kind of starting point for theological method. It does not erase Scripture from participation in the method but it does not give it precedence over the Spirit and human bodies. *Sola scriptura* is

---

1. Cunningham, *Faithful Persuasion*.

Homiletical Theology in Action

insufficient when located in a protected and sanctified theological silo that disregards the real messiness and mystery of human life and biblical interpretation in the Spirit. With this in mind, my confessional starting point attempts to reimagine what homiletical-theological method might be when it starts with the spirit(ual) as an embodied, cultural, and particular expression of interpretation for the task of homiletical theology.

"In the beginning" of creation, the spirit of God swept over the face of the waters (Gen 1). There was God and God's Word. The earth was a formless void and darkness was present. Nowhere does the writer of Genesis speak of the presence of a literary text, thus what we call "the Bible" was nowhere to be found. Yet, what is interesting to observe as it relates to the field of homiletics—its theory, theology, and practice—is the privileging of the Bible. The Bible prevails, perhaps even over human bodies, in homiletics. A quick glance of literature in homiletics will reveal that the Bible rules the day traditionally. This is not to say that biblical texts are not important for the interpretive task of homiletical theology. But it is to assert that interpretation in homiletics encompasses more than the Bible or texts. Scholars indicate this when discussing the various ideas surrounding exegesis as it relates to preaching—exegesis of the text, exegesis of the congregation or context,[2] exegesis of the self,[3] and even exegesis of God. These forms of exegesis are necessary in homiletical interpretation, but one of these, "exegesis of the text," makes headline homiletical news historically. This would seem to suggest that all one *really* needs to proclaim the gospel is a Bible.

The irony of this is that even the term *homiletical theology* leads one to think about "God talk" more broadly, which may or may not include the Bible. To engage in "God talk" means to discuss God, who was before, is beyond, and will be forever after the sacred text called "the Bible." "Homiletical theology" also means that preaching does theological work in all of its varied tasks, including engagement with the Holy Spirit and not solely the Bible.

God the Spirit was in the beginning, before texts, and although she seems to be on the borderlands of homiletical theology in contemporary discourse, this essay is an attempt to bring the spirit(ual) to the foreground in a conversation about the interpretive task of homiletical theology and explore what that means for biblical interpretation in preaching. Though I am at times wary of the heavy-handed use of the Bible in homiletics, a

---

2. See Tisdale, *Preaching as Local Theology and Folk Art*.
3. Farris, *Preaching That Matters*.

spirit(ual) approach to interpretation still includes the Bible for preaching; however, it will become clear that it is much more than the Sunday school song indicates—"the B.I.B.L.E., yes that's the book for me, I stand alone on the Word of God, the B.I.B.L.E.!"

To foster a conversation, I will first discuss what I mean by "spirit(ual)" in this particular essay as an entry point to exploring other themes in relation to "the spirit(ual)" and homiletical interpretation: bodies and the Bible; contextual community; fluid interpretive performance; phenomenology of interpretation; and the end of interpretation. I will conclude with some reflections on implications for the development of homiletical theology. I hope to spark a pneumatological dialogue through this suggestive essay by the articulation of how a spirit(ual) approach may impact the interpretive task of homiletical theology; it is by no means exhaustive in nature but is more of an intellectually musing gesture toward interpretive possibilities within homiletical theology. Through this exploration, it should become apparent that though there is a relationship to the Bible for the practice of homiletical interpretation, the Bible is not God, thus bibliolatry in the interpretive task of homiletical theology can and must be avoided as spirit(ual) interpretation is *extra Biblia*. The Bible is taken seriously but not necessarily literally.

Meaning of Spirit(ual)

There has been an ongoing "spiritual turn" in homiletical literature with works on spirituality and pneumatology in more recent years even as spiritual formation becomes more popular in theological education. For the purpose of this essay, I continue an intellectual exploration of the theme of spirit for homiletics, which is my own homiletical scholarly bias. A spirit(ual) approach to interpretation suggests the prioritization of the spirit(ual) as a lens to explore the topic; this coincides with the notion that the spirit was present at the genesis of creation whereas the Bible was not. For this paper, spirit(ual) has a twofold meaning. First, it refers to the Spirit of God or the Holy Spirit, the third person of the Trinity. To be spiritual refers to how one lives or walks in the Spirit every day and in a community (1 Corinthians). The Spirit is the *fons vitae*, thus without the Spirit, there can be no life, including no life in our interpretations. The Spirit is the presence and power of God thus essential for the interpretive task of homiletical theology, especially if we follow the teaching of the Apostle Paul (1 Cor

2:1–16); there can be no understanding or revelation through our practices of interpretation if the Spirit is not at work. A spirit(ual) approach keeps all of this in mind and places the homiletical theological priority on the Spirit.

The second meaning of "spiritual" at work in this essay involves the cultural musical genre known as spirituals. I have made the case elsewhere[4] that these songs are not only expressions of the Holy Spirit but are musical sermons that preach, thus doing interpretive homiletical work as well. I will not reiterate those arguments here but only present what an ex-slave said: "they calls 'em spirituals, case de Holy Spirit done revealed 'em to 'em."[5] Thus, these spirituals represent the Holy Spirit at work and homiletical theology in action. The spirituals will provide a concrete example of a spirit(ual) approach to homiletical interpretation throughout this essay.

The Spirit(ual), Bodies, and The Bible

Through a spirit(ual) lens for interpretation, the Spirit takes priority but this also implies that human beings do, too. In particular, bodies are important. The wind, breath, or spirit (*ruach*) hovered over the waters at creation, thus breath is a beginning point for all human action. To emphasize this shifts attention to the breath of God, the same breath flowing through human bodies. This means that the interpretive task of homiletical theology begins with the human person, body, and voice, not a Bible passage. The Bible is secondary to the human being in relation to interpretation. The spirituals demonstrate this in their performance because even when attempts were made to silence the enslaved, perhaps even through Bible verses, the homiletical body was used to "swing"[6] and sway as a form of resistance to oppression. Melva Costen highlights the somatic sensibility of the spirituals when she writes, "'silent songs' were expressed in kinesthetic movements and rhythms."[7] Slavery, upheld even by Christians, tried to control the black body, but the spirit(ual) would not allow that to happen. Some body had to interpret, suggesting that homiletical theology is body talk.

In addition, a discussion about pneumatology implies embodiment or materiality. The incarnation provides an example of this, since the Spirit is the agent of the incarnation of God in Jesus Christ. When God wanted to

---

4. Powery, *Dem Dry Bones*.
5. Callahan, *The Talking Book*, 61.
6. Johnson and Johnson, *The Books of American Negro Spirituals*, 28–38.
7. Costen, *In Spirit and In Truth*, 131.

demonstrate love, God became a body, implying the embrace of the body for the spirit(ual) life and a spirit(ual) approach to interpretation. Although there is a theological rationale for the inclusion and primacy of the body in homiletics, through the influence of Western philosophical traditions the body has been viewed historically with suspicion, which is why biblical texts were used to terrorize human bodies during slavery. This pneumatic and somatic connection is important because it reminds preachers that their calling is not to solely reiterate a text of the Bible without any attention to real human bodies and context. As Jana Childers notes, "without bodies, preaching is not worth talking about."[8] A spirit(ual) approach keeps us honest about embodiment in preaching and the fact that without bodies, preaching would be impossible. There must be some body to interpret and preach a gospel.

This is not to demonize sacred Scripture or to suggest that we cease conversing with the Bible for the purpose of preaching. That would be an unnecessary absurdity, especially in light of the fact that the Bible is considered to be an important source for the spirituals, so important that some have called the spirituals a "third testament." A spirit(ual) approach does not obliterate the Bible but it does not worship it either. It aims to avoid scriptocentrism because the Spirit is before and beyond it. Spirit(ual) preaching utilizes the Bible but is not confined to it. A glimpse of some titles of spirituals reveals the biblical linkage: "Joshua Fit the Battle of Jericho," "Go Down, Moses," "We are Climbing Jacob's Ladder," "Ezekiel Saw De Wheel," "Calvary." As one person notes, there is a "deep biblicism"[9] in the spirituals. A spirit(ual) approach to homiletical interpretation stays close to *and* keeps a distance from the Bible.

Yet, a spirit(ual) approach still possesses a hermeneutics of trust as revealed by this spiritual:

> Holy Bible, Holy Bible,
> Holy Bible, book divine, book divine—
> Before I'd be a slave, I'd be buried in my grave,
> And go home to my Father and be saved.[10]

The Bible was considered to be a holy book during slavery while simultaneously for slave preachers the biblical "text served mainly as a starting point

---

8. Childers, "The Preacher's Body," 224.
9. Walker, *Somebody's Calling My Name*," 52–54.
10. Lovell, *Black Song*, 263.

and often had no relation to the development of the sermon. Nor would the old-time preacher balk at any text within the lids of the Bible."[11] There was closeness and distance. In *God's Trombones*, James Weldon Johnson notes how a preacher "closed the Bible" and then proceeded to preach. Johnson writes, "after reading a rather cryptic passage [he] took off his spectacles, closed the Bible with a bang and by way of a preface said, 'Brothers and sisters, this morning—I intend to explain the unexplainable—find out the undefinable—ponder over the imponderable—and unscrew the inscrutable.'"[12] The preacher begins with the Bible but closes the Bible when he begins to preach. A spirit(ual) lens asserts that the Bible is important for preaching, but even more so are human bodies.

This interpretive angle rises from the notion that there was breath, dust, and human flesh before the Bible. Even the gospel was before the Bible,[13] the gospel embodied in Jesus Christ. Before decisions were made to form a canon, the gospel was being preached by human beings to human beings. Just as Jesus Christ, the anointed one, is not trapped in the pages of Scripture, the gospel message always requires more than articulating the Bible or any text. The gospel is more than the Bible thus not synonymous with it. A spirit(ual) approach to interpretation reveals that one could preach a text and never preach the gospel. The Bible may be included in proclaiming the gospel and helpful in doing so, but to reach the gospel through the interpretive task of homiletical theology requires moving beyond the Bible many times.

The spirit(ual) is so much more than text. As one scholar notes, "[T]he Spirit does speak and has more to say than just Scripture. . . . The voice of the Spirit cannot be reduced to simple recitation of Scripture, nonetheless it will be connected to and concerned with Scripture."[14] Through this spirit(ual) perspective, the Spirit helps integrate the biblical text with context such that the gospel can be proclaimed in any given situation. The gospel can only be heard when it hits the ground in real life in order to be received as *pro nobis*. It is not just *pro me*, "for me," but is necessarily for a community.

---

11. Johnson, *God's Trombones*, 4.
12. Ibid., 4–5.
13. See Farley, *Practicing Gospel*, 71–82.
14. Archer, *A Pentecostal Hermeneutic for the Twenty-First Century*, 182–83.

Nobody Knows the Trouble I See

The Spirit(ual) and Community in Context

In the context of the spirit(ual), the gospel and any interpretation of it, is for "the folk." A spirit(ual) approach includes individuals and communities, all of whom are a part of one body. Both, a la Paul, are temples of the Holy Spirit (1 Cor 3 and 6), thus a spirit(ual) approach to interpretation for homiletics should be mindful of individuals and communities. To be spirit(ual) means attachment to, not escape from community. Also, the spirituals are folk music, music by the folk for the folk. They are a community's musical sermons created by unknown ones within the community. We do not know the author or the exact time or place of the spirituals' origins, which accentuates the communal ideal for interpretation. In this mind-set, interpretation is not an individual affair; it is corporate. This is the nature of folk music that grows out of a people's needs.

A spirit(ual) approach means that interpretation in homiletical theology occurs with others in mind. John Lovell, in his classic book, *Black Song*, affirms this idea when he writes of how folk music reflects communal feelings and tastes and that "its creation is never completed; 'at every moment in history, it exists not in one form but in many.'" He states further, "There is no original in traditional art; no virtue in the 'earliest known version.' Later versions are developments, not corruptions."[15] What he speaks of was evident in the civil rights movement of the 1960s in the United States. He points to not only the communal lens of the spirit(ual) but the ongoing nature of development of the Spirituals and its fluid nature, of which I will say more in the next section. At this juncture, it is critical to note that the spirit(ual) makes interpretation a communal enterprise across time.[16] Culturally, this has been called an "ethics of antiphony" by Paul Gilroy in his work on the black Atlantic.[17]

The spirit(ual) works within a community and this community is rooted in particular situations and contexts over time and space. If the Spirituals are by the folk for the folk, then a spirit(ual) approach to interpretation pays attention to the needs of the community from which they arise. Interpretation does not happen in a vacuum but is textured and touched by the realities of the collective body. This means that before approaching any biblical text to interpret it, one reads the human community and

---

15. Lovell, *Black Song*, 13.
16. Fee, *Listening to the Spirit in the Text*, 15.
17. Gilroy, *The Black Atlantic*, 200.

Homiletical Theology in Action

its needs. After this communal reading, one reads the Bible with the eyes of the community. James Cone affirms this by writing, "black preachers have never been enslaved to the words of scripture. The texts of the Bible served as starting points for an interpretation consistent with existence of the folk."[18] The pressing realities of the folk is central for the interpretive task of homiletical theology through the spirit(ual) lens.

This "folk gaze" leads Brian Blount, drawing on Rudolf Bultmann, to stress the preunderstanding of readers as influential to interpretation. He writes, "We cannot establish this preunderstanding by looking at the text of the spirituals, because the texts give mixed signals.... We must instead look at the people themselves."[19] Reading the folk takes precedence over reading the Bible because it is the people who are alive with needs in the present moment. A spirit(ual) sensitivity requires a contextual sensibility such that what is proclaimed is for a particular people at a particular time and place who hopefully can receive the word in their "own native language" (Acts 2). Attention to the community in the interpretative task affirms the Spirit's work of translation such that a people can truly understand within their historical setting. As Blount writes:

> The interpretive move is from experience to biblical image, not the other way around. The slaves' critical starting point is their historical human circumstance. The biblical images become a means of understanding and enduring the pivotal reality that is their present moment.... Their key intent is not so much to understand the Bible as it is to understand their historical circumstance. The Bible becomes an interpretative means rather than an interpretive end.[20]

The aim of a spirit(ual) interpretation is to handle the biblical text in a manner that aids the context, not the other way around. The Bible does not need saving; people do. Whether in sorrow and suffering, as experienced by the enslaved who created the spirituals, or in ecstatic joy, spirit(ual) interpretation tunes its ears and heart to what the community needs in real time. What is in front of the text with its associated needs is primary. The *Sitz im Leben* of the folk in conjunction with that of the Bible converge on the interpretive highway of the spirit(ual) such that this approach parallels midrashim.[21]

18. Cone, *The Spirituals and the Blues*, 37.
19. Blount, *Cultural Interpretation*, 61.
20. Ibid., 56.
21. See Troeger, *Wonder Reborn*, 32.

One classic example of keeping in mind the needs of the community is the spiritual "There is a Balm in Gilead," which interrogates the prophet Jeremiah's question, "Is there no balm in Gilead? Is there no physician there?"(Jer 8:18–22). In this particular interpretative scenario, the Bible raises a question but the spiritual interpreter/preacher answers it for the community in need. The Bible does not have the final say but the homiletical interpreter fashions the biblical text in such a way to provide hope and healing for the folk. Jeremiah was joyless and heartsick in the biblical context but rather than read that biblical setting in such a way as to proclaim lament, the spirit(ual) approach discerns the need for hope in a dehumanizing setting and straightens "the question mark in Jeremiah's sentence into an exclamation point: 'There *is* a balm in Gilead!'"[22] Because the Bible itself and a mere repetition of its words are insufficient to preach the gospel, the homiletical interpreter in this case asserts, "There is a balm in Gilead to make the wounded whole/There is a balm in Gilead to heal the sin-sick soul." The folk needed to know that healing was possible and a spirit(ual) approach to homiletical interpretation understands the importance of humanity over against bibliolatry. The Bible is taken seriously even as the spiritual utilized the biblical imagery of balm, yet it was not interpreted literally. This context-sensitive interpretation gestures toward the overall fluidity of a spirit(ual) lens for interpretation.

The Spirit(ual) and Fluid Interpretive Performance

The interpretive framework of the spirit(ual), as discussed above, reveals an emphasis on the human, whether it be individual bodies or the needs of the folk community, without the total negation of the Bible. In what follows, I will explore this spirit(ual) approach of interpretation in further detail by revealing its nature in homiletical action. The Gospel writer John says, "The wind blows where it chooses, and you hear the sound of it, but you do not know where it comes from or where it goes." (John 3). Wind is spirit in this biblical setting and points to the movement and freedom of the spirit(ual) in its interpretive approach.

It is important to note that when talking about the spirit(ual) I am referring to something that moves and performs through material means like bodies. A spiritual performs a biblical text through voices and bodies in community as an interpretive act. "Performance" literally means "form

22. Thurman, *Deep River and the Negro Speaks of Life and Death*, 15.

coming through." Thus, when a spiritual is sung it is embodying the form of a particular biblical text. Traditionally, literary criticism or historical criticism rules the day in biblical interpretation; however, the Spirituals represent what is called performance criticism, that is, how a text is performed is an interpretation of that text. More than words, a spiritual is body and music, somatic and sonic. It is an oral-aural interpretive performance.

In one account James Weldon Johnson writes about an experience in a preaching moment that depicts the eventfulness of a homiletical interpretive performance.

> [The preacher] appeared to be a bit self-conscious, perhaps impressed by the presence of the "distinguished visitor" on the platform, and started in to preach a formal sermon from a formal text. The congregation sat apathetic and dozing. He sensed that he was losing his audience and his opportunity. Suddenly he closed the Bible, stepped out from behind the pulpit and began to preach. He started intoning the old-folk sermon that begins with the creation of the world and ends in Judgment Day. He was at once a changed man, free, at ease and masterful. The change in the congregation was instantaneous. An electric current ran through the crowd. It was in a moment alive and quivering; and all the while the preacher held it in the palm of his hand. He was wonderful in the way he employed his conscious and unconscious art. He strode the pulpit up and down in what was actually a very rhythmic dance, and he brought into play the full gamut of his wonderful voice, a voice—what shall I say? not of an organ or a trumpet, but rather of a trombone, the instrument possessing above all others the power to express the wide and varied range of emotions encompassed by the human voice—and with greater amplitude. He intoned, he moaned, he pleaded—he blared, he crashed, he thundered. I sat fascinated; and more, I was perhaps against my will, deeply moved; the emotional effect upon me was irresistible.[23]

Johnson captures the musical performance of a homiletical event between a preacher and congregation. The preacher starts with the Bible but then closes it while his preaching moves into a heightened realm of orality and embodiment. In that moment, there is the fluidity of electricity within the community. We do not know what the biblical text was but the performative moment interprets the word for the people. His intoning, freedom of expression, rhythmic movement, "the full gamut" of his trombone-like

---

23. Johnson, *God's Trombones*, 6–7.

voice and the congregation's "quivering" represent an interpretation of the Bible and current situation in that historical moment. For them, the sermon performance *is* the spirit(ual) meaning in that time and place.

The meaning comes not only through words or lyrics but through sounds—pitch, rhythm, pace, phrasing, volume—and the "participant proclamation"[24] of the community. How the word is performed is the interpretation and the spirit(ual) nudges us in this direction. There is distance from the Bible as in the previous account but that is the nature of a spirit(ual) approach as noted earlier. This distance opens up to a fluid and free hermeneutical stance. The distance is there not only because spirit cannot be equated with text but because "The 'texts' the slaves drew upon were orally transmitted Bible stories. The fact that the spiritual is an oral phenomenon opens it all the more to contextual influence; the literary controls that exist in written works are absent . . . The music and its accompanying words, in order to interpret effectively the historical moment, adapt themselves to that moment."[25] Oral interpretation is distinct from literary interpretation in that it only happens in a particular moment in real time and the times impact how the interpretation happens and its content. No two performance of music are ever the same and cannot be the same because time has changed, even if the interpreters remain the same. A spirit(ual) approach acknowledges that interpretations are always changing just as sermons are always new because every day is new.

Singers of the spirituals in the past "had no qualms about changing the music so that it would more appropriately fit a new sociohistorical circumstance." One account details the following:

> One day when the writer [James Miller McKim] was seeking to note on paper the melody of a "Sperichul" from the singing of a Negro of some musical cultivation he said to the singer; "you didn't sing it that way the first time." "Oh, no," said the singer, "that's the way we do. We don't sing it alike ev'ry time."[26]

Spirit(ual) interpretations are not static but improvisational in character within a community, ever-changing and fluid. Music and lyrics are adjusted to fit the setting. Interpretive outcomes are not fixed but ongoing based on communal needs. The Bible is used to make sense of particular circumstances and circumstances change constantly.

24. Crawford, *The Hum*, 15.
25. Blount, *Cultural Interpretation*, 57.
26. Ibid., 57–58.

Homiletical Theology in Action

An example of a spirit(ual) interpretive approach within a community is the spiritual "Go Down, Moses." It is an obvious communal performance of the famous Exodus story. Just the performance itself implies that the Exodus happened to a people, not an individual. It is a call and response song. For instance, a leader may sing: "Thus saith the Lord, bold Moses said," and then the community will respond, "Let my people go." The verses are antiphonal and though verses change, one aspect of the verses remains the same—the communal response "Let my people go." That emphasis brings attention to that particular part of the biblical story. It is stressed in the oral-aural performative interpretation to highlight the liberatory call of God to Pharaoh. As musical preachers with a spirit(ual) approach, it is not about getting it right or literally stating the Bible. It is about making sense of tragedy and triumph as honestly and faithfully as possible.

This is why the Exodus story, exemplified by this spiritual, functioned as a metaphor for those who were oppressed. The enslaved viewed themselves as Israel, God's chosen people, who were suffering. Pharaoh represented the oppressors. Moses could represent any one of the leaders in the community. Thus, this biblical story could be viewed as their story, reflecting their circumstances. It could be viewed as a mirror of their lives.[27] At the same time, it is critical to notice the fluidity of the interpretation. The spiritual is a compressed version of the story thus it is not an exact reiteration of the Bible story. In fact, the biblical story says that God commands Moses to tell Pharaoh, "Let my people go, so that they may worship me" (Exod 4:23; 7:16); however, in the spiritual, we only hear "let my people go." There is no mention of the worship of God because their spirit(ual) approach was attuned to their situation on the ground and what was critical for them was the freedom offered by God and not necessarily the worship of God; the latter part was ignored or muted.[28] One reads the world situation and the Bible to preach; some details will be stressed while others will not even be mentioned. Lyrics can be used or not based on the situation at hand. One version of "Go Down, Moses" lists eighteen verses while other printed versions of the spiritual only lists three verses.[29] This implies how one can add or delete verses to interpret the current circumstance. Interpretations are adaptable to concrete situations. Spirit(ual) interpretation is not chiseled in stone, which means that homiletical theology is not either.

---

27. Powery, *Dem Dry Bones*, 117–18.
28. Ibid., 122–23.
29. See *Songs of Zion*, 112; Work, *American Negro Songs*, 163.

Rather, the interpretative task of homiletical theology is improvisational and free. Vincent Wimbush writes of several spirituals, including "Go Down, Moses," and argues that they

> reflect a hermeneutic characterized by a looseness, even playfulness, vis-à-vis the biblical texts themselves. The interpretation was not controlled by the literal words of the texts, but by social experience. The texts were heard more than read; they were engaged as stories that seized and freed the imagination. Interpretation was therefore controlled by the freeing of the collective consciousness and imagination of the African slaves as they heard the biblical stories and retold them to reflect their actual social situation, as well as their visions for something different.[30]

The enslaved were not enslaved to the words of the Bible. They heard the text but listened for the story, which allowed freeing interpretations. These musical sermons have been called "story theology."[31] Wimbush is also helpful on this point. He writes:

> The sacralization of the Bible among white evangelical Protestants, North and South, could hardly have been ignored by the Africans. The young nation officially defined itself as a "biblical nation"; indeed, popular culture was also thoroughly biblical. It would have been difficult not to take note of the diversity of views that reading the Bible could inspire, not only between North and South as cultural, political readings, but also among evangelical communities—Baptist, Methodist, Presbyterian. The lesson that the Africans learned from these evangelicals was not only that faith was to be interpreted in light of the reading of the Bible, but also that each person had freedom of interpretation of the Bible. Given differences between individuals and different religious groups, the Africans learned that they, too, could read "the Book" freely. They could read certain parts and ignore others. They could and did articulate their interpretations in their own way—in song, prayers, sermons, testimonies, and addresses. By the end of the century "the Book" had come to represent a virtual language-world that they, too, could enter and manipulate in light of their social experiences. After all, everyone could approach the Bible under the guidance of the Spirit, that is, in his or her own way.[32]

30. Wimbush, "The Bible and African Americans," 88.
31. Kirk-Duggan, *Exorcizing Evil*, 59.
32. Wimbush, "The Bible and African Americans," 86.

Wimbush suggests the freedom that comes with the spiritual as it relates to interpretation. The imagery of rocks in the spirituals and how their use shifts depending on the need at hand is an example of the freeing fluidity. Rocks may be framed positively or negatively depending on the exact situation. Lovell writes, "The figures with rocks are usually quite striking. If one deliberates, a home in a rock is far more picturesque and incisive than it seems at first blush. But examine the 'rock' figures from Revelation. All John . . . gives is a picture of kings, mighty men, free men, and bondmen hiding themselves in the dens and in the rocks of the mountains, and saying to the mountains and rocks, 'Fall on us, and hide us from the face of him that sitteth on the throne, and from the wrath of the Lamb.'"[33]

But there are other interpretations in which the image of rocks are feared. For example,

> O rocks, don't fall on me,
> O rocks, don't fall on me,
> O rocks, don't fall on me,
> Rocks and mountains, don't fall on me.

Or,

> Went to the rocks for to hide my face,
> Rocks cried out, "No hiding place,"
> There's no hiding place down here.
>
> The rocks may even say,
> I'm burnin', too,
> I want to get to heaven just as much as you.

Whether it be rocks or other images like trains or water, spirituals adapt biblical imagery to their situation. They are free to explore the life-giving approaches to the Bible because what a spirit(ual) approach does is attempt to interpret the Bible for the purpose of life and hope because "the Spirit is life" (Rom 8:10). The flexible, fluid, and free interpretations of the Bible imply a distance from the "holy book." It is not the destruction of the Bible but an honest assessment of the Bible in relation to the Spirit and human beings, including their bodies.

Despite the overwhelming freedom that a spirit(ual) approach promotes for the interpretive task of homiletical theology, it is also clear that

---

33. Lovell, *Black Song*, 216–17.

there is still a closeness, a proximity, to biblical texts. There is a close relationship between the Spirit and Word, thus, a spirit(ual) lens for interpretation comes near the Bible in such a way that there is a fusion of the past, present, and future. "When the slave talks about the past deeds of God or looks to the future deeds of God, the slave is not attempting to escape into another time. The opposite is true: the slave, in the moment of his or her singing, brings that time and its liberating meaning and effect into the present. In the spiritual the lines between dimensions of time and place are collapsed; past and future become present."[34] In the spirit(ual), God is always on time or as the enslaved might say, "an on-time God."

This way of reading Scripture implies leaning into the notion of Emmanuel, that "God is with us." Therefore, the various characters of the Bible were not necessarily historical figures when appropriated because the people saw themselves in the Old Testament figures like Moses and Daniel. The same was true in the New Testament. For instance, "Po' ol' Lazarus, po' as I, / W'en he died, he had a home on high" puts the spiritual interpreter on the same level as Lazarus, who had a promised future home after death. The singer sees his worth through Lazarus and places him/herself in his shoes. In addition, when one sings, "I got a home in dat rock, don' you see?" it is a present situation as evidenced by the "I." One has a home in that rock now and waiting is not necessary. The biblical story is fused with their existential story in the present as horizons converge. One can declare, "Go, tell it on the mountain that Jesus Christ is born" because one is there in the story of the birth of Jesus. This spirit(ual) fusion allows the ancient stories of Scripture to come alive and make the spiritual ones feel a part of the larger story of the history of God in the world. This is why one will say, "*We are climbing Jacob's ladder.*"

Through a spirit(ual) lens, the main concern is not with an ancient figure but with a present one, thus the story of God continues in and through homiletical interpretation. This story is never truly fixed but it is fused with specific circumstances in time and space. A spirit(ual) approach to homiletical interpretation maintains both a fluid and fused relationship with the Bible; yet, this is not the ultimate *telos* of a spirit(ual) approach to interpretation.

---

34. Blount, *Cultural Interpretation*, 64.

The Spirit(ual) and the Phenomenology of Interpretation

Before discussing what I consider to be the ultimate end of interpretation, it may be useful to flesh out briefly what this spirit(ual) interpretive approach presented above looks like phenomenologically. Historically, and deeply rooted in the Protestant tradition, is the Word-Spirit relationship in which there is a sense of the interconnectedness of the Word of God and the Holy Spirit as evident throughout the biblical witness. The spirit(ual) approach explored in this essay is in alignment with this tradition but in an inverse manner in which the relationship is presented as Spirit-Word, with priority given to the Spirit. This is the case because the Spirit is the midwife of the Word. Within the Christian tradition, the Spirit is the agent of the incarnation and is the one who anoints Jesus making him the Christ and empowering him for ministry. This theological inversion is the reason for beginning with human bodies and the breath, that is, the spirit that flows through humanity from God.

Starting with the Spirit means that (1) one starts with human breath and life and embodied human beings in time and space. Beginning with breath is beginning with spirit, *ruach*, divine breath. One might say that to breathe is to pray from and for the Spirit, which makes the initial move of this approach to interpretation a prayer, an *epiclesis*, from a human being. Once one affirms the human breath as perpetual prayer from real human bodies animated by the Spirit then (2) one can acknowledge that human bodies are part of a communal body, a community of people in a certain context. A person is part of a people in a place, thus the interpretation process is really a communal experience, whether made explicit or not. A community has a history, a history of embodied cultural memory. Thus, in the interpretation process, we read ourselves and acknowledge our humanness as being created in the image of God but then we also read the communal context and the people within it. This is significant because a spirit(ual) approach affirms individual and communal identities before moving toward the reading of sacred texts.

After reading humanity, individually and communally, and discerning human need, then (3) one reads or interprets the Bible through the lenses of a community because we interpret on behalf of a community and its needs. As noted already, before we reflect on a biblical text, we reflect on who and where we are as embodied human beings and the needs of those to whom we belong and love in community. Yet, the spirit(ual) approach still engages Scripture without shame. There is closeness to and distance from the Bible. A spirit(ual) interpreter keeps enough distance between him/herself and the Bible such that the human community is "in between" the interpreter and sacred text so that the interpreter reads the Bible *through* the life of a community. As interpreters, we are too close if we only quote Bible verses or reiterate a text without reference to communal need because we do not see the community at all, perhaps having our view blinded by the "holy book." At this stage, one engages the Bible for hermeneutical insight that may bear fruit for those who will hear the proclaimed word; thus, one searches for the intersection of the Bible with human need because that is where the gospel will be heard, all the while recognizing that revelation is a gift of the Spirit (1 Cor 2).

After making interpretive decisions in relation to the people and their needs, (4) one then has to determine what and how to say what one has discerned as fitting and faithful to proclaim for the life of a community; the aim, through the spirit(ual), is that the community may hear the gospel in their "own native language" (Acts 2). Thus, engaging the Bible leads eventually toward the community to which we proclaim the gospel. The interpretive task has direction and it is directed toward a people in need, implying that the context of spirit(ual) interpretation of the Bible is the people of God who are hungry for eternal bread. Finally, at this point, once the word is interpreted and delivered to a community, the future of the Word, that is, how it is received by and what it does to the hearers in question, is in the hands of God who creates new life through the interaction of Spirit-Word as God did in the beginning. This means, just like at the beginning of this spirit(ual) interpretive process, (5) we end with holy breath, a prayer for the Spirit to bless the word so that God's redemptive purposes can be fulfilled for the life of the world.

The Spiritual and the End of Interpretation

The bookends of prayer as critical in the above phenomenology point to the underlying final goal of a spirit(ual) interpretive approach in homiletics, namely, praise and love of God. The act of loving praise is never complete, but the continual vocation of believers. Just as the Spirit enables us to pray (i.e., worship), "Abba, Father" (Rom 8:15; Gal 4:6), and love (Rom 5:5), when talking about a spirit(ual) stance of interpretation, this implies that homiletical theology's aims are also prayer, praise, and love. The highest form of preaching as theology is doxology. This affirms the idea that the

Spirit works to combine everything in doxology, including interpretive work. This does not negate the reality of suffering of the enslaved nor the groaning Spirit. As Cone writes, "In the spirituals, the black slaves' experience of suffering and despair defined for them the major issue in their view of the world."[35] As I have argued elsewhere, lament is a critical homiletical voice[36] and one should interpret truthfully such that one can sing,

> Oh, Lord, Oh, My Lord!
> Oh, My Good Lord! Keep me from sinkin' down.

The way the spirituals interpret Jesus is unavoidable. "He suffered, He died, but not alone—they were with Him. They knew what He suffered; it was a cry of the heart that found a response and an echo in their own woes. They entered into the fellowship of His suffering. There was something universal in His suffering,"[37] "Were you there when they crucified my Lord?" The inference is that the interpreter is there at the cross; thus, a *telos* of praise or love does not mute the suffering and sorrow of a people.

We see this clearly in the spiritual "Nobody Knows the Trouble I See":

> Nobody knows the trouble I see
> Nobody knows my sorrow.
> Nobody knows the trouble I see,
> Glory, Hallelujah!

The trouble is most prominent in this spiritual as it is in the world, yet the climax, the end, is praise signifying the end goal of interpretation by the spirit(ual). Though spiritual interpretation is truthful, trouble does not have the final word. God does, through the eyes of faith. Isaac Rufus Clark taught that "Just as [the] sun never fails [to rise or set], God never fails. Morning always comes."[38] In his study of the spirituals, Howard Thurman echoes this faith-filled trajectory and says, "[The spirituals] express the profound conviction that God was not done with them, that God was not done with life. The consciousness that God had not exhausted His resources or better still that the vicissitudes of life could not exhaust God's resources, did not ever leave them."[39] God is never quite finished with us and very

---

35. Cone, *The Spirituals and the Blues*, 57.
36. See Powery, *Spirit Speech*.
37. Thurman, *Deep River and the Negro Speaks of Life and Death*, 21–22.
38. Cannon, *Teaching Preaching*, 181.
39. Thurman, *Deep River and the Negro Speaks of Life and Death*, 37–38.

present in the time of trouble because the extent of God's love can never be exhausted.

Thus, to speak of love as an end of interpretation does not only suggest an interpreter's love for God through the Spirit, but it suggests that through interpretation we meet the eternal love of God. This interpretive approach points us beyond the Bible, which is not the goal, to what is unseen, to God, who is the goal. The spirituals are cultural hymns and thus provide a hymnic reading or hymnic hermeneutic whose goal is ultimately the praise of and love for God. A spirit(ual) approach to the interpretive task of homiletical theology leads to the worship of God and not the worship of the Bible because the Bible cannot love; it is not a loving subject like God. If love is an end of interpretation, this will keep real bodies within the community in the homiletical picture because without love, there are only objects or texts and not living subjects, like humanity or the Spirit. The spirit(ual) is a way to reclaim one's own life and love. Paul says that "love never ends" (1 Cor 13), thus interpretation will continue and preachers will keep proclaiming the love of God and interpreting for love, by love, in love, with love, because "God is love" (1 John 4:8). This love leads to a surplus of praise in the end because it acknowledges that nothing "will be able to separate us from the love of God in Christ Jesus our Lord" (Rom 8).

The spirit(ual) lens brings us to love and though the reader may not love this essay, it has been an attempt to stir conversation about a spirit(ual) approach to the interpretive task of homiletical theology. The wind blew this essay down the path of discovery in relation to topics about bodies and the Bible, contextual community, interpretive oral-aural performance, phenomenology of interpretation, and the goal of interpretation. Like a sermon, this essay is never really finished because more can always be said. This is a beginning and hopefully just as the Spirit moved over the waters "in the beginning" to create beauty, something beautiful may arise from my efforts here, even as I conclude with some reflections on what all of this may mean for the development of homiletical theology.

Implications for the Development of Homiletical Theology

In light of this spirit(ual) approach to interpretation, there are at least four implications to consider for homiletical theology. First, this turn to the spirit(ual) is a turn to the human, that is, real human bodies and experiences. The privileging of the Spirit leads to a privileging of personhood, not the muting of one's humanity. Rather, just as God embraced human flesh for salvific purposes, the Spirit embraces humanity to give life to homiletical theology. This emphasis on the human also recognizes that the biblical writers are themselves human beings, preachers, and interpreters of God's action in the world. Homiletical theology is definitely a human enterprise under the aegis of the Spirit. This spirit(ual) lens affirms theological anthropology because pneumatology affirms humanity and materiality. Underlying this approach is the fact that humans are made in the image of God although the image can become distorted by sin.

Nonetheless, this approach suggests that some authority resides with humanity when dealing with homiletical theology. It is not purely a divine action but is deeply human; thus, in terms of the interpretive task of homiletical theology, it is vital to consider a hermeneutics of humanity, one in which the human is affirmed from the very beginning, even before we get to exegesis of Scripture. Starting with the Spirit is intertwined with starting right where we are as human beings. Through this human lens or hermeneutics of humanity, interpretation should be guided by the rule of love, including love of God and love of neighbor. Placing some authority with humanity is a form of love and a reminder that even the Bible is a human document, though the tradition of the church confesses it to be inspired. To love and affirm humanity and its breath is to suggest that all homiletical interpretations should be a loving gesture toward the other. This does not mean that this is only about reader-response; the writers of Scripture were human too, therefore, this is about all humans striving to be faithful to the gospel of God in light of their particular situations in time and space. A spirit(ual) approach humanizes the process of interpretation and where there is no human, there can be no meaningful interpretation in the Spirit.

A second implication of the spirit(ual) approach to the interpretive task of homiletical theology has to do with the role of memory. Particularly, dealing with the spirituals reminds one of how human memory shapes interpretation and how interpretation is rooted in the body, individually and collectively. Scripture is a memory book through which the writers and readers remember God's mighty acts throughout history, but human bodies also remember. For example, Howard Thurman tells the now-famous story about his grandmother who raised him. She was a former slave who could not read or write and lived on a plantation until the Civil War. She would not listen to any of Paul's letters except 1 Corinthians 13. When Thurman was older, he finally had the courage to ask his grandmother why she would not let him read any of Paul's letters to her. Her response to him reveals the importance of memory for biblical interpretation. She said:

> During the days of slavery . . . the master's minister would occasionally hold services for the slaves. Old man McGhee was so mean that he would not let a Negro minister preach to his slaves. Always the white minister used as his text something from Paul. At least three or four times a year he used as a text: "Slaves, be obedient to them that are your masters . . . as unto Christ." Then he would go on to show how it was God's will that we were slaves and how, if we were good and happy slaves, God would bless us. I promised my Maker that if I ever learned to read and if freedom ever came, I would not read that part of the Bible.[40]

When it comes to interpreting for homiletical theology, the spirit(ual) points to the history of the enslaved and it is a history of inhumane suffering and oppression. The undeniable assault of terror on black bodies influences how and what one remembers for interpretation. There can be select memory or even amnesia. One may remember rightly or wrongly but memory, individual and collective, is inescapable. As in the case above, what we remember, want to remember, or what we want to forget, shapes the contour of what we hear and see in Scripture.

Bodily memory affects homiletical interpretation. If that memory has been bruised and broken, this history of calamity will shape how one reads texts. A spirit(ual) approach does not neglect memory because the Spirit helps us remember (John 14:26), even if it includes traumatic memories. A spirit(ual) lens affirms tragedy, agony, wilderness experiences, and life endured in a valley of dry bones. Pain is inescapable and one approaches texts through the lens of suffering. With this approach, the interpretive task of homiletical theology includes the viability of a blues sensibility of life. Painful memories influence the preaching of the gospel and the spirit(ual) assures homiletical theology remains rooted in the suffering of the world, humanity, and God. This approach does not negate the oppressed and disinherited but reads Scripture alongside the dispossessed, those who may not even be able to read for themselves. This interpretive lens always remembers wounds, which means that it may be thought of as a hermeneutics of trauma; for homiletical theology to be useful for the life of the world, it must travel this rough terrain.

---

40. Thurman, *Jesus and the Disinherited*, 30–31.

A third implication for the development of homiletical theology is that interpretation is never final. Homiletical theology must be freed from the bonds of enslavement to the Bible or at least the idea that everything that can be said about God has already been said in Scripture. This has been noted above, but it is important to highlight that in terms of homiletical theology and practice, the Bible is only one aspect of it. It is important but it is not God. The Bible is a collection of "sermons" by various contextualized preachers in community who desire to get their point across about God in relation to humanity through a variety of sermon genres. This means that the interpretive task of homiletical theology can really embody *homiletos* and be a conversation between and among preachers, interpreters, humans, and their (con)texts. Thus, one may view the interpretation process as a form of intertextuality, between our world as living texts and the textual world of Scripture. As conversation, there is a call and response, a back and forth, in the Presence, which suggests that interpretive meaning is never closed but perhaps always fresh for the present moment.

This spirit(ual) lens leads to variegated ways to read or interpret the Bible because there is no one right way. As questions posed vary, answers received will differ because the questions one asks of the Bible shapes the answers one receives and the questions themselves have been implicitly shaped by one's communal ecology and memory. This is why homiletical interpretation is never final: the questions and approaches have not been exhausted in the Spirit. There will always be surprises when dealing with the spirit(ual) as the conversation continues in such a manner that there is a mutuality between interpreter and Scripture. As a conversation, at times, the spirit(ual) interpreter may engage in a "muted reading" in the case of Thurman's grandmother or a "responsive reading" in which one talks back to the biblical text.[41] This approach is grounded in human freedom under the guidance of the Spirit who keeps the wind of conversation blowing.

A fourth, and final, implication for the development of homiletical theology is the way the spirit(ual) calls homileticians to prayer. This spirit(ual) approach brings back to remembrance a fundamental idea and practice, especially when considering breath. Breath and prayer reminds us that life and homiletical theology is a gift from God and because of this, preachers and teachers of preaching work, but should also pray, for positive fruit to be borne from our interpretations. Thus, homiletical theology is always a calling on God to bless our fragile mess. It is a lifelong, loving

---

41. See Powery, *Dem Dry Bones*, 122–25.

epiclesis. With that in mind, the interpretive task of homiletical theology is always provisional and although this turn to the spirit(ual) is a turn to the human, humans must recognize that we are stewards of breath, but not the Creator of breath. Therefore, we may always pray and approach the homiletical-theological task as "empty pitchers [coming] to a full fountain/ with no merits of our own."[42]

---

42. Johnson, *God's Trombones*, 13.

—5—

Promise and Cross

Homiletical Theology, the Vocative Word *Extra Nos*, and the Task of a Revisionist Eschatology

—DAVID SCHNASA JACOBSEN

Introduction: Toward Homiletical Theology in a Confessional Mode

For me homiletical theology is an interested activity. It occurs at the intersection between gospel and culture, even while there is something of gospel that pushes preachers into dialogue *with* culture. This is to say that for me, the beginning of homiletical theology is a confessionally invested understanding of the gospel's starting point that by its very nature brings me already in conversation with culture and context. It is precisely such moments that demonstrate the struggle to name God again: the confessional starting point is not an ending point; it does not settle matters. It is, in fact, much more likely to *unsettle* them. At the same time, such gospel speech does not exist apart from culture, certainly not as timeless truth or essence, but in its speaking brings theological conversation with culture into motion—and in such a way that culture talks back. Because gospel is not a fixed, timeless entity, it needs culture not only to incarnate itself, but on occasion also to enlarge and enhance itself. Homiletical theology occupies this very interested and local space for the way it does theology. In its most obvious and recurring sense in the life of the preacher, homiletical theology is theology in the form of sermon preparation. By extension, homiletical theology in a scholarly mode explores surrounding questions that help frame the kind of theological work required to connect gospel and life that is both rhetorical and conversational. In short, homiletical theology is a form of doing theology that names the gospel in light of preaching's contexts, theories, and practices.

Homiletical Theology in Action: Preaching and the Unfinished Task of Eschatology

In this essay I want to bring this theological approach to bear to a vexing gospel problem for the twenty-first-century, white, mainline pulpit: the struggle with eschatology.[1] While much of the black church has never really lost sight of the importance of eschatology for its own theological reflection and ethical engagement, and conversely fundamentalistic groups have managed to perpetuate literalistic eschatological timelines, the mainline church has struggled to figure out how to speak gospel in a cogent way with respect to eschatology. Recently, Tom Long has made the case in *Preaching from Memory to Hope* that a recovery of eschatology is important to the contemporary mainline pulpit.[2] This essay seeks to find a way forward that both retrieves largely white mainline Protestant traditions and revises them in living conversation with other contemporary contextual perspectives. For that reason, my main way of rehabilitating eschatology will be through the center of Reformation theologies: the place of promise, a central notion for Protestant theologies of Word and Sacrament. Yet I will seek to be plu-

---

1. Several essays in this volume envision homiletical theology in what Charles Bartow called the pedagogical and professional modes. The essay here will be different from some in that it pursues homiletical theology in its scholarly mode, as he describes in his article, "Homiletical (Theological) Criticism," 154. All three are vital parts, I believe, for the unfinished task of homiletical theology.

2. Long, *Preaching from Memory to Hope*, 111ff. For an insightful read about how this might happen given present cultural realities and changes in scientific paradigms see McClure, "Preaching, Eschatology, and Worldview." I wish to thank Professor McClure for his willingness to engage in conversation about the topic in preparing this work for print.

ralistically contextual by expanding that theology of promise and bringing it into conversation with homiletical theologies from other cultural contexts, especially black and Asian American homiletical theologies as well as liberationist ones. To aid in this, I will also seek to place a theology of promise in relation to a theology of the cross—and in a way that a theology of promise also is evident in lament as a deep manifestation of the same eschatological commitment *in context*. The theology of the cross will thus provide a deep, anti-triumphalistic frame to the rehabilitation of eschatology for the white, mainline context.[3] It is the *extra nos* of the promise and its sacramental rootage that keeps promise grounded and pointed toward God's good, eschatological purposes even while it bespeaks God's presence in absence.

Background: Prolepses of Today's Unfinished Eschatology

Of course, in the history of Christian theology it is hard to think of any doctrinal locus that has undergone more revision than eschatology. Within the canon itself, there is a struggle over the nature of eschatological hope that is played out over one of the central issues about the gospel proclamation. If Jesus is indeed proclaimed risen, then the general resurrection is in the offing and the new age is dawning. The end is near. Within a couple of generations, however, the scope of the promise is already being redefined in profound ways in 2 Peter 3:8–9:

> But do not ignore this one fact, beloved, that with the Lord one day is like a thousand years, and a thousand years are like one day. The Lord is not slow about his promise, as some think of slowness, but is patient with you, not wanting any to perish, but all to come to repentance.

The promise of eschatology is clearly both something radically given and yet brings with it hermeneutical entailments. In the course of the canon itself, these promises are named and recalled as early as Paul's first letters in the middle first century—that is in the shadow of Roman cross—and reiterated and reinterpreted in the dust of the destruction of the second temple in the final third of that century. All this is to say that promise both grounds faith and mixes it up ever new in contexts that require theological naming

---

3. See Beaudoin and Turpin, "White Practical Theology," 251ff.

of the gospel, what I have come to call homiletical theology. Eschatology belongs therefore to the center of homiletical theology's unfinished task.

Because of the crises that lurk behind these varying contextual moments in the first century, we might begin by affirming with Mary McClintock Fulkerson that theology, indeed all homiletical theology, begins with a wound.[4] Precisely these circumstances should remind us generally of the limits of homiletical theological reflection. Although eschatology does not stand still in the tradition, the contexts in which eschatology and the gospel are named are even more fluid and variegated. It would be a mistake of the first order to assume that we can arrive at a kernel of absolute eschatological truth *apart* from the different times and places that call forth homiletical theological reflection. Luther argues that promise is what we hold on to even as we are cast into hell. Martha Simmons adds that the function of eschatology is to speak the sweet by and by in the nasty here and now.[5] There is an underside, a *contextual* underside to uttering eschatological promise in the pulpit. Where it is named homiletically is something that matters deeply. Eschatology and the gospel itself are named again and again where theology begins: with a wound.

For me the wound is complicated, but certainly encompasses the white, mainline church's struggle with cultural disestablishment and its attendant dislocations.[6] The Protestant mainline church does not occupy the same space that it once did. It holds much relative power and benefits even now from privilege of race. Its institutions are still bastions of male authority and Eurocentric cultural leanings. I say this not because these realities are out there, but because they are also in me and shape my work as a homiletician. To try to do work as a mainline homiletician and practical theologian today is, explicitly or implicitly, to be coping through this wound in a way that opens up little hope for immediate wholeness, but can begin to glimpse, in bits and pieces, through the broken shards of our stained glass world, some healing *together*. In fact, whatever it is, the prom-

---

4. Fulkerson, *Places of Redemption*, 12ff. Paraphrasing Charles Winquist, she notes that creative thinking originates at the site of a wound, or as she describes it, from an inchoate sense that something must be addressed.

5. Simmons, Introduction, x.

6. Beaudoin and Turpin, "White Practical Theology," 257–58, locate the crisis of white privilege and Eurocentric scholarship in part in this historical and cultural shift of disestablishment. For the role of disestablishment in forming the North American discourse of practical theology generally see Cahalan, "Three Approaches to Practical Theology, Theological Education, and the Church's Ministry," 63–65.

ise should be sufficient to generate a different kind of *praxis* going forward, a shared praxis of faith animated by promise. And this is that to which this particular essay tends—a more eschatological faith *praxis*.

And yet it is precisely woundedness that gives life to the struggle with the promise.[7] We mainliners, and our traditions in the Bible, continue to be inscribed with it. Indeed the problem of eschatological promise is lived precisely in the breach of the wound: where the overflow of promise meets the undertow of failure. It is here in this anomic breach where theological work is done. The fact that promises and the eschatologies of the Scriptures are repeated and verbalized in church lead to the recurring need to work through the discrepancies. Yet it is here, in all the struggle with eschatological promise, that it both lives and calls forth revision. It does so chiefly by what eschatological promise provides both positively and negatively: a powerful vision of hope and an accompanying realization that things are not what they should be. For this reason, I bring a theology of promise in close relation to another feature of some classical, Reformation theologies: a theology of the cross.

Promise and Cross as Related Eschatological Theologoumena

In one important sense, there is little new to such a project. The linking of a theology of promise to a theology of the cross is a recurring feature even in contemporary, contextualized theological discourse in the North American and European contexts. One thinks immediately of Jürgen Moltmann's *Theology of Hope,* in which an eschatology of promise is so central, and in short order the appearance and subsequent impact of his *The Crucified God*. Douglas John Hall's work in North America has also helped to recontextualize these classic markers of Reformation theology for a new, more self-consciously contextual approach to doing theology in a disestablished church too often tempted to cultural hegemony and triumphalism, especially in his *The Cross in Our Context* and *Waiting for Gospel*.[8] Since Luther

---

7. Here I am drawing on the work of philosopher Richard Kearney, who seeks to transfigure by means of catharsis the wound into the mark of the scar, in his address "Narrative and Catharsis in Joyce, Homer, and Shakespeare." Narrative catharsis for Kearney is the way of working through the scar as trace—the wound is timeless, the scar is an engraved wound that may or may not heal. Perhaps as we work through eschatology in light of promise, in those places where the theological tasks for whatever reason are still unfinished, we need to come to terms with this reality.

8. It is important to note that the cross, like the promise to which it is linked, is also

Promise and Cross

in particular, the cross and the promise belong together. A theology of the cross is not so much about atonement theory, but a theology of revelation: seeing God not in triumph and glory, but in the scandal of the cross. A theology of the cross does not gussy things up homiletically. In the words of the *Heidelberg Disputation*, it calls a thing what it really is.[9] Conversely, a theology of promise understands faith and church in relation to a given promise, a sense of divine presence and grace given in Word and Sacrament—all in the shadow of that very cross.

I do not think this is far from the way Ted Smith speaks so beautifully about eschatological memories. Drawing on the work of Walter Benjamin, Smith points to eschatology as a profound place of hope *and* failure.

> Exile becomes an occasion for God's deep, wily fidelity. In the cross the world's rejection of God makes manifest God's boundless love for the world. This world finds itself joined most intimately to the Spirit of God not in its perfection, but in its longing, its deepest need, its cries too deep for words.[10]

While these theologoumena may still be confessed as, in the words of the Small Catechism, most certainly true, the preacher knows that they do not disclose everything that could be said in the practice of promise in today's pulpit. There is still more that can be preached. I would like to unpack this practiced reality in two different ways: the vocative nature of the promise in worship and the ever-changing nature of context in which such a vocative promise is uttered. Here homiletical theology retrieves the tradition and yet transforms it by setting it in relationship to preaching's contexts and practices.[11]

---

ever recontextualized. Theologies of the cross are not the province solely of male Teutonic scholarship, as the work of James Cone, Marit Trelstad, Mary Solberg, and Deanna Thompson make clear. They are ever reinterpreted through contexts. For a homiletically astute situational and contextual reappropriation of the cross, see Brown, *Cross Talk*.

9. Luther, "Heidelberg Disputation," 31.

10. Smith, "Eschatological Memories of Everyday Life."

11. Portions of what follows are themselves something of a retrieval! Elements below are reworkings and further refinement of material I wrote in an earlier *Forschungsbericht*, "The Promise of Promise."

Homiletical Theology in Action

The Vocative Promise in Worship

In Luther, the notion of promise is not merely conceptual, but rooted quite concretely in the practice of Word and Sacrament. The thereness and validity of the promise is not based on the plausibility in the self-conscious subjectivity of the believer, but on its utterance especially in worship. As philosopher Phillip Cary points out, the problem with a promise of the gospel that goes unbelieved may not lie in the inability of someone to testify or confess that persons know that they believe (the classic Reformed position of Calvin), but in the very concreteness of the promise's utterance.[12] The refutation of the promise is not that it doesn't correspond to the reality that I believe, testify to, or otherwise confess, but that, as Luther so often puts it, God is a liar. A promise that goes awry at the point of its vocative utterance, as speech act theory tells us, is not its inability to correspond to reality or the way we perceive that reality, so much as an infelicity of speech.[13] Luther expresses confidence in the promise for this very reason. Its utterance in preaching and sacraments is the promise—it is not some concept of promise that refers to a corresponding object that we in our subjectivity can either perceive or not perceive, testify or not testify, confess or not confess.

While philosophical and theological investigations of the illocutionary force of promise in speech act theory have been powerful for the development of such notions,[14] I would like to place this important claim about the vocative nature of promise in the context of worship itself. What makes promise interesting, to my mind, is its utterance in the worship community. As liturgical theologian Graham Hughes has pointed out, worship is the place where the task of meaning making is brought into a vocative context where we address God and God addresses us.[15] In fact, if Nicholas Wolterstorff is correct, it is in just such a context where promise takes its unique contextual and vocative form in a kind of double agency, where divine locution becomes human illocution.[16] It is for this reason, I believe, and not because of some ontological claim about promise or reality or

---

12. Cary, "Sola Fide," 266.

13. Searle, *Speech Acts*, 54.

14. Austin, *How to Do Things with Words*, and Evans, *The Logic of Self-Involvement* are key examples of the philosophical interest. Bayer, *Theology the Lutheran Way*, and Morse, *The Logic of Promise in Moltmann's Theology*, represent consistent theological approaches to the same.

15. Hughes, *Worship as Meaning*, 282–83.

16. Wolterstorff, *Divine Discourse*, especially 67, 71.

even our perceptions about reality, that the power of promise to convey presence becomes important. As Donald Evans points out, part of the illocutionary force of the promise is the self-involvement of the promiser.[17] Philosopher Richard Kearney claims that what promise offers is a kind of future-present self-giving of the traversing divine, not a disclosure of being, both an ontological-eschatological impinging on the present.[18] This in itself is a promising retrieval of the Reformation notion of promise in a non-foundationalist revision. Promise may therefore be about the future presence of God through vocative double agency in a contemporary context of Word and Sacrament.

The Ever-Changing Nature of the Context of the Vocative Promise

And yet there is a surplus of meaning that accompanies the promise's utterance in ever new contexts. A promise uttered vocatively is not the same in shifting moments in time. It is at this point that the promise itself necessarily morphs in ways that cannot be contained in a pure correspondence of terms sense. The utterance of promise does something *unsettling* in that it pries open reality in its speaking. Moltmann talks about this in quasi-Barthian terms in his *Theology of Hope*. For Moltmann, promise is not an event in reality, but *creates* reality. My claim is not that promise exerts this kind of force in a kind of *creatio ex nihilo* sense, but rather does so precisely in its relation to its concrete utterance. What promise opens up, ever anew, is a new way of being in the world in front of it. It is this that makes the retrieval of promise important in way that opens up the promise coming *otherwise*.

Here we might also consider the post-structuralist notions of John Caputo in his books *The Weakness of God* and, most recently, *The Insistence of God*. In both works Caputo argues for a joining together of his notion of divine weakness, which he assimilates to the tradition of a theology of the cross, to an unsettling notion of promise that points beyond the fixed reality of language to something that *comes*, in a kind of Derridean, eschatological sense. Here, there is no sense of presence, but pure futurity and

---

17. In his work on the self-involving language of creation, Evans builds on earlier philosophical work on performative utterances to clarify in particular the notion of self-involvement in the use of commissive utterances, *The Logic of Self-Involvement*, 27–32.

18. Kearney, *The God Who May Be*, 20–38.

an unsettling of being and fixedness. While I am not willing to pursue a kind of poststructuralist theology of the word for its own sake (whatever that would mean!), I recognize as a homiletical theologian pursuing a kind of unfinished task that lurks in the tradition, that the retrieval and revision that I am suggesting operates at a very provisional level that cannot be identified solely with the givenness of what is alone. In this way, the ever changing nature of context pushes my own Reformation traditions beyond themselves to a kind of eschatology that operates at the edge of experience, what is known, and begins to touch on mystery.

Promise, Eschatology, and Homiletical-Theological Method

The approach that Robert Kelly and I set out in *Kairos Preaching* involves bringing the gospel as unconditional promise, understood within Reformation traditions as salvation by grace through faith, into close proximity with situations.[19] This move, which begins with a classic understanding of promise, sets the conversation in motion between gospel and context/culture. Promise is thus not the endpoint of gospel reflection, though it is its starting point. While many sermons dealing with eschatology are likely to emerge not in immediate relation to a situation, but with some strange, eschatological text, Edward Farley points out that not even textually focused sermons emerge situation-free. Situations, says Farley, are the in light of which any text's eschatology is set to the task of proclaiming gospel.[20] With that in view, we then turn to the homiletical-theological method that Kelly and I presuppose can open up eschatological revision.

As one considers the situations that we reflect on contextually in *Kairos Preaching*, one also notices how frequently an utterance of that gospel promise turns to another gospel commonplace, a theology of the cross.[21] To name the promise in proximity with a situation is simultaneously to recall the strangeness of God's revelation in the cross of Jesus. Why is this so? I can think of two reasons, both of which are important for our homiletical-theological reflection here.

First, the gospel commonplace of justification is itself already eschatologically determined. Its announcement and promise of radical grace is

19. The brief summary draws from Jacobsen and Kelly, *Kairos Preaching*, chapters 1–3.

20. Farley, "Preaching the Bible and Preaching the Gospel," 73.

21. Jacobsen and Kelly, *Kairos Preaching*, 21.

understood in relation to eschatological judgment and salvation. As we assert in the book, because of this eschatological promise, you are free—your destiny is good.

There is also, however, a second sense in which a theology of the cross, as a frequently related gospel commonplace, also sets eschatology in motion. In the cross of Jesus we experience that eschatological gift in the midst of suffering and *Anfechtung*. This realization is important also as a *qualifier* of eschatological expectation. Eschatology is not simply about triumph, and in fact embodies in its cruciform shape anti-triumphalistic tendencies. The cross is an apocalyptic moment of disclosure both of profound divine love and solidarity and human oppression and injustice. It is this dynamic that keeps eschatology real and rooted in calling a thing what it really is. Again, as Martha Simmons puts it, eschatology is where the sweet by and by meets the nasty here and now.[22]

Precisely this homiletical-theological tension, and one focused on the promise as an external utterance in context, is what is so productive for the revisionist work of reclaiming eschatology in the contemporary white, mainline church. For where it rejects or ignores a theology of the cross, and fails to call a thing what it really is, the full-orbed language of promise is vitiated. Where the two are held together, a theology of promise and a theology of the cross, it is here where the overflow of promise meets the undertow of failure. Here is precisely the wound where theology is done and eschatology renamed—yet again—as part of the unfinished theological task that is preaching gospel. It is also here, in the breach that is the wound, where it becomes possible to hear the gospel on the lips of others—and in a way that allows promise to pry open a different future.

Overhearing the Promise . . . Again

And yet such profound notions of radical grace and traversing presence, especially if viewed as Kearney suggests, onto-eschatologically, also point to a deep desire for justice.[23] With Kearney, therefore, we need to overhear those homiletical-theological voices that possibilize the present. If classic, Reformation conceptions of promise exist to underline divine grace and sacramental presence, another aspect of promise, and one that is decisively eschatological, concerns the relation of God's promised future and our

---

22. Simmons, Introduction, x.
23. Kearney, *The God Who May Be*, 37–38.

present especially in the face of injustice and oppression. While there is a profound sense in which God's justifying grace, proleptically given in the cross and resurrection of Jesus, frees *for the neighbor(s)* and for engagement for justice, the promise viewed eschatologically does more than that. God's future, I am claiming, also calls the present order into question, especially its inevitability, and offers an alternative vision that eschatologically acts on the present to possibilize it, to pry it open. What it does is not to predict the future, but to dis-close the present.[24]

Here I find myself attending to the voices of other homiletical theologians. In particular, I hear the promising speech of Eunjoo Mary Kim, Kenyatta Gilbert, Dale Andrews, Christine Smith, Dawn Ottoni Wilhelm, and Olin Moyd—all of whom relate an interest in eschatology to their contextual-theological work as homileticians.[25]

In *Preaching the Presence of God* Kim writes this about the place of promise in preaching in the Asian American context: "The struggle between the powers of good and evil, the universal reign of the one true God, and the message of comfort with hope and promise for the future to the faithful in their times of most bitter suffering are its major concerns. . . . The expectation of the future is now grounded in the promise of God, the second coming of Christ."[26] In this way, she clearly places eschatology at the center of her project of a contextual theology of preaching by taking seriously Asian spirituality's concern for critical transcendence.

In his book *The Journey and Promise of African-American Preaching*, Kenyatta Gilbert helps to develop his practical-theological agenda for trivocal African American preaching by touching on the importance of promise for his own homiletical-theological vision: A good sermon is a theological conversation about what it means to speak of a promise-bearing God who addresses the real needs of real people.[27] Notice here the connection between promise and present realities, between eschatology and life as lived.

A significant part of Dale Andrews's project in *Practical Theology for Black Churches* aims to reconcile Black liberationist and survivalist/refuge

---

24. I develop this notion of the resurrection as apocalyptic dis-closure in connection with a homiletical-theological reflection on the puzzling ending(s) of the Gospel of Mark, in *Mark*, 221–30.

25. See the works cited below. Dale Andrews also argues that eschatology is one of the four key elements for preaching within a black ecclesiology of refuge in "Ecclesiology, Preaching and Pastoral Care in the African American Church Tradition."

26. Kim, *Preaching the Presence of God*, 60.

27. Gilbert, *The Journey and Promise of African-American Preaching*, 80.

Promise and Cross

approaches to suffering and oppression. In this light, he notes the following about promise: Survival may in fact be part of humanity's proactive participation in the redemptive activity of God. It is, rather, God's promise in Jesus Christ to work redemptively even in suffering.[28] His careful placement of eschatology at the center of faith identity becomes a means of bringing into dialectical relationship both this-worldly and other-worldly perspectives. To this end, Andrews writes further, "The culmination of salvation history in the Kingdom of Heaven ultimately fulfills the gospel promise of complete freedom for the African slaves and early free blacks. Eschatology is the theological vision of that hope . . . ; otherworldly promise translates into this-worldly hope and ways of being."[29] Again, eschatological promise reaches into the present to pry it loose.

Across three important works, Christine Smith speaks of a powerfully eschatological sense of promise joined to life lived now. In a chapter in her edited volume, *Preaching Justice: Ethnic and Cultural Perspectives*, Smith unpacks Ezekiel 34 to help disclose a promised place for marginalized gay and lesbian persons.[30] Smith writes, "we may just find God's incarnation power in ways we have never been able to imagine. In this world, where gender ceases to rule and heterosexism ceases to control, God's promise . . . might well become a promise for us all." In *Risking the Terror*, where Smith connects promise with a liberation perspective on the resurrection, she develops this theme even further. In part building on the radical critique of the web of oppression in *Preaching as Weeping, Confession, and Resistance*, Smith returns to the prophetic task of justice preaching with a desire to name God more fully by means of resurrection's promise: "I found myself urgently turning to the possibility of resurrection as that promise in the Christian faith that is strong enough to counteract and transform death itself. . . . As a practical theologian and preacher, I needed new language, new images, and new understandings that would enable me to be a more faithful proclaimer of God's resurrection life."[31] Smith's vision of promise in the resurrection blurs the line between divine and human agency by locating it incarnationally in the people of God now. Yet the promise is itself rooted in the resurrected Jesus in a way that offers the promise and helps us

---

28. Andrews, *Practical Theology for Black Churches*, 46.
29. Ibid., 47.
30. Smith, *Preaching Justice*, 144.
31. Smith, *Risking the Terror*, 1.

claim the power of the resurrection among us.[32] Of course, it is not about Jesus alone; the reign of God is an overarching vision that expresses what God desires and promises and to such a degree that it gives us a glimpse of God's ultimate promise.[33]

In her article "God's Word in the World," Wilhelm understands prophetic preaching in deep relation to the notion of promise.[34] Although prophetic preaching sometimes runs the risk of forgetting divine agency, Wilhelm places human and ecclesial engagement within the purposes of a sovereign God. Here Wilhelm builds somewhat on Walter Brueggemann's prophetic imagination and its connection to a community with an alternative consciousness. In doing so, she locates the issue of prophetic preaching within the countercultural witness of Anabaptist communities in connection with an overarching vision of God's passion and God's promises which *ground* the possibility of engaging prophetically. The proclamation of the promise in prophetic preaching can function for Wilhelm in two key ways. First, such prophetic proclamation recalls the one who promises.[35] God is the source of justice, love, and the very reign to which the promise points. Second, the promises of God are about invoking the futurity of God's realm. Wilhelm notes, "the prophetic preacher who is passionate about God's Word in the world is not simply concerned with renunciation of evil but listens for God's promises echoing in every generation and relates instances of faith, hope, and love as they are found in the church and world. As surely as sin is at work among us, so are the promises of God and the prophetic preacher is responsible for identifying and naming the ways in which God's intended future is realized in the present."[36] In this way, the promises even now name the future of God in the present.

In *The Sacred Art* Olin Moyd develops a practical-theological vision of preaching that speaks deeply of promise in the sense we are describing. Moyd describes the deep connection in the African American tradition between salvation from sin *and* the hope for freedom, justice, and redemption,

32. Ibid., 67.
33. Ibid., 73.
34. Wilhelm, "God's Word in the World," 76–93.
35. Ibid., 87.
36. Ibid., 88. Despite the reliance on Brueggemann's countercultural categories, I have placed Wilhelm's work on promise here rather than among the postliberals in the neo-Barthian camp above. Her view of promise is open to its echoes as well as evocations and naming both in the church and world, and thus breaks open the exclusively ecclesial orientation of the postliberal options.

a connection that embodies for him the whole counsel of God.[37] Moyd elaborates on the idea: Preaching the whole counsel included the telling and retelling of biblical incidents of God's self-revelation in human history and God's promise and plan for continued involvement in the redemption of his people.[38] In Moyd's understanding promise extends to the core of the gospel itself: "The mission of the preacher is to be the bearer of the gospel—the Good News of redemption. . . . [P]reaching always included a message of exhortation and promise—guidance and hope."[39] Moyd takes up this notion yet again as he thinks about eschatology, God's redemptive and liberative purposes, God's activity and our participation. Exhortation and promise belong together: "Exhortation was the calling upon the people and the nation to adjust and to readjust their lives spiritually and socially in order to achieve a just society. And promise meant preaching hope for the inbreaking of a just society—the coming into genuine confederation and community of the people of God."[40] This is how Moyd sees preaching giving a capacity for empowerment and motivation.

It is important to note that a theology of promise here is only sometimes at the center of these disparate homiletical-theological projects. Some take a more covenantal view of promise, for example. What one does see among these homileticans, however, is a way of embracing the language of promise that draws deeply from the often neglected eschatological sense for the present. In some cases, it does so by drawing deeply as well on the connection of promise to the presence of the one who promises, too—a key notion shared by the those with a more vocative understanding of promise from the traditions of dialectical theology.

Tom Long complements this notion in his work on eschatology in *Preaching from Memory to Hope*. The third of his statements on preaching and eschatology is as follows:

> [P]reaching eschatologically today means helping our people know that the eschatological and apocalyptic language of the Bible is not about predicting the future; it is primarily a way of seeing the present in the light of hope.[41]

---

37. Moyd, *The Sacred Art*, 53.
38. Ibid., 55.
39. Ibid., 57.
40. Ibid., 121–22.
41. Long, *Preaching from Memory to Hope*, 129.

According to Long, eschatology should not be left to the kind of futuring that the culture likes to dabble in. Eschatological vision is about seeing the present aright, and furthermore in the presence of a theology of the cross, seeing the present *order* for what it really is. Perhaps an inability to live with this particular eschatological sense in preaching says more about the accommodation of the mainline church to the present order than anything else. Already, eschatological language helps to pry mainliners loose in the sense of seeing the present aright.

However, there is also a second important sense to this eschatological vision. Part of its possibilizing work is caught up in seeing God's purposes and even God anew. This is also a feature of newness that emerges in ever new recontextualizations of gospel, an evangelical surplus of meaning that accompanies its rearticulation, as Ed Farley has named:

> Gospel is not a thing to be defined. Is is not a doctrine, a delimited objective content. The summaries in Acts and in Paul of what is proclaimed, the formulas of the kerygma, attest to this. Phrases like the kingdom of God, Jesus as Lord, Christ crucified do have content, but that content is not simply a quantity of information. To proclaim means to bring to bear a certain past event on the present in such a way as to open the future. Since the present is always specific and situational, the way that the past, the event of Christ, is brought to bear so as to elicit hope will never be captured in some timeless phrase, some ideality of language. Preaching the good tidings is a new task whenever and wherever it takes place.[42]

Richard Kearney even speaks of a kind of possibilizing of God in such moments in his onto-eschatological perspective, by which the epiphanic God of the burning bush is named: I am who I will be.[43] Caputo, operating out of a Derridean perspective, speaks not so much of God's existence, but God's insistence and interprets promise as a kind of Deleuzean event that is always (eschatologically) coming.[44] At the very least, homiletical theologians might also have to acknowledge, as part of their constructive task, the possibilization of gospel itself. Eschatology keeps the good news new and in the wrestling with gospel in context holds up bits and pieces of the promise to light in a way that discloses the present by possibilizing it. It is, I

---

42. Farley, "Preaching the Bible and Preaching the Gospel," 80.

43. Kearney, *The God Who May Be*, 34–37.

44. Caputo, *The Weakness of God*, 5–7. He carries these notions further with his idea of the perhaps of God precisely as a form of weak rather than strong theology in *The Insistence of God*, 8–14.

suspect, this very theological moment where preaching indeed moves from memory to hope. It is, in bits and pieces, where homiletical theology does its most constructive work.

Theological Implications for a Revisionist Homiletical Eschatology

Eschatological Reservations

And yet to do so is to operate under important theological limitations. As Paul himself says in 1 Corinthians 13 (KJV), "for now we see through a glass darkly." In this sense a hesitation about eschatological speech is an act of wisdom. Whatever homiletical theology is, it is not speculative. It may have at its core the mystery of the gospel, but the gospel is a mystery *being disclosed*. Luther gets at this with his distinction between the God preached and the God not preached. Whatever we say about God, we begin with what we know, which for Luther starts with the death and resurrection of Christ. This discloses God's love for us, God's being *for us*. We may not always know everything of the divine counsel, but we do know this: this central piece of God's love disclosed in Jesus.

Consistency with a Wounded, Risen Christ

This means, as a theological starting point, that a homiletical eschatology must somehow square with its Christology. Whatever it is we claim about God's promise, the transversing presence it offers and the possibilizing space that it pries open must be consistent with Christ crucified and risen. This is not to make eschatology Christomonist, or even exclusively christocentric. It is, however, a shaping of the arc of homiletical eschatology in a way consistent with the one who was wounded and risen. This is important, also, for the wound that we have claimed contextually conditions a revisionist homiletical eschatology. At the core of Christian proclamation is not a disappearance of scars, or an absence of tears, but rather their acknowledgment in the presence and purposes of God and wiping away of tears that have really been cried. Apart from this eschatology is not only unreal, but not yet fully Christian. If the gospel is set in eschatological motion by the life, death, and resurrection of Jesus, its promise should at least in some sense be consistent with that. Jesus Christ is the prototype of God's ultimate, eschatological purposes. He, the crucified and risen one, is the yes to all of God's promises.

Recognizability

Ron Allen in his chapter in *Homiletical Theology: Preaching as Doing Theology* makes the plea that homiletical theology be recognizable theology.[45] As a way of recognizing its ties to hearers, homiletical theology must do theology in a way that is recognizable and in connection with tradition—even at those points where it tends toward the constructive-theological task. A recognizable, revised homiletical eschatology will be sure to do its constructive work in a way that dialogues deeply with the tradition(s) as given. Eschatology cannot be severed from memory, even as it seeks to revise eschatology in light of the wound that calls forth its theological reworking.

Systematicity

Theologian Ted Peters makes the case that eschatology is actually a bundled set of theological reflections that entails personal, corporate, and cosmic eschatologies.[46] This is also to say, to my mind, that any revision of eschatology in contemporary homiletical theology cannot be done so piecemeal as to ignore the wider landscape of eschatology. Somehow our personal eschatology cannot be revised in a way that does not account for the way eschatology impinges on corporate life and God's purposes for creation/cosmos. While homiletical theology is certainly not systematic theology, it ignores the implications of systematicity at its own peril.

Rationality

German theologian Gerhard Sauter in his work on eschatology makes a case for the logos or rationality of eschatology. Sauter argues that eschatology should be rational to the extent that it is capable of giving account for hope.[47] For me, a further implication is that our eschatology should be conducted in such a way that it opens dialogue with others. Eschatology

---

45. Allen, "Preaching as Spark for Discovery in Theology," 147.
46. Peters, "Where Are We Going?," 347–48.
47. Sauter, *What Dare We Hope?*, ix–xvi.

need not be only for in-house church consumption, but should have some sort of public dimension to it. This does not mean an utter abdication of its particular language—in fact, the language of eschatology has its cultural correlates as well, if nothing else in the world of art and the literary imagination. The point here rather is that our revised eschatology should not forget to be rationally and publicly engaged.

Revised Eschatology for a Renewed Faith Praxis

A revised eschatology of promise does more than move just to move the furniture of heaven around. A revised homiletical eschatology also helps to sponsor a new way of being in the world, a different kind of praxis. In his book *Faith: A Practical-Theological Reconstruction*, Gerrit Immink speaks of *faith* praxis in connection to promise.[48] In part, this means a new kind of reflective action in the world that emerges from faith in connection to promise. While the accent of promise is still on grace, it is a kind of grace that pries open fixed, oppressive systems and sponsors engagement toward God's promise even now in the present. A revised, homiletical eschatology needs to be cognizant of a shared faith praxis that its promise animates. This is also part of the conversational vision of homiletical theology that I have begun to articulate: a conversation in faith toward action.

Because the eschatological vision is contextual, because the utterance of promise is woundedly situational, it is not always to describe what this promise looks like. In this way a homiletical theology of promise can never operate in some pure ideality of language, but must be named in the midst of struggle, in both the overflow of promise and the undertow of its failure. And yet, as promise tends toward an eschatologically reconstructed faith praxis, it begins to show itself in bits and pieces—in signs that gesture incarnationally toward cruciform hope.

Where promise is uttered again in community it already begins to reveal connections and provoke with them new, impinging solidarities. The strangeness of uttering promise, bearing as it does the self-involvement of the promiser, betokens what otherwise seems a hidden network of relations. What startles about promise is the realization of our being addressed by a crucified, risen other and the odd second-person plural network that is our interhuman reality. In other words, by its very utterance promise is a relationship: a promise that hearers can hold and that hearers can even hold

---

48. Immink, *Faith*, 18–21.

back to God in lament to the Promiser. Within the vocative environment that is worship, a new set of relationships is being revealed as a kind of unfolding mystery. There's a beautiful scene in the HBO miniseries *Deadwood* where Preacher Smith speaks of the cantankerous, foul-mouthed, even murderous community of Gold rush-era Deadwood as a kind of visionary disclosure of the body of Christ. The reality of this muddy mess of saloon operators, claim jumpers, and addicts would seem to belie such a claim in absolute starkness. And yet, when Preacher Smith in an almost mystical voice begins to name the connections that reveal the body's emerging reality, it begins to dawn on the viewer just what he is seeing. The promise is both strange and revealing in the way it unveils hitherto hidden relationships and fragile solidarities of newness. In faith praxis such relationships are both surprising gift and possibilizing call.

Yet there is more to this faith praxis. For the promise is not only uttered, it is spoken in strange proximity to a sacred meal. The Reformers held that promise was the glue that held Word and Sacrament together. They did not agree how this did so, but did sense that Word and Sacrament belonged together—even if the subsequent history of Protestant worship was to undo that binding. At the church where I attend in Woburn, Massachusetts, the worshiping community gathers to celebrate Word and Sacrament every week. The way Christ becomes present through the promise is embraced in liturgy and action, with standing bodies and words of vocative response: "Praise to you, O Christ," as the Gospel is about to be read aloud. Yet for all this promise-centered, vocative liturgy, when it comes time for the Eucharist to be shared, the communion servers come up first to receive. One of the servers, a person of great faithfulness and standing in the congregation, lays hold of the top and front of the lectern where the Gospel had been read aloud and pushes the heavy, wooden lectern back from the edge of the elevated, marble chancel. She knows that in order to serve and receive the promise in flesh, room must be made along the chancel's edge for open hands, wounded persons of every sort, and, I would assert, space for a promise-empowered reconstructed faith praxis. Even now, Paul asserts in 1 Corinthians 15, Christ already begins to hand over the kingdom to God, so that God might be all in all.

There is no timeless essence to promise; nor is there a real way of talking about the gospel as promise apart from concrete contexts and the wounds of situations. Yet, they exist not solely at the level of the potential. Even now, the crucified, risen Lord goes out ahead. His promise is illuminating, but is in fact a traversing presence, a presence in absence whose promise opens up the reality of our lives in the cross's shadow and the sustaining relationships and the already embodied foretaste that is disclosed in its utterance in Word and Table, and gestures beyond to new creation.

Implications for the Development of Homiletical Theology

I have been arguing that a gospel of promise is the starting point for a homiletical theology. Yet when promise is seen in deeper connection with gospel, and in light of a cultural context in which, as Tom Long points out, memory and hope have both been problematized, the homiletical theologian needs to be ready to dialogue in ever deeper ways with culture to discern how such eschatological promise can be uttered again. This essay has focused on the relation of the promise and the cross, both of which require contextualization, and which together aim to call into question the mainline resistance to disestablishment. Because homiletical theology is dialogical, a conversation with other homiletical theologies of promise has both affirmed a tradition of dialectical presence of promise in the invested presence of commissive promissory speech *and* critiqued its excesses by highlighting the many ways promise helps to possibilize the future in a way consistent with the Promiser. This happens in part through the contextualization that the vocative nature of the double-agented promise entails in actual communities in specific contexts. It happens as well by attending to, and dialoguing with, the homiletical theologies of other communities that help to keep communities open to hearing promise in an unfolding and contextual praxis of faith.

As homiletical theology in the confessional mode, it offers a unique form of homiletical theology in action. While it is the struggle with eschatology that is the presenting issue here, how we get to the struggle is important. It is, for me, the nature of the gospel itself that drives me into theological reflection. Elsewhere, I have characterized the gospel as having a starting point in justification by grace through faith and taking the shape of promise.[49] In this case, it is the nature of promise itself and its deep connection to a theology of the cross that pushes me as a theologian into ever more contextualized reworkings of the gospel and precisely at that gap, the place where the overflow of promise meets with the undertow of failure. What eventuates is not pie in the sky, but a more profound sense of gospel hope forged in suffering, but for the sake of opening a new praxis of faith.

49. Jacobsen and Kelly, *Kairos Preaching*.

Section III: Homiletical Theology in the Analytical Mode

—6—

Doing Bible

When the Unfinished Task of Homiletical Theology Pushes the Envelope of Canonical Authority

—O. Wesley Allen, Jr.

Introduction: Toward Homiletical Theology in an Analytical Mode

In the introduction to this volume, David Schnasa Jacobsen describes the analytical mode of homiletical theology as "exploring [homiletical theology's] premises or the validity of its first theological judgments in the hope of refining and clarifying its processes of reflection." In this essay, I play with a prominent assumption that appears in the first volume, *Homiletical Theology: Preaching as Doing Theology* and is central to the framing of this second volume. That assumption is that homiletical theology performs an *unfinished* task of theology in service to the church's proclamation. I use the language of "playing" with this assumption to describe my approach in this essay as a way of confessing from the outset that I push the term "unfinished" far beyond what the editor and conversation partners intended as a means for testing its limits.

Homiletical Theology in Action

The first gathering of (and volume published by) the Consultation on Homiletical Theology strived to delineate the nature of homiletical theology as a unique theological endeavor in its own right and not simply a rhetorical, practical endeavor that draws on and applies the work of other theological disciplines (e.g., hermeneutics, exegesis, systematic theology, apologetic theology, ethical reflection) in order to communicate the faith to the church through the medium of sermons. While there was, in the end, little consensus in the first group of presenters in describing *how* homiletical theology is a different way of "doing theology," the wonderful conversation among those of differing opinions focused the uniqueness around this element of "unfinished" work. Thus following that initial conversation, Jacobsen posed the following question for the authors writing for this second volume:

> The default position is that the task of preaching is simply about applying a fixed deposit of tradition, whether of scripture or doctrine, to contemporary life. In contrast, Ronald Allen has argued that even when preaching a text like Acts, preachers are actually writing its "29th chapter" (*Acts of the Apostles for Preaching*, 2013). Barbara Lundblad in her published Beecher lectures (*Marking Time: Preaching Biblical Stories in Present Tense*, 2007) argues that this unfinished theological task is built in to the mutual relationship of marking time, which guards both our interpretations and the words of scripture as the witness of the other. *How can we conceive homiletical theology's role with respect to the sources and norms of Christian theological reflection?* [Emphasis added.] Papers with a view toward envisioning homiletical theology as practical theology, constructive theology, or theological method in light of specific theological problems posed by scriptural texts and doctrinal traditions are welcome.[1]

Ronald Allen's suggestion that when preaching a text like Acts, preachers are actually writing its 29th chapter is intended to be a provocative way to claim that preaching Acts continues the story of Acts, with its open ending. He is clearly not suggesting that preachers should add material to Acts. But why not? Why doesn't the view that homiletical theology is doing the unfinished work of the author of Acts instead of simply applying Acts as a fixed tradition to the life of the contemporary church precisely call for amending the canon in the pulpit in some midrashic form?

---

1. Jacobsen, "Research Questions," Homiletical Theology Project web site.

Doing Bible

Barbara Lundblad's *Preaching Biblical Stories in the Present Tense* is also cited in the invitation. In this work, she notes that passages of the Bible "are marked by the time in which they were written, marked also by editors who reworked the texts at a later time."[2] For Lundblad, this element of Scripture invites us to look to it for new revelation in our day. But if we push her words beyond what she intends in the same way we did with Ronald Allen's, we should ask: Given the call to do theology in a way that moves beyond applying a fixed tradition, why should we not rework the text for our time as ancient redactors did for theirs so that it contains gospel appropriate for our context (e.g., the way Luke redacted Mark)?

Thus, in this essay I propose to test the limits of how far we should be willing to go down the path of homiletical theology as doing the "unfinished" business of *Scripture* by asking explicitly: instead of only "applying" exegetical results to the purpose and practices of preaching, should we consider Scripture as not "fixed" when it comes to the church's proclamation? Should the nature of the authority of the canon for the church's proclamation be that of a fixed deposit of tradition to be interpreted or an "unfinished" collection to be finished? Should "*doing* the unfinished work of theology" include "*doing* Bible"? This playful question will help us, I hope, explore how far we are willing to expand the boundaries of homiletical theology as a *unique* endeavor beyond simply interpreting and applying the given tradition, as well as test my own notions concerning biblical authority.

Canonical Content and Preaching

Edward Farley is surely the grandfather of the Consultation on Homiletical Theology. His classic work *Theologia: The Fragmentation and Unity of Theological Education* serves as the starting point for arguing for a more constructive task for homiletical theology than is often seen in our guild or recognized around our faculty tables.[3] He has also asserted that biblical preaching has lost its way in its focus on preaching a biblical passage ("bridging" a specific text and a specific contemporary situation) instead of preaching the gospel ("to bring to bear a certain past event [the event of Christ] on the present in such a way as to open the future").[4] Although

---

2. Lundblad, *Marking Time*, 7.
3. Farley, *Theologia*.
4. Farley, "Preaching the Bible and Preaching the Gospel," 101; see also his "Toward a New Paradigm for Preaching." This line of argument is followed as well by Farley's

he would not agree with my assessment, I would argue that Farley simply substitutes one bridge for another, substitutes a construct of a core *kerygma* for a concrete text. Still his critique has much merit. The Sunday morning pulpit is filled with sermons that comment in detail on a text and never seem to arrive at a/the word of God for the people of God. And he is certainly correct in asserting that not every passage chosen by a preacher or assigned by the lectionary contains preachable content worthy of the descriptor "good news."

In a sense what I would argue Farley is doing is calling preachers to preach their canon-within-the-canon (gospel) instead of preaching the snippets from the canon regardless of whether they cohere with or communicate this claim(s) of the canon-within-the-canon. This view that some prima facie, biblically informed (but perhaps not biblically limited) understanding of the character, actions, and will of God-in-Christ should serve as the authority over preaching the Bible itself is common, even for those who would disagree with Farley's critique of pericope preaching. Indeed, I have made a similar proposal myself. While I have certainly been comfortable with and commended pericope (e.g., lectionary) preaching, I have also argued that the preacher should not focus on the text as the sermon's subject matter but see the text as a lens to view the sermon's subject matter—God's hide-and-seek presence in the world and the implications of that presence.[5] This description may give more authority to individual passages to compose the view of God's presence than Farley would, but it still presumes the preacher has some *a priori* understanding of God's good news for which the preacher searches when looking through the passage.

Similarly, Ronald J. Allen and Clark M. Williamson, out of a process theological perspective, developed three criteria with which to evaluate all elements of the preaching task: appropriateness to the gospel, intelligibility, and moral plausibility.[6] These three (or at least the first and third) criteria assume the preacher must have a prior understanding of what counts as "the gospel" in order to evaluate whether or not a biblical passage contains it.

---

colleague, David Buttrick; see especially "Preaching and Bible." A good review of this position that includes both elements of agreement and disagreement can be found in Allen, "Why Preaching from Passages in the Bible?"

5. Allen, *The Homiletic of All Believers*, 44–52.
6. Williamson and Allen, *A Credible and Timely Word*, 71–90.

Mark I. Wallace, who has a more evangelical perspective than Farley, Allen, and Williamson, or me, might be expected to take a different stance on biblical content. He, however, agrees with this basic orientation:

> A reader does not uncover the hidden or latent sense of the Bible buried deep within its pages but rather creates meaning through a sort of gestalt process of making sense of one passage in relation to others by appealing to a third general principle that relativizes all other readings. Biblical reading, then, is a largely contextual affair. It consists of weighing the relative merits of this or that interpretation in relation to some higher principle that helps one make sense of the individual medley—or sometimes cacophony—of the pages in question. Biblical reading always operates by means of a canon within a canon. Every reader tacitly or openly operates with a "working canon" concerning what she thinks is the correct hermeneutical yardstick by which to measure the relative merits of this or that construal of a particular passage.[7]

Similarly, in an essay describing his understanding of the authority of Scripture from the perspective of Reformed theology, Walter Brueggemann says:

> The inherency of evangelical truth in the Bible is focused on its main claims. From that it follows that there is much in the text that is "lesser," not a main claim, but a lesser voice that probes and attempts, over the generations, to carry the main claims to specificity, characteristically informed by particular circumstance and characteristically in the text open to variation, nuance, and even contradiction. It is a primal Reformation principle, given main claims and lesser voices in the text, that our faith is evangelical, linked to the news and not Biblicism, thus recognizing the potential tension between good news and lesser claims.[8]

From these few examples, we can conclude that there are many, from very different theological perspectives, who would recognize in ways similar to Farley that biblical interpretation and preaching are shaped by a canon-within-a-canon or a gospel-within-the-canon.[9] Therefore, preachers do not (that is, should not) simply preach the content of whatever passage is

---

7. Wallace, "The Rule of Love and the Testimony of the Spirit in Contemporary Biblical Hermeneutics," 67–68.

8. Brueggemann, "Biblical Authority," 11–12.

9. Of course, the recognition that not all texts are "gospel" texts is not new. Certainly, the interpretive move of looking for four senses of Scripture—literal, allegorical, moral, and anagogical—was an attempt to "make" meaning where little was found.

before them on a given Sunday as if it must contain the gospel simply because it is in the canon.

Canonical Methodology and Preaching

The Question

Does this conclusion simply end with the recognition that we do and should have a canon-within-the-canon or might it open the door further than any of the above writers intended? In his contribution to the first meeting of the consultation, David Schnasa Jacobsen argues that homiletical theology is "unfinished business" in a number of ways.[10] The matter of special interest in relation to this essay deals with the fact that Scripture itself is unfinished in that parts of it were written in response to traumatic events, such as the destruction of the temple in 70 CE. He says,

> In many ways, New Testament writings from Mark onward are trying to work through this trauma and grief through their narrative theologies. Sensitive interpreters of the New Testament struggle with some anti-Jewish elements that may have emerged in early New Testament narratives precisely because of these traumatic events. If so, the task of an unfinished theology is even more complicated than we might first imagine. . . . The issue is not just how we interpret Mark, or Matthew, or Luke, or any New Testament writer. *The issue may also be whether we can "take up" their theological task again, beside them.* It is in this extra sense in which I wish to talk about homiletical theology's unfinished task. As preachers we are continuing to take up the theological task of the tradition even while our responses are themselves provisional. The task of homiletical theology is not merely unfinished because of new times and new places, nor is it unfinished solely because of tensions between texts and doctrinal traditions; it is also unfinished because the good gifts of Scripture and tradition came to birth, at least in part, amidst grief and trauma.[11]

Later, after asserting that preaching should usually be concerned with "how to speak the gospel and not to say something else," Jacobsen adds,

---

10. See also his "Preaching as the Unfinished Task of Theology."

11. Jacobsen, "The Unfinished Task of Homiletical Theology," 44–45; emphasis added.

> Homiletical theology also occasionally bumps into moments when Scripture, tradition, or situations bring to the fore unfinished theologies which call forth a different kind of engagement: *to say more when one needs to.* In those occasions homiletical theology entails constructive, conversational moments where, in the interaction between gospel and experience/culture something new is named—perhaps even just new in this time and place.[12]

Jacobsen speaks of the "unfinished" work of Scripture to name its open-ended nature and the way it invites readers, preachers, and theologians to continue struggling with its struggles. But, again, I, playfully, want to push this language further than he intends in order to see how far the uniqueness of homiletical theology can be pushed in relation to the authority of Scripture as a fixed tradition.

Thus the need for a sense of the gospel prior to interpreting and critiquing a text in relation to homiletical theology broadly and preaching more narrowly, combines with the evocative naming of Scripture as unfinished in a way that at times calls us to say more than has been said in or by it, and leads to us to the question: Why should preachers not edit, omit, or add to the passages of the Bible in our preaching when they fail to cohere with the sense of the gospel we believe is central to the canon and is needed by our congregation?[13] I am not raising the question of opening the canon (although that question clearly follows from the smaller one I am asking). Instead I am pondering the role that continued redaction of Scripture might play in Christian preaching.

In part this idea is suggested by language found in the invitation for this consultation as cited above. How far are we willing, or should we be willing, to go in *moving beyond* "applying a fixed deposit of tradition [in this case Scripture] to contemporary life"? Clearly the invitation is asking how far we should move beyond the task of simply "applying," but I would like to push those words to ask how far we can move beyond "fixed." In other words, when it comes to Scripture, just how fixed is "fixed"?

---

12. Ibid., 46–47.

13. It is not surprising that the plethora of books dealing with the authority of Scripture focus on the question of how the text should be read (i.e, what type of authority should be granted to Scripture), simply assuming the collection and its content to be fixed.

Homiletical Theology in Action

The Canonical Model

What Lundblad names descriptively—that pieces of texts we consider Scripture have been thoroughly edited to be more appropriate to the needs of later readers—has been a long-term prescriptive concern for me. How far does the nature of the authority of the canon extend beyond simply interpreting the content of the canon to reworking elements of the canon? This question could be posed differently: What authority do we as individuals or as communities of faith have to challenge or critique the canon? The Wesleyan Quadrilateral places Scripture as the primary criterion for theological reflection but does not allow it to stand without answering to tradition, reason, and experience. Historical criticism attempts to read the text as a product of its time, challenging its historical and scientific relevance at times. Reader-oriented hermeneutics recognizes that readers *make* meaning of the biblical text instead of discovering meaning that is "objectively" there. And ideological readings call out the biblical text for ways it fosters patriarchal, economic, heterosexual, ethnic, and political forms of oppression. All of these perspectives would seem to open the door for preachers to edit Scripture *for the sake of the gospel*.

I, however, am more interested in whether the canon itself, that is *internally*, authorizes a redactive approach to Scripture in proclamation than the confrontation of external sources of authority in relation to the canon.

The church has primarily emphasized that the *content* of Scripture is what is considered authoritative for the church. For example, the Second Helvetic Confession says,

> We believe and confess the canonical Scriptures of the holy prophets and apostles of both Testaments to be the very true Word of God, and to have sufficient authority of themselves, not of men. For God Himself spoke to the fathers, prophets, apostles, and still speaks to us through the Holy Scriptures.
>
> And in this Holy Scripture, the universal Church of Christ has all things fully expounded, whatsoever belong both to a saving faith, and also to the framing of a life acceptable to God: in which respect it is expressly commanded of God that nothing be either put or taken from the same.[14]

---

14. Dennison, comp., *Reformed Confessions*, 810.

Doing Bible

This understanding of Scripture has contributed to the understanding of preaching in the application mode being challenged by this consultation. The Confession continues:

> Wherefore when this Word of God is now preached in the church by preachers and received of the faithful; and that neither any other Word of God is to be feigned nor to be expected from heaven.[15]

This stance asserts that to preach a word one must preach the Word. The *content* of Scripture is what is authoritative for the church and its proclamation. Preachers and homileticians, however, are certainly willing to claim scriptural authority in ways that go beyond simply its interpreting its content. Jesus' sermon in Nazareth in Luke 4 and the sermons in Acts are often lifted up as models for the purpose and approach to Christian preaching. We commonly use the prophets' postures and approaches to power (and not just the content of their oracles) as a biblical model for prophetic preaching. We might speak of Paul's pastoral, occasional approach in his letters as a model for pastoral, theological preaching today. Indeed, in the first set of consultation papers, Alyce McKenzie suggests a sapiential homiletic rooted in the model of the biblical sage.[16]

So why not a *redactional homiletic* based on the biblical model of reworking texts for new situations faced by new communities in new days? To borrow the United Church of Christ's recent marketing campaign: should we not see the canon as closed with a comma instead of a period, listen for God "still speaking," and redact scriptural passages as needed to speak the gospel instead of simply applying that passage as "fixed"?

The biblical models for such a redactional homiletic are numerous. Examples include:[17]

- Huge amounts of the narratives of the Hebrew Bible were passed down orally through generations of storytellers who remolded the material even as they preserved it. Scholars assume most of these traditions were brought together, edited yet a final time, and written down for the radically new situation of the Babylonian exile.

---

15. Ibid., 811. I have struggled with the hierarchical concept of preaching as the Word of God expressed here in *The Homiletic of All Believers*, 38–44, but I did not at the time extend my concern to how we construct Scripture as the Word of God.

16. McKenzie, "The Company of Sages."

17. This list is far from exhaustive.

- Redactors shaped the arrangement of Proverbs and the Psalter to contextualize individual pieces or smaller collections that they inherited into a larger whole, and thus offer readers a different experience through the collection than the individual pieces offered.
- Redactors compiled, combined, and changed the oracles of the prophets both to form prophetic "books" that speak in a new way and to allow the oracles to speak in a new day.
- Followers of Paul both edited his letters (e.g., in creating a composite of multiple letters in 2 Corinthians) and adapted his theological language and topoi when they wrote letters under his name.
- The Gospel writers used midrashic portrayals of Jesus to convey their Christology (e.g., the use of a Moses typology).
- The New Testament writers generally used Hebrew scriptures to interpret the Christ event in ways that had little to do with the original context of cited proof texts or the author's original intent behind them but instead served the needs of their current communities of faith.[18]
- The Gospel writers thoroughly revised the oral and written sources available to them to create a narrative they considered more theologically, existentially, ecclesiastically, and socially appropriate to their situations (e.g., Matthew and Luke's use of Mark and "Q" shows both an appreciation of these sources and a critique of them).

If we use not just the content but also some methodologies found in Scripture to justify other sorts of homiletical approaches and theologies, why should preachers not also, for the sake of unfinished business of preaching the gospel instead of simply applying the text, affirm a redactional homiletic that follows from the canon's own redactional approach to proclamation?

Biblical writers consistently have been found to have redacted earlier materials for four main reasons:

1. They corrected elements of original texts they identified as problematic in some fashion (be it stylistic or theological).
2. They perceived the existential, situational needs of their audience as being different than the needs of earlier audiences the original text addressed.

18. Contra those who argue the New Testament writers used Hebrew Bible quotes consistently aware of their context. See Hays, *Echoes of Scripture in the Letters of Paul*.

3. They adopted hermeneutical methods of their day in using texts from earlier periods developed in relation to other methods.
4. And, perhaps most importantly, new experiences of the divine and of divine revelation led them to bring texts into accord with those experiences.

Consider, for example, some of the redactional elements in the stories of Jesus' entry into Jerusalem in the Synoptic Gospels (Mark 11:1–10; Matt 21:1–9; Luke 19:28–40).

- Mark shapes (creates?) the earliest version of the story we have as a midrash on Zechariah 9:9, implicitly transforming the Zechariah text into a prophecy concerning Jesus as the messiah.
- For Matthew, implicit is not enough. In accordance with his hermeneutical approach throughout the narrative, he cites the Zechariah text explicitly as a formula quotation (Matt 21:5). Once he does so, however, Matthew also wants to make sure the story coincides with the prophecy precisely, so (not understanding Hebrew parallelism) he goes so far as to have Jesus ride two animals—a donkey and a colt—at the same time. Moreover, whereas Mark simply has Jesus enter the temple, look around, and leave (hardly triumphal), Matthew changes the story to have Jesus enter the temple immediately to "cleanse" it (cf. Mark 11:1 and Matt 21:12).
- Luke does not cite Zechariah to emphasize the importance of the scene, but instead changes the anonymous crowd to a crowd of his disciples explicitly exclaiming Jesus as the Son of David (to remove any ambiguity as to whether Mark's crowd intended to proclaim Jesus to be the Son of David or only did so ironically as they sang a pilgrimage hymn; cf. Mark 11:9–10 and Luke 19:37) and adds an exchange with the Pharisees in which Jesus says that if his disciples were silent "the very stones would cry out" (Luke 19:39). Moreover, Luke (like Matthew) changes Mark's story to have Jesus enter the temple to "cleanse" it immediately upon entering Jerusalem, but first has Jesus weep over the city in accordance with the importance placed on the city throughout Luke-Acts and with the explicit way in which he has had Jesus predict the siege of Jerusalem in 70 CE (Luke 19:41–46).

The Gospel writers' different interpretations of Jesus fund the manner in which they shape and reshape this story in significant ways. All four of the types of redactions we noted above are found here in this very short scene.

This small example of redactive tendencies in the canon could be multiplied thousands of times over had we the time and space to chronicle it all. Such a thoroughgoing method behind the proclamation of the canon at least suggests that an analogous approach might be warranted in the church's ongoing task of proclaiming the gospel. Instead of simply bridging the ancient text and the contemporary situation, are preachers not allowed, or even called, to redact texts to correct problems found in them in terms of current theologies, to meet directly the existential needs of our situations, to follow contemporary hermeneutical sensitivities, and especially to bring the text into accordance with contemporary understandings and experiences of the divine?

Arguments against a Redactional Homiletic

I must confess that I am quite uncomfortable with affirming this sort of "doing Bible" that I have suggested. A number of arguments against a redactional homiletic easily come to mind. Not all, however, stand on as solid ground as I might wish.

First, I hear Fred Craddock's voice ringing in my ears as he warned his students against preaching "almost Bible."[19] But is almost Bible that offers actual gospel not better than actual Bible that is almost gospel?

Second, I remember my own debates with my colleague in Hebrew Bible, Lisa Davison, in which she argued for midrash to include more women's voices in the text that claims to offer liberation but in truth had silenced women.[20] I agreed with her concern completely, but I argued for critiquing without modifying the text, especially given the fact that with biblical illiteracy few people in the pews would recognize that the text was intentionally being changed. But why is preaching against the text for the sake of preaching the gospel a more legitimate approach than redacting the text (following the model found in the canon itself) in order to preach the gospel?

Third, I am also aware that the redactional examples I named above as part of the writing and compiling of Scripture were employed *before* the writings that were redacted had been canonized. Matthew did not redact a

---

19. See Craddock, *As One without Authority*, 135.
20. See Davison, *Preaching Women of the Bible*.

document that had been canonized and read "as is" for generations. Matthew used a ten-year-old Gospel of Mark as a primary source, among other sources, in writing his own Gospel early in the life of the church. So should redaction, Christian midrash, or doing Bible disappear into the apostolic age in the same manner that miracles did?

This last argument against a redactional homiletic can be expressed from the other side of the coin: contemporary redaction is simply incompatible with the way the church has understood the authority of and used the canon over the course of its life. The last redactions were concluded in the first century (or so). While most of us would not recognize all of the words in the Bible as God's Word, we do recognize that the church has historically considered the content of Scripture to contain the Word of God. Are we not breaking covenant with the communion of saints if we modify the very content that has grounded the church and its preaching for two millennia?

I take this concern very seriously. Scripture is the church's book, the church gets to determine in what manner it is authoritative, and the tradition of the church is overwhelming in considering the content of the canon fixed. So my approach has been to let scriptural content stand as is but to interpret and critique it through the use of tradition, reason, and experience even as I strive to allow Scripture to interpret and critique me. When my preaching students add details to a text, I often find myself repeating to them what Christopher Seitz said to me when I did the same as a student, even though I do not share his canonical-critical reasons for saying it: "The Bible is written on a need-to-know basis."

It is not that simple, however. We have already noted the lesson given by reader-oriented hermeneutics—that interpretation is not an objective process by which meaning is discovered in a text but through which meaning is constructed using a text. But there is more. If we are honest, the Christian pulpit throughout its 2,000 years has been filled with as much allegory, almost Bible, eisegesis, lectio divina, and midrash as it has with critical readings based on the plain, theological, historical, or ethical sense of the text. While we (I) might not approve of such precritical or uncritical interpretation of Scripture from a scholarly perspective, it has been a constant practice of the church. I use the word *practice* here intentionally, in relation to its contemporary theological use, to suggest we might even view the sustained practice as authoritative for a more critical redactional homiletical practice. So in addition to the redactional model lying behind the canon, a nearly redactional model also lies before it. It is damn near ubiquitous! Why should the rise of historical criticism dismiss the practice instead of reforming it in the direction of explicit, informed redaction?

The fourth and most substantial argument against a redactional homiletical approach to Scripture, it seems to me, is related to the ambiguity of the content of "the gospel." We often use the phrases, "the gospel, "God's good news," or "the good news of Jesus Christ," as if the content of that news is self-evident (and as if these terms are synonymous). The tens of thousands of Christian denominations and theological schools is evidence to the contrary. Were we to argue, using Allen and Willamson's language, that redactions to a text for the sake of preaching the gospel instead of preaching the text is fitting so long as the changes are "appropriate to the gospel," evangelicals, liberals, process thinkers, revisionists, and liberation theologians would all make significantly different judgments about what is "appropriate" because they understand "the gospel" differently.

Would that this were the end of the problem, but the issues related to the ambiguity of "the gospel" increase exponentially when we move from the level of theological traditions to individual preachers. In the individualism of our modern and postmodern cultures, often preachers throw off the mantle of their roles as representatives of a tradition and speak only out of their own individual experiences and theology. In such a situation there is no limit to the range of redactions that could be made to the biblical text in the name of various understandings of "the gospel." Given that deconstructionists have taught us that every communication is some sort of exertion of power and status, the lack of a "fixed" text would offer no boundary at all beyond which preachers could not tread in the name of their individual understanding of the gospel, even if that text itself is an exertion of power and status.

Of course, it is undeniable that on any given Sunday morning, we already have limitless interpretations of the gospel even while the canon and its content is considered fixed. And certainly, our different interpretations of "the gospel" are based on self-serving circular reasoning—we choose the canon-within-the-canon that determines the core of the good news and then use that canon-within-the-canon to confirm it and critique other parts of the canon. Yet as long as the text remains fixed, it at least has the status of an authoritative Other with which we (that is, all Christian individuals and communities) can enter into conversation and debate. Our interpretations may make meaning in ways that go against the text (for good and bad reasons), but we should not give ourselves authority over the text to the point of changing it and taking away its Otherness. In worship, it is our practice not simply to preach on a text. We *read* a text and then preach on it. Whatever form of allegory, almost Bible, eisegesis, lectio divina, or midrash our sermons might take, they follow on the heels of reading the text "as is." The text stands on its own as a (possibly) flawed but faithful witness to the gospel before flawed but (possibly) faithful preachers make what they will of it in service to the gospel.

Implications for the Development of Homiletical Theology

The central question posed for this second volume in the series on homiletical theology is: *How can we conceive homiletical theology's role with respect to the sources and norms of Christian theological reflection?* The question grows out of a rejection of the idea that the "default position is that the task of preaching is simply about applying a fixed deposit of tradition, whether of scripture or doctrine, to contemporary life." This essay has challenged how far in answering the question we should really be willing to move beyond the default position, at least in one aspect. In other words, I have investigated whether the problem with the default position is that the tradition (specifically Scripture) is fixed.

Of course, as I highlighted earlier, none of the scholars I cited to justify my investigation were really asking the question whether the canon should not be considered fixed. I, however, contend that the way the consultation has framed the conversation and the language used by the different scholars to describe the role of preaching broadly and homiletical theology specifically legitimates, perhaps even necessitates, putting such a question on the table.

As named above, I consider the strongest argument for authorizing preachers for "doing Bible" in the way we speak of "doing theology," that is for redacting biblical texts to better serve the task of proclaiming the gospel, to be that such redactional work is modeled in the canon itself. The very canon that would be altered seems to authorize the practice. This argument, however, is outweighed by the church's canonization of the content of the Scriptures as *a fixed Other* with which the church (and its preachers) enter into conversation to proclaim the gospel. To consider the content of the canon fixed in no way implies that God's revelation is once and done. Our *conversation* with Scripture must never be allowed to be fixed, even though the tradition itself is fixed. Biblical interpretation, like every theological undertaking, is an eschatological enterprise. "God said it, I believe, and that settles it for me" is the worst kind of bibliolatry. Yet to change elements of the Bible, even for the best of reasons, risks engaging in an idolatry of the always unfinished. The tension between *the already* of the fixed biblical text and the *not yet* of the consummation of "the gospel" is where preaching and homiletical theology must reside.

Thus this paper argues for limiting homiletical theology's role with respect to the sources and norms of Christian theological reflection at one end of the spectrum of possibilities in the sense of claiming that that role does not include the *redaction* of those sources.

The consultation has placed as a limit at the other end of the spectrum in rejecting the *application* of the ancient traditions to contemporary situations. While I would tend to agree with this rejection, I would also question whether this position has been assumed but not tested within this consultation itself. Surely, each of us would argue that some texts or traditions, on the basis of our different a priori understandings of the gospel, can (should?) appropriately be "applied" in some contemporary homiletical contexts. (Of course, this assertion depends on how one defines the word *apply* in this context—also something the Consultation needs to clarify.) If it were agreed that application is at least a worthy endeavor for preachers and homiletical theologians at times, then the question is not what role should *replace* application in homiletical theology, but, given the unfinished tasks of theology, what role or approaches should be included *alongside* application up to but not including the redaction of the fixed tradition. In other words, a task for the Consultation that this author would find instructive is to define *the boundaries of the spectrum* of legitimate roles of homiletical theology over against the range of illegitimate roles that lie outside that spectrum.

—7—

"Surely There is a God Who Judges on Earth"

Divine Retribution in Homiletical Theology and the Practice of Preaching

—Rein Bos

Homiletical theology is constantly challenged from two sides. On the one hand new and fresh reflections on Scripture and the Christian tradition of faith cause us to rethink our preaching constantly. Altering an expression from the early period of the Reformation about the necessity of constant reformation of the church, we can also say that *Predicatio reformata semper reformanda*—as church we must continually reexamine our practice of preaching and our homiletical reflection to be true to our calling. The second challenge comes from the reality of life, the search to interpret real-life experiences in the light of Scripture and tradition. New situations, crises, cultural tensions, opportunities, and questions cause us to continually rethink and re-envision the church's preaching and proclamation. In this essay I will take up the challenge to explore premises for homiletical reflection and the practice of preaching on "uncomfortable words." Because I in the end argue for taking an objectionable tradition seriously over against our usual homiletical reluctance, I consider it an example of homiletical theology in the analytical mode. This is to say that this reflection on God's judgment pushes homiletical theology to hold on to an uncomfortable theological locus, a "hard saying," as a way of exploring the limits of its task.

God's Wrath, Judgment, and Vengeance

The words *revenge, retribution, vengeance, judgment*, and *wrath of God* call forth uncomfortable feelings. During the last few decades these "uncomfortable words" or "hard sayings" have disappeared slowly and silently from the vocabulary of the proclamation in many mainline churches—that is at least true for Europe and North America. In present times it seems that these uncomfortable words are unacceptable from social, juridical, ethical, political, and psychological points of view.

For comfortable middle-class European and American Christians the "hard sayings" sound cold and forbidding and even have the odor of religious extremism. It is said that, in the face of multiple crises, the word to be spoken in and by the church needs be the voice of pastoral attentiveness.

From a theological point of view, the "uncomfortable words" also are not given much room to stand. At one end of the spectrum one can hear voices saying that vengeance belongs to "primitive" societies, such as ancient Israel is believed to have been. And a "primitive" avenging God does not fit with the God-talk of modern times.[1] At the other end of the theological spectrum voices can be heard saying that Christ in his suffering carried God's judgment so that divine vengeance is not relevant for Christians anymore.

When we take a short look at some notable textbooks on the theology of Old and New Testament we learn—hardly surprisingly—that divine retribution is rarely treated as an independent theme.[2] It also is absent from the accepted rhetoric of homiletics as demonstrated by the fact that major textbooks and encyclopedias on preaching pay no attention to this subject.[3]

---

1. Noort, "Vengeance is Mine," 159.

2. von Rad, *Old Testament Theology, Vol. 1 and 2*, Westermann, *Elements of Old Testament Theology*, Zimmerli, *Old Testament Theology in Outline*, and Kaiser, *Theologie des Alten Testaments* are notable in their omissions. See Brueggemann, *Theology of the Old Testament*, 318–19, for a brief mention of this.

3. For example, see Willimon and Lischer, *Concise Encyclopedia of Preaching*, Duduit, *Handbook of Contemporary Preaching*, and Wilson, *The New Interpreter's Handbook of Preaching*; and Tisdale, *Prophetic Preaching*.

Only a few books pay more attention to these "uncomfortable words than a few paragraphs."[4]

The Retouch of the Uncomfortable Words Needs a Retouch

This ecclesial, theological, and homiletical avoidance of the "hard sayings" is understandable and to a certain degree even justifiable in the light of the judgmentalism and moralism associated with much traditional preaching that involves those hard sayings. The unnecessary fear caused by such preaching was and is surely in need of reconstruction.

But, as with every reaction, this retouch brought also some unwanted side effects—hence the need for analytical work for the homiletical theologian. In avoiding the "hard sayings" we are left with a benign and toothless God who can be compared to a lion in a circus. The lion looks dangerous through children's eyes, but adults know it is tame. Indeed, this domesticated God does not threaten anymore. But this toothless God cannot comfort, bring liberation, or establish justice. H. Richard Niebuhr criticized this "therapeutic Christianity" sharply: "A God without wrath brought men without sin into a Kingdom without judgment through the ministrations of a Christ without a cross."[5] There are therefore several reasons that invite us to retouch the retouch.

First, Scripture testifies substantially in both the Old and New Testament about God's judgment and retribution. Second, if preachers focus solely on pastoral needs for grief and comfort, they run the risk of leaving the deeper issues of evil and injustice unnamed and unexplored.[6] Third, we have to counter irresponsible and unhealthy applications of divine judgment that may and do occur in certain areas of theology and preaching. And last but not least a consideration from pastoral practice: in conversations with members of my congregation, I sense a peculiar mix of fascination, recognition, and fear for words like *divine judgment* and *vengeance*. On the one hand these words ignite hope for restoration in the hearts of

---

4. See Heschel, *The Prophets*, Brueggemann, *The Practice of Prophetic Imagination*, and Davis, *Biblical Prophecy*.

5. Niebuhr, *The Kingdom of God in America*, 193.

6. "As important it is to provide a safe refuge and home cooked meals and all the care and support that we can muster, that is not enough. The root causes of poverty persist.... If these realities go unchanged, families will continue to be thwarted when they attempt to escape homelessness and want.... More and more clergy of every faith must speak out against these injustices" (Olson, Preface, xvii).

victims of maltreatment. On the other hand, these words cause "fear and trembling" because they shed divine light in the dark areas of our soul.

Scripture's Substantial Testimony

Scripture speaks substantially about divine judgment. What might be the reason or background for that? The prophets of the eighth and seventh century BCE saw the Lord's judgment as inevitable "because they recognized that their society was profoundly out of sync with the reality of YHWH, so out of sync that it could not endure."[7] The prophets speak sharply about the unbearable nature of Israel's transgressions. Things are "not the way it's supposed to be."

The commandments of the Lord set non-transgressible limits: "Thou shall not." These commandments are meant for the good of creation and creatures. If and when these limits are nevertheless transgressed, misfortune and disaster will be the result. The prophets do not predict an unavoidable fate but anticipate "logical consequences" of the transgression of the Lord's given limits. The prophets say that the results are not to be seen or interpreted as "just" economic misfortune or "only" military bad luck. The prophets interpret this disaster as the Lord's judgment, executed by both human and nonhuman agents.

The Deeper Issue of Evil and Injustice

Scripture has a word for the transgression of non-transgressible limits: sin. This word has also not much standing in the vocabulary of the proclamation in many mainline churches—that is at least true for Europe and North America. We run thus the risk of a *Verharmlosung* (belittlement) of the reality of sin and injustice. "The awareness of sin used to be our shadow. Christians hated sin, feared it, fled from it, grieved it. But the shadow has dimmed. Nowadays the accusation you have sinned is often said with a grin, and with a tone that signals an inside joke."[8] *Temptation* is a TV gameshow, "Chocolate Sin" is a dessert with substantial calories, and adultery is amusement in daily episodes of soaps.

"When was the last time you had a good conversation about sin?" was already two decades ago the challenging headline of an advertisement in

---

7. Brueggemann, *The Practice of Prophetic Imagination*, 45.
8. Plantinga, *Not the Way It's Supposed to Be*, ix.

The New York Times. The most remarkable thing was that this was not an advertisement of a religious organization but of the *Wall Street Journal*,[9] the medium of the place where greed and self-gratification is fuel and elixir.[10] "Sin isn't something that many people, including most churches, have spent much time talking about or worrying about. . . . But we will say this for sin: it at least offered a frame of reference for personal behavior. When the frame was dismantled, guilt wasn't the only thing that fell away; we also lost the guide wire of personal responsibility."[11] Picking up the challenging headline, Thomas G. Long asks, "how long has it been since those of us who stand in the pulpits of polite and educated mainline churches have stimulated such a conversation?"[12]

And, for sure, we have to exercise restraint in considering the contemporary meaning of the proclamation of divine judgment of Israel's prophets. We must certainly be cautious when we interpret the results and consequences of the "Habits of the Heart,"[13] "The Impulse Society,"[14] and the "Greed is Good" mentality.[15] But Ellen Davis is right when she says "Nonetheless, when we take seriously prophetic understandings of the covenantal triangle, with the multidimensional interresponsiveness that obtains among God and both human and nonhuman creatures, then the situation becomes complicated. We may have to entertain questions about causality that do not come readily to contemporary Westerners."[16]

Countering Irresponsible and Unhealthy Applications

In the course of history a wide variety of events were labeled as divine judgment by so called "prophetic preachers," from Black Monday to Swine influenza, from 9/11 to the Fukushima nuclear disaster. But we enter a field bristling with all kinds of pitfalls when events or experiences are labeled as

---

9. *New York Times*, January 8, 1992.
10. See Lewis, *Flash Boys,* and Blinder, *After the Music Stopped.* Also see the movie, *Wolf of Wall Street.*
11. *New York Times*, January 8, 1992.
12. Long, "Learning to Speak of Sin," 92.
13. Bellah et al., *Habits of the Heart.*
14. Roberts, *The Impulse Society.*
15. Campbell, "Greed is Good," *The Guardian*, March 10, 2009.
16. Davis, *Biblical Prophecy*, 102.

divine retribution only to serve the personal moral agenda of a particular preacher.

These pitfalls were evidently present in the words of Jerry Falwell when he interpreted 9/11 as divine judgment.[17] On a broadcast of the Christian television program *The 700 Club*, Falwell made the following statement right after the attack on the World Trade Center towers:

> I really believe that the pagans, and the abortionists, and the feminists, and the gays and the lesbians who are actively trying to make that an alternative lifestyle, the ACLU, People For the American Way, all of them who have tried to secularize America. I point the finger in their face and say "you helped this happen."[18]

Jerry Falwell construed the 9/11 attacks as divine punishment. But his message sounded far too triumphant and Falwell was too eager to advertise only his own moral agenda at the expense of all the victims. It was no wonder that he had to apologize for his statement the same day as he made his accusations (the Thursday after 9/11).[19] A similar unhealthy and irresponsible reference to divine retribution was made by Pat Robertson when he suggested that the devastating earthquake in Haiti (2010) was God's judgment for the people's "pact with the devil."[20]

One major difference between the biblical prophetic oracles and utterances like that of Falwell and Robertson is that "Israelite prophets . . . characteristically suffered *along with* the people—their own people—even as they announced God's judgment upon them. . . . Real prophets suffer evil along with the people they address, and therefore they often plead for divine forbearance in the face of human frailty (see Amos 7:1–6)."[21] Preaching divine retribution can't be done from pretended high moral ground but requires the attitude of solidarity with those who face divine judgment. Talking like Falwell and Robertson is from this point of view to be seen as a derailment.

---

17. It was remarkable that one of the lectionary texts on the Sunday after September 11 was Psalm 51, which traditionally has been understood as King David's plea to God to have mercy on his sins.

18. "Falwell apologizes to gays, feminists, lesbians," CNN, September 14, 2001.

19. Ibid. Falwell told CNN: "I would never blame any human being except the terrorists, and if I left that impression with gays or lesbians or anyone else, I apologize."

20. "Pat Robertson says Haiti paying for 'pact to the devil,'" CNN, January 13, 2010.

21. Davis, *Biblical Prophecy*, 101–2 (italics original).

"Surely There is a God Who Judges on Earth"
The Challenge Remains Despite the Risks

These considerations underline that preaching about divine retribution is risky and faces complicated questions. Who of us can discern the hand of God in the events of history? There are no logical, translucent, or causal connections between a particular crisis on the one hand and God's revenge on the other. It is one thing to affirm that God acts in history, but quite another to claim to know exactly how, when, where, or why. Besides, the innocent rather than the guilty usually suffer most in times of crises. Further, categorizing a crisis as divine judgment runs the danger of justifying, or at least reducing, the culpability of the perpetrators. And there is also the well-known risk that preachers exploit Scripture's testimony about God's judgment to "upgrade" their own moralistic agenda with divine authority. Preaching about divine retribution is vulnerable because of the church's misuse and overemphasized accusatory tone.

But despite those serious risks, it is an important challenge to preach God's judgment in our contemporary situation, especially given the above-mentioned considerations. So we have to answer the question: if and when we take up the challenge, how do we do that? In this essay I will reflect on important pre-conditions or "boundary markers" for biblically sound, homiletical-theologically accountable, and mentally healthy preaching about divine retribution.

We encounter a network of these uncomfortable words especially in the books of the prophets and the Psalms, be it in a very different mode and from a different perspective. In the books of the prophets we hear words of judgment from God against Israel. In the Psalms we hear Israel asking God to act with revenge against Israel's enemies. The prophets see God's judgment as the inevitable consequence of Israel's wrongdoings. In the Psalms we hear prayers of the victims of evildoers.

Doing Justice to the Proclamation of Scripture as a Whole

The above-mentioned considerations cause homiletical theology to draw a clear biblical-theological and hermeneutical framework for the "boundary markers." In Scripture we meet an ingenious tapestry that came to existence in the course of a lengthy and complex process of tradition, redaction, and canonization. Originally independent texts became related to each other in the book of the community of faith. The new canonical whole creates a network of words, images, and motives where all kinds of internal connections were created between once independent but now inextricably related words and texts. Words like *revenge, punishment, retribution, vengeance,* and *judgment* can therefore not be proclaimed as independent issues or themes.

Canonical Shape of the Book of Isaiah

Judgment and grace are not independent words nor completely separated realities. They belong together and are inseparable because they are inseparably connected in the context of the canon of Scripture as a whole. This can both be illustrated and proven by means of the canonical shape of the book of Isaiah.

Critical scholarship has for over a century held to the view that we can discern three distinct parts in the book of Isaiah, each with its own historical circumstance, mode of literary articulation, and theological outlook. Chapters 1–39 anticipate the destruction of Zion, deportation, and exile. Chapters 44–55 anticipate return from Babel and the restoration of Zion. Chapters 56–65 reflect on life and the early Isaianic promises of God *after* the return.

This kind of critical scholarship had a double effect. On the one hand it contributed to a better understanding of the evolution of the book and a provided deeper appreciation of its parts. But this critical scholarship has, on the other hand, "atomized the book of Isaiah into a myriad of fragments, sources, and redactions which were written by different authors at a variety of historical moments. To speak of the message of the book as a whole has been seriously called into question."[22] That has led to a separated treatment of each of the three parts of the book. In well-known commentary series appear separated volumes on chapters 1–39, 40–55, and 56–65, written by different Old Testament exegetical scholars.

Recent scholarship makes a next move in the reflection. Depending on critical consensus, it moves to a more holistic and canonical understanding. For these scholars it is exactly the connection of anticipated judgment and deportation on the one hand and the anticipated return and restoration on the other "that give structure to the book of Isaiah . . . and that articulates the fundamental message of the book, namely, that the judgment of YHWH is real but penultimate and is followed by YHWH's will for restoration that will follow according to YHWH's plan."[23]

---

22. Childs, *Introduction to the Old Testament as Scripture*, 324.
23. Brueggemann, *An Introduction to the Old Testament*, 167.

"Surely There is a God Who Judges on Earth"

Taken independently and seen from an exclusive historical-critical point of view, First Isaiah speaks mainly of judgment to pre-exilic Israel. Seen from the same point of view, Second Isaiah's message is predominantly one of forgiveness and comfort. Seen from a more holistic, canonical approach, however, the words of judgment cannot be loosened from the words of forgiveness, comfort, and new beginning. Even when we hold the utterances of chapters 40–55 as originally addressed to exiles in Babylon, the present canonical shape of the book of Isaiah has furnished these chapters with a very different setting, i.e., a prophetic word of promise offered to Israel by the eighth-century prophet, Isaiah of Jerusalem.

The present setting into which the canon has placed chapters 40–55 is a highly reflective, theological context. In this new canonical context, the message of Second Isaiah "no longer can be understood as a specific commentary on the needs of exiled Israel, but its message relates to the redemptive plan of God for all history. The announcement of forgiveness to downtrodden Israel—'her warfare is ended, her iniquity is pardoned'—is not confined to a particular historical situation. Rather, in its canonical context it is offered to sinful Israel as a promise of God's purpose with his people in every age. Indeed, the loss of an original historical context has given the material an almost purely theological shape. In the context of sin and judgment, these chapters testify to Israel's real future."[24] The literary and even artistic achievement of the final shape of the book of Isaiah "constitutes the core Isaianic assertion concerning *inescapable judgment* reliably followed by *generous restoration*. Thus the two themes together constitute both Israel's lived memory and Israel's defining theological conviction."[25]

Canonical Shape of Other Parts of Scripture

The combination of inescapable judgment and generous restoration constitute not only the theological bone structure of the book of Isaiah, but Israel's defining theological conviction and therefore the theological bone structure of Scripture as a whole and can thus also be found in other parts of Scripture.

We can, for example, point to the book of Jonah. The repentance of the inhabitants of Nineveh brought God to change his mind and turn from

---

24. Childs, *Introduction to the Old Testament as Scripture*, 326.
25. Brueggemann, *An Introduction to the Old Testament*, 170 (italics original). See also Clements, "Patterns in the Prophetic Canon," 42–55.

his fierce anger about the calamity that he had said he would bring upon them. The ultimate horizon of this prophetic book is not divine judgment or destruction but the portrayal of the identity of God who is "concerned about Nineveh, that great city, in which there are more than a hundred and twenty thousand people who do not know their right hand from their left, and also many animals" (Jonah 4:11).

The same can be said of the place and role of "robust" texts in the Gospels. The Olivet Discourse in Matthew's gospel uses for instance tough language and imagery. The tough language and imagery of Jesus spoken on the Mount of Olives cannot be loosened from words spoken on another mountain, i.e., the Beatitudes. In the context of the Gospel of Matthew as a whole, both "mountain words" belong together and have to be read "stereophonically."

It is the cry for justice of the martyrs under the altar (Rev 6) that sets the tone of the violence in John's visions on Patmos. The violence in these visions cannot be disconnected from the vision of "there will be no more sea," and "God will dry all tears from their eyes."

Contemporary preaching of divine judgment has to respect this canonical framework of the proclamation of Scripture as a whole, i.e., the interconnected relation of judgment and forgiveness, repentance, and new beginning. Scripture does not isolate the threat of divine retribution from the promise of a new beginnings and the proclamation of grace. The announcement of the exile is connected with the promise of return to Jerusalem and the rebuilding of the temple (Isaiah). Judgment and vengeance are never God's exclusive or last words (Jonah). That means that divine judgment can never be an exclusive theme of a contemporary sermon. We can only deal with the "uncomfortable words" in combination with the proclamation of forgiveness, the call for repentance, and the promise of new beginning. Here are two illustrations how this canonical connection can be worked out.

Abraham Lincoln's Second Inaugural Address

The first illustration is taken from the inaugural address of President Abraham Lincoln when he took the oath of office for the second time in March 1865. The Civil War was drawing to a close. The states of the North stood on the brink of victory. Lincoln gave one of the most remarkable speeches in American history. In it he sought to explain the meaning of the Civil War and to establish a basis for restoring the Union.[26] Lincoln found a way of expressing that meaning using biblical language.[27] He said that all Americans knew that slavery was somehow the cause of the war. Lincoln went even a step further in labeling the war as divine judgment on the states of both North and South.[28] But Lincoln also points in another direction at the closing of his address:

> With malice toward none, with charity for all, with firmness in the right ... let us strive on to finish the work we are in, to bind up the nation's wounds, to care for him who shall have borne the battle, and for his widow, and his orphan—to do all which may achieve and cherish a just and lasting peace, among ourselves, and with all nations.[29]

Lincoln connects divine judgment, so to speak, canonically with the call "to bind up" and "to achieve and cherish a just and lasting peace."

Kaiser Wilhelm Gedächtnis Kirche (Berlin, Germany)

This bipolar character of Scripture's proclamation is also illustrated on the remains of the Kaiser Wilhelm Gedächtnis Kirche (Emperor William Remembrance Church) in the heart of Berlin, Germany. This neo-Gothic Protestant church was built in the 1890s by Germany's last emperor, Wilhelm II, and is dedicated to his grandfather, Kaiser Wilhelm I. In November 1943 allied air raids on Berlin reduced the church to rubble. An inscription on a plaque on the remains of the tower of the church tells why the council of the church decided not to rebuild the church after the war.

> This church has been destroyed during World War II in the night of November 23rd 1943 in an air attack. The (damaged) tower of the old church shall commemorate God's judgment that fell on our people during the years of the war.[30]

---

26. Goodwin, *Team of Rivals*, 696–701.
27. See White, *A. Lincoln*, 658–66.
28. Keillor, *God's Judgments*, 119–154, and White, *A. Lincoln*, 658–66.
29. Lincoln "Inaugural Address," March 4, 1865.
30. Summary and translation by the author. The same tone was heard in a message of the first synod meeting of the Bekennende Kirche (Confessing Church) after the war in July 1945. The opening line of that message was "Gottes Zorn war über uns" (God's wrath was upon us). See Walter and Link, *Die Dunklen Seiten Gottes*, 178. Karl Barth wrote a letter in a comparable tone to the congregation of Basel in 1945. "Wir können den

Even after so many years, these striking words move every visitor standing before the remains of what once was an impressive church. The words of the plaque utter a humble confession. A plaque at the other side of the former entrance hall makes clear that judgment is not God's last or exclusive word. That second plaque says:

> The remains of the church had been re-opened in 1987 as a memory hall and as a place of reminder against war and destruction and a call for reconciliation.[31]

The texts on these two plaques on either sides of the entrance hall illustrate that we can only preach the dimension of divine judgment when it is—in this case literally—juxtaposed with the call for repentance, the promise of reconciliation and the challenge to "achieve and cherish a just and lasting peace." This bipolar character of proclamation is an important pre-condition for "our contemporary prophetic mandate."[32]

The Prophets

The pre-exilic prophets announced the coming "day of the Lord" as a day of judgment and vengeance of God. However uncomfortably it may sound to present-day readers and listeners, permeated by the thinking of modernity and postmodernity, Israel's prophets reckoned with the possibility that natural disasters had to be interpreted as the protest of creation on behalf of the Creator against injustice and oppression.[33]

So many years later, we are hardly the first readers and listeners who have problems with the rough words of the prophets. The prophets themselves shiver also when they have to say "words like fire and like a hammer that breaks a rock in pieces" (Jer 23:29). Jeremiah tries to get rid of the words of the Lord. But God's words are too strong.

Ausbruch und das Ende dieses Krieges weder als blindes Schicksal und Naturgeschehen, noch als bloßes Menschenwerk verstehen. In diesen Ereignissen hat Gott geurteilt und gerichtet über bestimmte menschliche Fehlentwicklungen." See Barth and Koch, *Offene Briefe 1945–1968*, 45–46.

31. Summary and translation by the author.

32. See Brueggemann, *The Practice of Prophetic Imagination*, 132–33; 135.

33. See Marlow and Barton, *Biblical Prophets and Contemporary Environmental Ethics*, 146.

"Surely There is a God Who Judges on Earth"

> O Lord, you have enticed me,
> and I was enticed;
> you have overpowered me,
> and you have prevailed.
> I have become a laughing-stock all day long;
> everyone mocks me.
> For whenever I speak, I must cry out,
> I must shout, "Violence and destruction!"
> For the word of the Lord has become for me
> a reproach and derision all day long.
> If I say, "I will not mention him,
> or speak any more in his name,"
> then within me there is something like a burning fire
> shut up in my bones;
> I am weary with holding it in, and I cannot (Jer 20:7–9).

The prophetic preaching of God's judgment and vengeance is never the proclamation of a verdict of an unmoved, emotionless, or impersonal power. The Lord is a God who is compassionately committed to his creatures and creation. Judgment and vengeance do not take place outside God but rather he suffers himself. As Terence Fretheim correctly says "the Godward side of wrath is always grief."[34] The prophets of Israel "suffered along with the people—their own people—even as they announced God's judgment upon them."[35]

Speaking and preaching about judgment was often an unwanted task for the prophets. The prophetic mantle often fits only those who are called against their will. Moses claimed a speech impediment (Exod 4:10–13), Isaiah confesses the impurity of his lips (Isa 6:5), and Jeremiah appealed to his inexperience (Jer 1:6). He felt enticed and overpowered by the Lord and thus wanted to hold back God's word of judgment (Jer 20:7–9). We even hear that prophets "protest to God, not because of their own personal suffering, but on behalf of the doomed people. When God shows Amos the locust swarm that is about to devour the sprouting crops, he cries out:

---

34. Fretheim, "The Earth Story in Jeremiah 12," 101. See also Fretheim, *The Suffering of God*.

35. Davis, *Biblical Prophecy*, 101.

Homiletical Theology in Action

'My Lord YHWH, forgive! How can Jacob stand, since he is small?' (Amos 7:2)."[36]

Altering words of Jesus, we can say: "Let any preacher who is without sin, be the first to throw a stone of judgment at the congregation." When preachers see and notice evil only in others, there is a real danger that their sermons will cause either aggression or laughter among the listeners. At the end of a sermon in the Holy Week, Fleming Rutledge puts this theological reflection as follows in "sermon language."

> Yes, my pew will be thrown over—my pretensions, my props, my defenses, my masks, and, especially, my idols will all be stripped away. God is not going to let any of us continue indefinitely keeping him on the margins while we pursue our own idolatrous interests. But the good news, the joyous news, the liberating news is that the Messiah with the whip is "the Lamb of God, who takes away the sin of the world" (John 1:29). He has come to his temple, and in his blazing light we see ourselves as the guilty creatures that we are; but his coming in judgment is at one and the same time his offering of his body and blood for our true worship.[37]

A Wounded Healer

The proper attitude and tone in speaking judgment can be illustrated by the work of the *Truth and Reconciliation Commission* (1996–1997, hereafter TRC) in South Africa, marking the end of the period of Apartheid. Anybody who felt he or she had been a victim of violence could come forward and be heard at the TRC. The commission offered perpetrators of violence also the possibility to request for amnesty from prosecution. Archbishop Desmond Tutu says in the Foreword of the final TRC Report:

> We have been privileged to help to heal a wounded people, though we ourselves have been . . . "wounded healers." When we look around us at some of the conflict areas of the world, it becomes increasingly clear that there is not much of a future for them without forgiveness, without reconciliation. God has blessed us richly so that we might be a blessing to others. Quite improbably, we as South Africans have become a beacon of hope to others locked in deadly conflict that peace, that a just resolution is possible. If it

---

36. Ibid., 14.
37. Rutledge, *The Undoing of Death*, 57.

"Surely There is a God Who Judges on Earth"

could happen in South Africa, then it can certainly happen anywhere else. Such is the exquisite divine sense of humor.[38]

The awareness and the experience of being a "wounded healer,"[39] combined with an "exquisite sense of humor" are necessary characteristics for preachers when they want to deal with divine judgment in contemporary sermons.

Psalms

In the book of Psalms we hear the "uncomfortable words" not as words of judgment from God against Israel but as prayer of Israel asking God to act with revenge against its enemies. In more than a hundred Psalms one can hear a cry for vindication, revenge, retaliation, or retribution, as here:

> O God, break the teeth in their mouths;
> tear out the fangs of the young lions, O Lord!
> Let them vanish like water that runs away;
> like grass let them be trodden down and wither.
> Let them be like the snail that dissolves into slime;
> like the untimely birth that never sees the sun.
> Sooner than your pots can feel the heat of thorns,
> whether green or ablaze, may he sweep them away!
> The righteous will rejoice when they see vengeance done;
> they will bathe their feet in the blood of the wicked.
> People will say, "Surely there is a reward for the righteous;
> surely there is a God who judges on earth" (Psalm 58:6–11).

But who are we to repeat the just quoted words of Psalm 58? Christians are invited to follow Jesus who is "gentle and humble in heart" (Matt 11:29). Paul invites God's chosen ones to clothe themselves "with compassion, kindness, humility, meekness, and patience" (Col 3:12). And indeed, some human beings feel the freedom to live up to this standard. We can think of "icons" of justice, like Dr. Dietrich Bonhoeffer, Dr. Martin Luther King Jr., Bishop Desmond Tutu, or President Nelson Mandela. We can also think of the mother of Emmett Till. Cornel West draws an impressive portrait:

---

38. Tutu, Foreword, 2.
39. Nouwen, *The Wounded Healer*.

> The high point of the black response to American terrorism (or niggerization) is found in the compassionate and courageous voice of Emmett Till's mother, who stepped up to the lectern at Pilgrim Baptist Church in Chicago in 1955 at the funeral of her fourteen-year-old son, after his murder by American terrorists, and said: "I don't have a minute to hate. I'll pursue justice for the rest of my life." And that is precisely what Mamie Till Mobley did until her death in 2003. Her commitment to justice had nothing to do with naïveté. When Mississippi officials tried to keep any images of Emmett's brutalized body out of the press—his head had swollen to five times its normal size—Mamie Till Mobley held an open-casket service for all the world to see. That is the essence of the blues: to stare painful truths in the face and persevere without cynicism or pessimism.[40]

The reality of life is that only few of us can reach to the "high point" of Mamie Till Mobley. For the majority of human beings feelings of revenge are part of the reality of life. There are moments and situations that people not only long for revenge, but deserve that justice be restored. It is not the question whether people may or may not have those feelings and thoughts of revenge. Those feelings and emotions simply occur—sometimes without good reason or cause and there are situations that those feelings are at least understandable. The question is rather: if and when we have those feelings and thoughts, how do we deal with them?

The first option to deal with such feelings and thoughts is to execute them actively. In that case, newly liberated people take up arms and take revenge on their former oppressors. This option leads only to destruction and even more injustice, as history shows time and again. Keith Lowe describes for instance how this horrendous first option worked out in Europe in the two years after World War II. Individual collaborators were rounded up and summarily executed, concentration camps were reopened, and violent anti-Semitism was reborn. In monstrous acts of ethnic cleansing, tens of millions were expelled from their ancestral homelands.[41] We read and hear regularly about this option in the news reports from all over the world. These feelings and emotions can be felt on a smaller scale—but not less fierce!—on a daily basis in offices, homes, schools, and children's playgrounds.

---

40. West, *Democracy Matters*, 20–21.
41. See Lowe, *Savage Continent*, and Lendon, *Song of Wrath*.

The second option is that victims simply deny the longing for revenge and suppress feelings of wrath, for instance because we think that it is not appropriate for Christians to think that way. But suppressed and denied feelings resurface sooner or later in one or another destructive way, as we learn from psychology and psychiatry. The Dutch Dominican peace activist André Lascaris says that situations of ongoing and silenced injustice bear the risk to function as "the midwife of violence."[42] Silenced injustice will therefore only create a fertile matrix for "bathing the feet in the blood of the wicked."

There is a third option that avoids the risks of the first two options. This option makes the longing for revenge and the feelings of vengeance in prayer explicit, spreads them out for the Lord, and hands over those longings and feelings to God. King Hezekiah did that in the most literal sense when he went up to the house of the LORD and spread out the letters he received from messengers of the king of Assyria (2 Kgs 19:14–19). So do the psalmists spread out the whole frightening and terrible reality in the house of the Lord and say: "Lord, see what they do! Read what they write! It fills me with anger and feelings of revenge."

Preaching as the Preamble for Prayer

Exactly by making those feelings and emotions explicit in words, we can prevent that revenge and retribution from being executed in actions. When preaching does not silence or suppress those feelings, experiences, and emotions, it can become the preamble for prayers in the modus or "tonality" of the imprecatory psalms.

Preaching and liturgy thus offer the congregation the opportunity to rearrange and reframe their emotions in the context of the kingdom of God and his righteousness. Exactly by naming those feelings and longings explicitly, we admit that those emotions have a place in our hearts and minds. Sermons become a prayer and praying becomes proclamation when we say:

> Dear God,
> feelings of revenge and retribution make my heart restless
> and consume my soul.
> People who meditate treachery all day long
> imagine the worst for me,

---

42. Lascaris, "Vergelding en vergeving bij bijbels-theologisch perspectief," 30–34.

they seek my life and lay their snares.
Their lips flow over from mischief
and their acts hurt.

Even when I see their face,
I groan because of the tumult of my heart.
My heart is filled with fear
but also with feelings of revenge.

I lay all those feelings and emotions before you.
I hand them over to you.
Because vengeance is yours,
you will repay.[43]

We don't have to withhold, suppress, or deny any feeling or emotion, not even the darkest ones. The Psalms are the school of language for our prayers, especially in cases where we want to express and make explicit our (understandable) longing to get back at someone or something, the (reasonable) desire for vengeance, or the (sensible) yearning for retribution. Sermon and prayer offer the congregation the possibility to reframe these strong feelings and emotions in the curative context of cross and resurrection. It is exactly that context that reframes feelings of retribution into longing for justice, longing for the kingdom of God and the righteousness of that kingdom. Jesus connects the proclamation of God's kingdom with this reframing of our thoughts and mind. "Peplērōtai ho kairos kai ēngiken hē basileia tou theou—metanoiete kai pisteuete en tō euangeliō" (Mark 1:15). This context empowers and challenges us to work for justice.

"Merciful God, do not have mercy on those who had no mercy"

To express thoughts about retribution, feelings of revenge, and longing for retaliation can be curative for the victims. This can also be curative for the congregation as a whole because it contributes to keeping awake the morale and keeping morals vigilant. This is all the more necessary in a world where individuals and groups suffer from suppression, maltreatment, and torture, as Amnesty International reports regularly. And furthermore, countless ordinary people are bullied in their offices, classrooms, and factories.

43. Text by the author.

"Surely There is a God Who Judges on Earth"

Violence against children is especially repulsive.[44] And that is not only true for clear abuse like child labor[45] or child soldiers[46] far away. In the United States, a report of child abuse is made *every ten seconds*. More than *four children die every day* as a result of child abuse.[47] Such horrendous figures bring into memory notorious words of Psalm 137:7–9:

> Remember, O LORD, against the Edomites the day of Jerusalem's fall,
> how they said,
> "Tear it down! Tear it down!
> Down to its foundations!"
> O daughter Babylon, you devastator!
> Happy shall they be who pay you back what you have done to us!
> Happy shall they be who take your little ones and dash them against the rock!

Time and again every reader gasps for a breath reading those words. Dashing children against a rock, what do we do with those words? Even in this case, it makes no sense to say that victims are not allowed to speak or think that way. Just ask fathers and mothers of raped daughters what they really think and feel. There's a good chance that you will hear words and images comparable with Psalm 137. Those feelings and emotions will become dangerous exactly when they stay unnamed. When victims get the possibility to spell out what boils in their heart, it will loosen the isolation of their feelings and emotions. As J. Clinton McCann says, "The structure of Psalm 137 teaches us that the crucial act of remembering is energized by the strong and inseparable emotions of grief and anger. . . . In the face of monstrous evil, the worst possible thing is to feel nothing. What must be felt is grief, rage, outrage. In their absence, evil becomes an acceptable commonplace. To forget is to submit to evil, to wither and die, to remember is to resist, be faithful, and live again."[48]

In the face of monstrous evil and injustice, the most inhumane thing is to feel nothing. Preaching may not cover injustice with the so-called cloak of charity. The South African homiletician Cas Vos says: "The psalms also firmly express that the biblical God does not exhibit false neutrality when

---

44. See Jensen, *Graced Vulnerability*, 65–100.
45. International Labour Office, "World Report on Child Labour."
46. Child Soldiers International, "Louder Than Words."
47. US Department of Health and Human Services, *Child Maltreatment 2012*.
48. McCann, *A Theological Introduction to the Book of Psalms*, 119.

there is injustice and suffering. The psalms do not tell the oppressed to have brotherly love for their oppressors. Instead, the Psalter exposes the mechanisms of oppression and calls on God to change the lot of his people, so that his kingdom can grow in righteousness and solidarity."[49]

Words like Psalm 137 are calls to not submit to evil, calls to not keep silent in the face of wickedness. Words like this Psalm call us to break through the "state of denial," that leaves so many victims alone in their suffering, pain, and injustice. When we deal with those texts in preaching, our sermons can nurture the sensitivity of the listeners for justice and the righteousness of God's kingdom. Preaching and prayers can thus help "not to wage war according to human standards" but to take every thought captive to the obedience of crucified and risen Lord (2 Cor 10:3–6) and thus reframe destructive feelings and emotions in a salutary and curative way.

In his contribution of the commemoration of the liberation of concentration camp Auschwitz-Birkenau (January 1995), Elie Wiesel gave an impressive contemporary "imprecatory prayer":

> Although we know that God is merciful, please God do not have mercy on those who have created this place. God of forgiveness, do not forgive those murderers of Jewish children here. . . .
>
> Do not forgive the murderers and their accomplices. Those who have been here: remember the nocturnal processions of children and more children and more children, frightened, quiet, so quiet and so beautiful. . . .
>
> If we could simply look at one, our heart would break. Did it not break the heart of the murderers? . . .
>
> God, merciful God, do not have mercy on those who had no mercy on Jewish children.[50]

Wiesel invited the audience to remember the Jewish children. He ends his contributions as follows:

> And if you remember, as we try to remember, then hope is possible that, because of our memory, thanks to our Jewish memory, a better world might be built in which children could be happy-smiling, singing, taking each other's hands and saying to each other "Well, another morning, another day for humankind."[51]

49. Vos, *Theopoetry of the Psalms*, 40.

50. Adrian Bridge, "'God, have no mercy on them': Adrian Bridge with the survivors who gave testimony to the unfathomable crimes of Auschwitz," *Independent*, January 27, 1995.

51. Ibid.

"Surely There is a God Who Judges on Earth"

Preaching as Last Post Signal

From that perspective, the liturgy on Sunday morning can be compared to the simple yet moving daily Last Post ceremony in Ypres (Belgium). The Last Post is a bugle call at ceremonies commemorating those who have been killed in war. Every night at 8 PM this ceremony takes place under the Menin Gate in Ypres by buglers of the local volunteer Fire Brigade to commemorate the fallen of World War I. Every night the ceremony is ended with an Exhortation, read by a member or guest of the Last Post Association. The Exhortation is taken from Robert Laurence Binyon's poem "For the Fallen" published in *The Times* during the war. Standing under the arch of the Menin Gate the person will say the words:

> They shall grow not old, as we that are left grow old:
> Age shall not weary them, nor the years condemn.
> At the going down of the sun and in the morning,
> We will remember them. [52]

According to the tradition, all those who are present at the ceremony repeat the last sentence together: "We will remember them." When the congregation gathers on Sunday morning, we will not forget all the LORD's benefits (Ps 103:2). But we will also remember those who "shall grow not old," we will remember the injustice and the suffering in our world nearby and far off.

Vengeance Must Be Sweet

This essay took up the question: if and when we take up the challenge to preach divine judgment, how do we do that? I came to the following preconditions or "boundary markers" for biblically sound, theologically accountable, and mentally healthy preaching of divine judgment:

A. It is important that form and content of our contemporary preaching respect the canonical context of the "uncomfortable words." That means that we can only discuss judgment, vengeance, and revenge in their unbreakable connection with forgiveness, repentance, and new beginning.

---

52. Robert Laurence Binyon, "For the Fallen," *The Times*, September 21, 1914.

Homiletical Theology in Action

B. Dealing with divine retribution as found in prophetic utterances requires a compassionate stance of a "wounded healer" on the part of contemporary preacher, i.e., it requires an attitude and tone of authentic solidarity between preacher and congregation. Mark Buchanan is right when he says, "It's all in the tone with which we speak the truth. Truth can become falsehood if we don't get the tone right."[53]

C. The "imprecatory psalms" offer the language to deal in a priestly, prophetic way with experiences of injustice and feelings of revenge. Not in the sense that preaching invites or encourages the members of the congregation to revenge. But by naming those feelings explicitly in the public sphere of the liturgy, we offer the possibility to transfer those feelings and emotions out of the sphere of the anonymous silence and hand them over in prayer to the hands of the LORD.

D. Precisely because it is *God's judgment*, there is room for surprising and creative *human revenge*. That can be illustrated by means of a quote from the Abel J. Herzberg (1893–1989). This Dutch Jewish author wrote plays and novels, many about biblical characters. But he is best known for his highly personal essays and memoirs of his experiences in the concentration camp Bergen-Belsen during World War II. In his book *Letters to My Grandson*,[54] Herzberg tells about a beautiful Saturday afternoon after the war, in August 1945. He and some friends sat on the patio of the villa of a Jewish family in Amsterdam (the Netherlands). When the war started, the villa fell into the hands of member of the National Socialist Movement,[55] the most important Nazi party in the Netherlands. But those collaborators were imprisoned when the war ended in May 1945. Because they had lived in the villa for some years, the wife of the collaborator knew that there was a tree with green prunes in the garden of the Jewish family. She also knew that these prunes had to be ripe in August. She was ill and the doctor had prescribed her the eating of green prunes. So she sent her maid to the Jewish family with the request to bring her a basket with these prunes:

> Jews call that a *chotspe* (a brutality). This request caused a general and enormous indignation. But my father would have commented in this way. "Imagine that in the bitterest hours of the war, we went

---

53. Buchanan, "Preaching in the City of Man," 26.
54. See Herzberg, *Brieven Aan Mijn Kleinzoon*.
55. In Dutch, the Nationaal-Socialistische Beweging (NSB).

dreaming about our revenge after the liberation. One would have suggested a hatchet day and someone else suggested another, even more cruel revenge. But the most successful proposal would have been made by the one who described what we experience right now. It is peace. They are behind bars. His wife is ill and asks us for help. Why don't we give her the help she is asking for? Give her the best prunes you can find." And who knows my father would have been right? Because vengeance must be sweet, not bitter.[56]

The gift of the sweet prunes is "heaping of burning coals," mentioned by Paul in Romans 12. Altering the words of Desmond Tutu, we can say "Such is the exquisite sense of humorous retribution."

Homiletical Theology

The practice of preaching proclaims the Word of God in a specific situation of time and place. Preachers are time and again challenged to interpret particular situations in and of a congregation in the light of Scripture and vice versa. Every sermon is at the same time broadly based (in Scripture and tradition) and specifically focused (on a particular situation).

Homiletics and homiletical theology reflect on a more abstract level: when the practice of preaching is challenged by the reality of life, what are the hermeneutical and homiletical "boundary markers" for biblically sound, theologically accountable, and mentally healthy preaching? In this essay I answer this question by reflecting on the subject of divine retribution.

This subject is "provided" by the rising tension among peoples, religions, and groups in our world. We can think of recent events of racial unrest in New York and Ferguson, Missouri (2014) and the assassination of journalists and cartoonists in Paris (France). This tension evokes time and again emotions of revenge, as news reports tell us on a daily basis. How can preaching help to channel these burning emotions in a curative way so that feelings of retribution are reframed as longing for justice?

To answer this question I reflect on Scripture's testimony on divine retribution. It is clear that we cannot simply repeat or copy one to one the utterances on divine judgment of Israel's prophets of the eighth century BCE or use the same words as the "imprecatory prayers" in the Psalms. We are suspicious to label contemporary crises easily as divine judgment because these words are so often used to advertise a particular moral or

---

56. Herzberg, *Brieven Aan Mijn Kleinzoon*, 22. Translation by the author.

political agenda. And yet, the "uncomfortable words" of the prophets wait patiently to be heard. The reality of several widespread and deep-rooted crises and tensions invite and challenge us to reread the prophetic utterances on divine judgment. Ellen F. Davis is therefore correct when she says:

> Uncomfortable though it may be, the biblical view that the nonhuman creation warns of and somehow participates in God's judgment is an idea with clear theological import for our time. If we are to interpret it responsibly, then we must see the biblical writers consistently represent divine judgment as the fierce yet ultimate loving exposure of injustice, of oppressive practices that diminish or destroy the creation and thus fundamentally distort God's own intention for it.[57]

When we allow Scripture to disrupt our comfortable middle-class theology and preaching, we have to take into account the elliptic shape of Scripture's testimony. While the two foci of an ellipses are opposed, they are, nevertheless, always interrelated, interdependent. "Uncomfortable words" on Divine judgment need to be understood amidst the interplay with their antiphonal words. We find meaning in these "uncomfortable words" within the dialectical tension of opposites.[58] Israel makes bold and confident claims of the Lord as the gracious, sovereign, and steadfast God. Walter Brueggemann rightly says that on the other hand that "Israel's faith is a probing, questioning, insisting, disjunctive faith. The questions that Israel raises in its cross-examination are not of a speculative or theoretical nature. They are questions of a concrete, practical kind, arising out of life experience."[59] We hear people praying and questioning: "Why?" (Ps 22:1; Mark 15:34; etc.), "How long?" (Ps 6:3; 13:1–2; Rev 6:9; etc.), "Where are you?" (Ps 42:3; 79:10; Mark 4:38; John 11:21 etc.). In Brueggemann's words, the confident "core testimony" never exists without the questioning "counter testimony." Words of faith and trust are always accompanied by questions, doubts, and even complaints.

This essay sets out that talking about and preaching on divine judgment has to respect the bifocal canonical framework of the proclamation

---

57. Davis, *Biblical Prophecy*, 103.

58. Every theological issue in Scripture has a hermeneutical "helper, as his counterpart," or a hermeneutical "help-meet," within the rich variety of witnesses of Scripture. The expressions are taken from Genesis 2:18 in the translations of Rotherham, Young and the KJV.

59. Brueggemann, *Theology of the Old Testament*, 313, 318.

of Scripture as a whole, i.e., the interconnected relation of judgment and forgiveness, repentance, and new beginning. Scripture doesn't isolate the threat of divine retribution from the promise of a new beginnings and the proclamation of grace. To reduce the variety of the witnesses of Scripture to a single "core witness" in the center and to remove other voices to the periphery runs the risk of opening the door to all kinds of religious legitimized extremism and fanaticism (e.g., on the issue of the use of violence and armed force). Both poles of every ellipses keep each other in balance and prevent possible radical opinions that center the attention on one focus only. The ongoing task of homiletical theology is to reflect on the complex tension between the poles of the elliptical witness of Scripture on the one hand and the equal complexity of contemporary situations. In this way, homiletical theology in an analytical mode keeps our theology in preaching closer to its sources, even when it feels uncomfortable.

Afterword

—David Schnasa Jacobsen

This volume has taken great pains both to define and push the limits of a nascent homiletical theology. Many preachers and homileticians recognize, with the help of theologian Edward Farley, that the task of interpreting biblical texts for preaching cannot be done adequately apart from some clear sense of the theological purpose of preaching. Such a homiletical-theological purpose is grounded neither in a fixed gospel apart from texts and situations, nor in a uniformly available gospel distributed evenly across every conceivable scriptural pericope.[1] Once these parameters are recognized, however, the theological structure of the homiletical task presents itself more clearly. To preach is to be engaged in a theological task deeply connected with "gospel," and yet not just "gospel" in some stand-alone, reified sense, but understood in relation to context. This in turn has an impact as well on how preaching sees its task in relation to troublesome theological traditions. The result is a decisive move away from the notion that preaching is a place of application only. It is, profoundly, where theology is done in context.

Of course to say that the center of homiletical theology, whether in dealing with troublesome texts or difficult doctrines, is a theology of the gospel in context actually opens up a wider problem: that of the *relationship* between gospel and culture, gospel and *context*. Much of the literature in the field, and beyond, struggles to discern how we can speak of gospel at all, since even the gospel itself is a cultural product; on the other hand, how can we speak of culture in relation to gospel without in the end diluting or denying gospel? Faithful theological interpreters, whether preachers or

---

1. Farley, *Practicing Gospel*, 71–92.

homileticians, sense that this gospel/culture relation is most important of all. This is all the more true since it stands at the center of so much of the history of twentieth-century theology since Barth and Tillich. Just where do we who would claim a "theology of the gospel in context" as the center of homiletical theology position ourselves relative to this problematic?

Homiletician Ted Smith ventures an interesting notion in his own response to the cultural turn in theology and the problem of finding some point of leverage with which to engage culture and communities of practice. In his critical treatment of Stanley Hauerwas and Delores Williams in the introduction to his book *The New Measures*, Smith notes the way in which both a postliberal and a liberationist theologian embrace the turn to culture—especially as a way of loosing cultural traditions from the sway of a liberalism with certain theological "ideals" and its pretension to universality over cultural particularity.[2] Both Hauerwas and Williams seek to ground theology in the practices and lived experience of communities. At some point, however, Smith notes that it becomes necessary even for them to move from the "is" of communities, culture, and practice to the "ought" of theology and normativity. Both Hauerwas and Williams wish to lift up concretions of the gospel in communities and practices. However, there is a sense in which the creation of those *gemeinschaftlich* ideals requires a kind of *a priori* sifting of the practices of these imperfect communities—it is in other words critical, and yet engaged in an act of critical legerdemain in order to offer its point of critique: the best practices of ideal persons or idealized communities. Smith's alternative view is to see the relationship of "is" to "ought" as one like caption and picture. A caption names a picture, but does not exhaust it. There is a sense, as every preacher knows, that illustrations both carry the freight of what they illustrate and yet beget unintended entailments. It is this gap between picture (read: description) and caption (read: confession) that forces us to see this relationship of culture and gospel as one involving both embrace and critique (analysis).

Smith hopes to set up a dynamic through a retrieval of Benjamin's *rettende Kritik* that allows a description of cultural practices to be understood as a kind of eschatological memory that invites both judgment *and* redemption—a way forward past the strange gymnastics by which we try to reify a cultural practice in the name of "ought" or try to purify the "ought" by locating it in some cultural fulfillment in the "is." By contrast, I hope

---

2. Smith, *The New Measures*, 16–42. This paragraph represents a brief summary of some of the key features of Smith's argument in these pages.

Afterword

to see the enactment of this relationship in an ongoing and never-ending dialogue between the *provisionality* of any (confessional) ought and the mysterious un-graspability of any (descriptive) is. My own vision for homiletical theology is to place a confessional hunch about the gospel, our given "habitus" in the things of salvation, in conversation with ever-widening understandings of the actual "is" of cultures, communities, and practices in context.[3] For me it is precisely this dialogue that is the unfinished business of homiletical theology, an ongoing gap between caption and picture that both keeps us up at night and allows us to preach, however haggardly, at Sunday morning light.

In the next volume in this series, the Consultation on Homiletical Theology will go deeper precisely into this problem of gospel and culture. How do we articulate a theology of the gospel *in context*? At this point we press beyond matters of method in relation to theology in preaching to get at the heart of the theological work of the preacher and the ground for the theological reflection of the homiletician. Having seen homiletical theology in action, we stand here now on the threshold of a truly homiletical theology with a burning question: how can we speak of a theology of gospel-in-context? We will take this up in volume III.

---

3. The use of the term *habitus* here refers again to the work of Farley, *Practicing Gospel*, 3–13. In an article that took up Farley's earlier vision in *Theologia* and tried to relate it to methodological developments in practical theology, Don Browning argues that theology is always a negotiation between the *habitus* that is practical wisdom and the dialectic of theological method. See Browning, "The Revival of Practical Theology." Could it be that homiletical theology occurs at the intersection between confessional and descriptive work, with one or the other "taking the lead" in homiletical-theological reflection? In either event, reflection on a theology of the gospel in context becomes crucial.

Appendix A: Contextual Analysis

Carefully consider the following with regard to *both* your congregation and community:

1. Church demographics with regard to:
   - Geography and how the geography affects the cultural ethos
   - Number on roll
   - Average attendance in worship
   - Average church school attendance
   - Number in various age groupings
   - Economic welfare
   - Comparison of church demographics with larger community
2. Neighborhood and community demographics
3. Neighborhood and community values
4. How they spend their time
5. Where folks in both church and larger community work
6. Where folks live
7. What things are prominently displayed in houses
8. What they drive
9. What they do on their time off
10. How they relate to one another
11. How they communicate with one another
12. Their values, as indicated by how they spend their resources of time and money

13. What they think about God and the church
14. Their relationship to the larger world (community, world events)
15. Larger cultural values and their relationship to them
16. The church's kind of Christianity and the community's spiritualties
17. Their relationship to the larger denomination and its faith traditions/current issues
18. Their traditions (personal, community, and church)
19. What they think/feel about themselves
20. What they fear
21. Where the official power lies in the church and community
22. Where the real power lies
23. Their way of worshiping
24. Expectations for what constitutes a good sermon and pastor
25. Things you'd "better not" talk about in your church and community

Appendix B: Exegetical Questions for Preaching

Do all study of the Bible in prayer, asking the Holy Spirit for enlightenment and wisdom!

Textual Questions:

How does this particular Scripture fit into the whole of the biblical book? You need to have an understanding of the general outline and themes of the whole book a passage is in. You can do your own outline of the book, which may differ from ones scholars provide in commentaries. New readings will result in new outlines.

Consider your understanding of what the gospel is that all of the Bible proclaims. How does this Scripture relate to the whole of the gospel? How does it modify, nuance, or fall short of your understanding of the gospel? Does this text challenge or change your understanding of the gospel?

What is the sociocultural background of text? When was this written? Where? What was going on in history in general at that time? What was going on in that place at that time? How did the people of God respond? What's implied in how they should have responded?

Places are important. For example, like now, folks assumed certain things about you if you came from a certain place. In Jesus' day Galileans were known for being independent freedom fighters. Whether or not this perception was true is something you have to discern by reading between the lines, but it can help explain certain expectations people had. Find out everything you can about place names and what they meant to the folks then. How does geography figure into the meaning of a passage?

What do people's names mean? Where else do the people show up in Scripture and what function do they serve in the larger story?

What items are mentioned in the text and how/why were they ordinarily used? For example, in the passage, "I have set my face like flint" (Isa 50:7), when you ask what flint is and what it was used for, you will find flint was used to make altars and knives used to cut the covenant of circumcision. Flint is the rock Moses struck in the desert that had water flow out of it. Notice how these uses and connotations add dimension to the meaning of the text. Use a concordance to look up other places that such key items occur in the Bible and how they're used.

Consider the genre of the passage. Is this a letter, poetry, a story, or saying? If it's a story, what kind of story is it? We have certain expectations of literature based on what kind, or genre, we think it is. For example, when something starts with "Once upon a time," we think it's going to be a fairy tale with certain fantastical qualities. So consider: What are the normal expectations of the genre? Does this passage conform to them? Or does the passage play with our expectations to bend or break our assumptions? If so, where, how, and to what purpose?

Consider rhetorical audience expectations and who this text was written for. Much of what was written in the Bible was handed down orally before being written down. Was the written audience different from whom it was originally intended before being written? If so, how does that affect its meaning? What were the original audience's expectations underlying this text? How does this text deal with those normal expectations? Think through all these issues theologically: Are our expectations good, tainted, bad, incomplete? Are they met, judged, exposed, exceeded? How is the author playing with expectations in order to tell us something important about God?

What does this passage intend to do and how? Look carefully at the sequencing of structure of the particular passage and how it unfolds its

Appendix B: Exegetical Questions for Preaching

meaning. Is it a common literary/rhetorical form? With variations? Is it using a standard form ironically?

Look at the original language and do serious word studies! If you're a bit rusty linguistically, you can examine the passage in an interlinear Bible and look up key words in either *The Theological Dictionary of the New Testament* or *The Theological Dictionary of the Old Testament*. Note these key words' secular and sacred usages during their time and in times past. Where else are these words used? Consult a good concordance to see how the word is used elsewhere. Are there any unusual repeated words and cognates in the original language? Where, how, and why? Are there unusual technical/theological terms? Are there words being used in extraordinary ways through wordplay with associative meanings in the original language that don't come through in most English translations? How important are these in understanding what's going on and what's at stake theologically (i.e., with regard to God)?

Think about your own perspective toward this text. Where are the difficulties, perplexities, joys, etc., for you in this text and why?

Think about the way an abused, hungry slave or a person from a totally different culture might experience this text. Hear various people's responses to the text, especially people whose life experiences are very different from yours.

Think about the social position of those in the text. What is their socioeconomic status in their society, and what's that like today? How does that affect meaning? For example, bread means something a bit different to someone who hasn't had anything to eat in three days than it does to someone who has it at every meal.

Rewrite the text the way you remember it, noticing what you did and did not remember by comparing what you wrote to the actual text. Why did you notice what you did?

Think about how various parts of this Scripture are like something similar today.

Imaginative Readings:

Though we need to be careful in making every thought captive to Christ (2 Cor 10:5), our reading of Scripture may be enhanced by a more imaginative reading such as that espoused by Ignatius where you put yourself in the scene of a biblical narrative. (And this really works best with a story, not a letter or discourse.) Though you can let your imagination go for the exercise, the validity of what it brings up needs to be tested in accord with the aims of the text itself and the gospel.

What do you see, hear, smell, taste, touch, feel at various parts of the story? With whom do you identify? Why? Take the position of different characters and look at what's going on from their point of view. What do they see, hear, feel, touch, taste? If you were a director, how would you film the scene in order to get its meaning across?

Do a character study like an actor by asking basic questions of each character like:

- Who am I? (Do a basic biographical history, but also consider: How do I move? What animal am I most like?, etc.)
- Where am I?
- When?
- Why?
- What do I want?
- How will I get this?
- What obstacles must I overcome?
- How far will I go? Why?

Have each character do a monologue and listen to what they tell you.

Do an improvisation of the text with a group of actors/readers.

Block the scene like a director.

Draw it like a set designer/cinematographer.

Appendix B: Exegetical Questions for Preaching

Draw/paint/sculpt/collage your own version of text.

Image the text by starting with each factual image in the text to get it clearly in mind then free associate images that it brings to mind.

Sing it. What mood would this text be if it were music? What would its rhythm be? Its musical genre?

Dance or move to the text. Note what knowledge the body brings to the light.

The Big Questions:

So what (were/are) the purposes of this passage?

What does the passage tell us about God and/or the human relationship with the divine?

What is God saying through this Scripture?

What does the life promoted by this text look like and how does that relate to the gospel?

How will you need to change in order to live out this text?

How will life as a whole, including societal structures, need to change in order to live out this text?

What are we called to do/be as a result of this text?

Bibliography

Allen, O. Wesley, Jr. *The Homiletic of All Believers: A Conversational Approach.* Louisville: Westminster John Knox, 2005.
Allen, Ronald. "Preaching as Spark for Discovery in Theology." In *Homiletical Theology: Preaching as Doing Theology. The Promise of Homiletical Theology 1*, edited by David Schnasa Jacobsen, 129–52. Eugene, OR: Cascade, 2015.
———. *Preaching Is Believing: The Sermon as Theological Reflection.* Louisville: Westminster John Knox, 2002.
———. "Why Preaching from Passages in the Bible?" In *Preaching as a Theological Task: World, Gospel, Scripture; In Honor of David Buttrick*, edited by Thomas G. Long and Edward Farley, 176–88. Louisville: Westminster John Knox, 1996.
Andrews, Dale. "Ecclesiology, Preaching and Pastoral Care in the African American Church Tradition." Collected Papers of the Annual Meeting of the Academy of Homiletics, 1997, 12–21.
———. *Practical Theology for Black Churches.* Louisville: Westminster John Knox, 2002.
Archer, Kenneth J. *A Pentecostal Hermeneutic for the Twenty-First Century: Spirit, Scripture, and Community.* London: T & T Clark International, 2004.
Austin, J. L. *How to Do Things with Words.* Oxford: Oxford University Press, 1962.
Barth, Karl, and Diether Koch. *Offene Briefe 1945–1968.* Zürich: Theologischer Verlag, 1984.
Bartow, Charles. "Homiletical (Theological) Criticism." In *The New Interpreter's Handbook of Preaching*, edited by P. Wilson, 154–57. Nashville: Abingdon, 2008.
Bayer, Oswald. *Theology the Lutheran Way.* Edited and translated by Jeffery G. Silcock and Mark C. Mattes. Grand Rapids: Eerdmans, 2007.
Beaudoin, Tom, and Katherine Turpin. "White Practical Theology." In *Opening the Field of Practical Theology: An Introduction*, edited by Kathleen Cahalan and Gordon Mikoski, 251–70. Lanham, MD: Rowman and Littlefield, 2014.
Bellah, Robert N., Richard Madsen, William M. Sullivan, Ann Swidler, and Steven M. Tipton. *Habits of the Heart: Individualism and Commitment in American Life.* Berkeley, CA: University of California Press, 1985.
Blinder, Alan S. *After the Music Stopped: The Financial Crisis, the Response, and the Work Ahead.* New York: Penguin, 2014.
Blount, Brian K. *Cultural Interpretation: Reorienting New Testament Criticism.* Minneapolis: Fortress, 1996.
Brown, Sally. *Cross Talk: Preaching Redemption Here and Now.* Louisville: Westminster John Knox, 2008.

Bibliography

Browning, Don. *A Fundamental Practical Theology: Descriptive and Strategic Proposals*. Minneapolis: Augsburg Fortress, 1991.

———. "The Revival of Practical Theology." *The Christian Century* 101:4 (February, 1–8, 1988) 134–44.

Brueggemann, Walter. *An Introduction to the Old Testament: The Canon and Christian Imagination*. Louisville: Westminster John Knox, 2003.

———. "Biblical Authority: A Personal Reflection." In *Struggling with Scripture*, by Walter Brueggemann, William C. Placher, and Brian K. Blount, 5–31. Louisville: Westminster John Knox, 2002.

———. *The Creative Word: Canon as a Model for Biblical Education*. Philadelphia: Fortress, 1982.

———. *The Practice of Prophetic Imagination: Preaching an Emancipating Word*. Minneapolis: Fortress, 2012.

———. *Theology of the Old Testament: Testimony, Dispute, Advocacy*. Minneapolis: Fortress, 1997.

Brueggemann, Walter, William C. Placher, and Brian K. Blount. *Struggling with Scripture*. Louisville: Westminster John Knox, 2002.

Buchanan, Mark. "Preaching in the City of Man." In *Prophetic Preaching*, edited by Craig Brian Larson, 19–28. Peabody, MA: Hendrickson, 2012.

Buttrick, David. *A Captive Voice: The Liberation of Preaching*. Louisville: Westminster John Knox, 1994.

———. *Homiletic: Moves and Structures*. Philadelphia: Fortress, 1987.

———. Foreword to *Homiletics*, by Karl Barth, translated by G. Bromiley and D. Daniels, 7–11. Louisville: Westminster John Knox, 1991.

———. "Preaching and Bible." In *A Captive Voice: The Liberation of Preaching*, 5–32. Louisville: Westminster John Knox, 1994.

Cahalan, Kathleen. "Three Approaches to Practical Theology, Theological Education, and the Church's Ministry." *International Journal of Practical Theology* 9:1 (2005) 63–94.

Callahan, Allen Dwight. *The Talking Book: African Americans and the Bible*. New Haven, CT: Yale University Press, 2006.

Cannon, Katie Geneva. *Teaching Preaching: Isaac Rufus Clark and Black Sacred Rhetoric*. New York: Continuum, 2002.

Caputo, John. *The Insistence of God: A Theology of Perhaps*. Bloomington, IN: Indiana University Press, 2013.

———. *The Weakness of God: A Theology of the Event*. Bloomington, IN: Indiana University Press, 2006.

Cary, Phillip. "Sola Fide: Luther and Calvin." *Concordia Theological Quarterly* 71:3–4 (July 2007) 265–81.

Child Soldiers International, "Louder than Words: An agenda for action to end state use of child soldiers. http://www.child-soldiers.org/global_report_reader.php?id=562.

Childers, Jana L. *Purposes of Preaching*. St. Louis: Chalice, 2004.

———. "The Preacher's Body." *The Princeton Seminary Bulletin* 27:3 (2006) 222–37.

Childs, Brevard S. *Introduction to the Old Testament as Scripture*. Philadelphia: Fortress, 1979.

Chopp, Rebecca. *The Power to Speak: Feminism, Language and God*. New York: Crossroad, 1991.

Bibliography

Clements, Ronald E. "Patterns in the Prophetic Canon." In *Canon and Authority: Essays in Old Testament Religion and Theology,* edited by George W. Coats and Burke O. Long, 42–55. Philadelphia: Fortress, 1977.

CNN. "Falwell apologizes to gays, feminists, lesbians," September 14, 2001. http://edition.cnn.com/2001/US/09/14/Falwell.apology/.

———. "Pat Robertson says Haiti paying for 'pact to the devil.'" January 13, 2010. http://edition.cnn.com/2010/US/01/13/haiti.pat.robertson/

Coats, George W., and Burke O. Long, eds. *Canon and Authority: Essays in Old Testament Religion and Theology.* Philadelphia: Fortress, 1977.

Cone, James. *The Spirituals and the Blues: An Interpretation.* Maryknoll, NY: Orbis, 1991.

Cooper, Burton Z. and John S. McClure. *Claiming Theology in the Pulpit.* Louisville: Westminster John Knox, 2003.

Costen, Melva. *In Spirit and In Truth: The Music of African American Worship.* Louisville: Westminster John Knox, 2004.

Craddock, Fred B. *As One without Authority.* Nashville: Abingdon, 1971.

Crawford, Evans. *The Hum: Call and Response in African American Preaching.* Nashville: Abingdon, 1995.

Cunningham, David S. *Faithful Persuasion: In Aid of a Rhetoric of Christian Theology.* London: University of Notre Dame Press, 1991.

Davies, W. D., and Dale Allison. *A Critical and Exegetical Commentary on The Gospel According to Saint Matthew: Matthew 19–27,* vol. 3. International Critical Commentary. Edited by J. A. Emerton, C. E. B. Cranfield, and G. N. Stanton. Edinburgh: T & T Clark, 1997.

Davis, Ellen F. *Biblical Prophecy: Perspectives for Christian Theology, Discipleship, and Ministry.* Louisville: Westminster John Knox, 2014.

Davison, Lisa Wilson. *Preaching Women of the Bible.* St. Louis: Chalice, 2006.

Dennison, James T., Jr., comp. *Reformed Confessions of the 16th and 17th Centuries in English Translation: Volume 2, 1552–1566.* Grand Rapids: Reformation Heritage, 2010.

Dube, Musa W. *Postcolonial Feminist Interpretation of the Bible.* St. Louis: Chalice, 2000.

Duduit, Michale. *Handbook of Contemporary Preaching.* Nashville: Broadman, 1992.

Evans, Donald. *The Logic of Self-Involvement.* London: SCM, 1963.

Fairey, Shepherd. "Manifesto." http://www.obeygiant.com/about.

Farley, Edward. *Ecclesial Man.* Philadelphia: Fortress, 1975.

———. *Ecclesial Reflection: An Anatomy of Theological Method.* Philadelphia: Fortress, 1982.

———. *Practicing Gospel: Unconventional Thoughts on the Church's Ministry.* Louisville: Westminster John Knox, 2003.

———. "Preaching the Bible and Preaching the Gospel." *Theology Today* 51:1 (April 1994) 90–103.

———. *Theologia: The Fragmentation and Unity of Theological Education.* Philadelphia: Fortress, 1983.

———. "Toward a New Paradigm for Preaching." In *Preaching as a Theological Task: World, Gospel, Scripture; In Honor of David Buttrick,* edited by Thomas G. Long and Edward Farley, 165–75. Louisville: Westminster John Knox, 1996.

Farris, Stephen. *Preaching That Matters: The Bible and Our Lives.* Louisville: Westminster John Knox, 1998.

Fee, Gordon. *Listening to the Spirit in the Text.* Grand Rapids: Eerdmans, 2000.

Bibliography

Fiorenza, Elisabeth Schüssler. *But She Said: Feminist Practices of Biblical Interpretation.* Boston: Beacon, 1992.

———. *In Memory of Her: A Feminist Theological Reconstruction of Christian Origins.* New York: Crossroad, 1983.

Fretheim, Terence E. "The Earth Story in Jeremiah 12." In *Readings from the Perspective of Earth*, edited by Norman C. Habel, 96–110. Sheffield: Sheffield Academic, 2000.

———. *The Suffering of God: An Old Testament Perspective.* Philadelphia: Fortress, 1984.

Fulkerson, Mary McClintock. *Places of Redemption: Theology for a Worldly Church.* New York: Oxford University Press, 2007.

Fung, Ronald Y. K. *The Epistle to the Galatians.* Grand Rapids: Eerdmans, 1988.

Gadamer, Hans Georg. *Truth and Method.* 3rd ed. New York: Continuum, 2004.

Gench, Frances Taylor. *Back to the Well: Women's Encounters with Jesus in the Gospels* Louisville: Westminster John Knox, 2004.

Gilbert, Kenyatta. *The Journey and Promise of African-American Preaching.* Minneapolis: Fortress, 2011.

Gilroy, Paul. *The Black Atlantic: Modernity and Double Consciousness.* Cambridge, MA: Harvard University Press, 1993.

Goodwin, Doris Kearns. *Team of Rivals: The Political Genius of Abraham Lincoln.* New York: Simon & Schuster, 2005.

Harrington, Thomas W. "The Way to God or God's Way to Us: The Theologies of Edward Farley and James McClendon in Critical Dialogue." PhD diss., Marquette University, 2011.

Hays, Richard B. *Echoes of Scripture in the Letters of Paul.* New Haven, CT: Yale University Press, 1993.

Heidegger, Martin. *Being and Time.* Translated by John J. Macquarrie and Edward Robinson. New York: Harper & Row, 1962.

Herzberg, Abel. J. *Brieven Aan Mijn Kleinzoon: De Geschiedenis van Een Joodse Emigrantenfamilie.* Den Haag: Bakker and Daamen, 1964.

Heschel, Abraham. *The Prophets.* New York: Harper and Row, 1962.

Hölderlin, Friedrich. *Poems and Fragments.* Translated by Michael Hamburger. Oxford: Anvil, 2004.

Hughes, Graham. *Worship as Meaning: A Liturgical Theology for Late Modernity.* Cambridge: Cambridge University Press, 2003.

Immink, F. Gerrit. *Faith: A Practical Theological Reconstruction.* Studies in Practical Theology. Grand Rapids: Eerdmans, 2005.

International Labour Office. "World Report on Child Labour." http://www.ilo.org/ipec/Informationresources/WCMS_178184/lang--en/index.htm.

Jacobsen, David Schnasa. *Mark.* Fortress Biblical Preaching Commentaries. Minneapolis: Fortress, 2014.

———. "Preaching as the Unfinished Task of Theology: Grief, Trauma, and Early Christian Texts in Homiletical Interpretation." *Theology Today* 70:4 (January 2014) 407–16.

———. "Research Questions." Homiletical Theology Project Web Site. http://www.bu.edu/homiletical-theology-project/research-questions/.

———. "The Promise of Promise: Retrospect and Prospect of a Homiletical Theology." *Homiletic* 38:2 (Winter 2013) 3–16.

Bibliography

———. "The Unfinished Task of Homiletical Theology: A Practical-Constructive Vision." In *Homiletical Theology: Preaching as Doing Theology. The Promise of Homiletical Theology* 1, edited by David Schnasa Jacobsen, 39–55. Eugene, OR: Cascade, 2015.

Jacobsen, David Schnasa and Robert Allen Kelly. *Kairos Preaching: Speaking Gospel to the Situation*. Minneapolis: Fortress, 2009.

Jensen, David Hadley. *Graced Vulnerability: A Theology of Childhood*. Cleveland: Pilgrim, 2005.

Johnson, James Weldon. *God's Trombones: Seven Negro Sermons in Verse*. New York: Penguin, 1976. First published 1927.

Johnson, James Weldon, and J. Rosamond Johnson. *The Books of American Negro Spirituals*. New York: Da Capo, 1969. Originally published in two volumes 1925, 1926.

Johnson, William Stacy. "Making Grace Real: Barth and Beyond." *The Christian Century*, 118:14 (May 2, 2001) 16–20.

Kaiser, Otto. *Theologie des Alten Testaments*. 2 vols. Göttingen: Vandenhoeck & Ruprecht, 1993, 1998.

Kearney, Richard. "Narrative and Catharsis in Joyce, Homer, and Shakespeare." Keynote address at Boston College, March 23, 2012.

———. *The God Who May Be: A Hermeneutics of Religion*. Bloomington, IN: Indiana University Press, 2001.

Keillor, Steven J. *God's Judgments: Interpreting History and the Christian Faith*. Downers Grove, IL: IVP Academic, 2007.

Kim, Eunjoo Mary. *Preaching the Presence of God*. Valley Forge, PA: Judson, 1999.

Kirk-Duggan, Cheryl. *Exorcizing Evil: A Womanist Perspective on the Spirituals*. Maryknoll, NY: Orbis, 1997.

Lascaris, André. "Vergelding en vergeving bij bijbels-theologish perspectief." In *Tergukeer van de wraak?: een tijd verscheurd tussen revance, vergelding en verzoening*, edited by Roger Burggraeve and Johan De Tavernier, 28–42. Averbode: Averbode, 1996.

Lendon, J. E. *Song of Wrath: The Peloponnesian War Begins*. New York: Basic, 2010.

Lewis, Michael. *Flash Boys: A Wall Street Revolt*. New York: W. W. Norton and Co., 2015.

Lincoln, Abraham. "Inaugural Address," March 4, 1865. Gerhard Peters and John T. Woolley, *The American Presidency Project*, http://www.presidency.ucsb.edu/ws/?pid=25819.

Long, Thomas G. "Learning To Speak of Sin." In *Preaching As a Theological Task: World, Gospel, Scripture; In Honor of David Buttrick*, edited by Thomas G. Long and Edward Farley, 91–103. Louisville: Westminster John Knox, 1996.

———. *Preaching from Memory to Hope*. Louisville: Westminster John Knox, 2009.

———. *The Witness of Preaching*. 2nd ed. Louisville: Westminster John Knox, 2010.

Long, Thomas G., and Edward Farley, eds. *Preaching as a Theological Task: World, Gospel Scripture*. Louisville: Westminster John Knox, 1996.

Lose, David. *Confessing Jesus Christ: Preaching in a Postmodern World*. Grand Rapids: Eerdmans, 2003.

Lovell, John, Jr. *Black Song: The Forge and the Flame*. New York: Macmillan, 1972.

Lowe, Keith. *Savage Continent: Europe in the Aftermath of World War II*. New York: St. Martin's, 2012.

Lundblad, Barbara K. *Marking Time: Preaching Biblical Stories in Present Tense*. Nashville: Abingdon, 2007.

MacPhee, Josh. *Stencil Pirates: A Global Study of the Street Stencil*. Brooklyn, NY: Soft Skull, 2004.

Bibliography

Marlow, Hilary, and John Barton. *Biblical Prophets and Contemporary Environmental Ethics: Re-Reading Amos, Hosea and First Isaiah.* Oxford: Oxford University Press, 2009.

Martyn, J. Louis. *Galatians: A New Translation with Introduction and Commentary.* Anchor Bible Series 33. New York: Doubleday, 1997.

McCann, J. Clinton. *A Theological Introduction to the Book of Psalms: The Psalms as Torah.* Nashville: Abingdon, 1993.

McClure, John S. *Other-Wise Preaching: A Postmodern Ethic for Homiletics.* St. Louis: Chalice, 2001.

———. Post. Homiletical Theology Project Facebook Group Page. https://www.facebook.com/photo.php?fbid=10202520909218647&set=gm.757286587651924&type=1&theater.

———. "Preaching, Eschatology, and Worldview." *Journal for Preachers* 13:1 (1989) 2–10.

———. *The Four Codes of Preaching: Rhetorical Strategies.* Rev. ed. Minneapolis: Fortress, 2004.

McClure, John S., and Burton Z. Cooper. *Claiming Theology in the Pulpit.* Louisville: Westminster John Knox, 2003.

McKenzie, Alyce M. "The Company of Sages: Homiletical Theology as a Sapiential Hermeneutic." In *Homiletical Theology: Preaching as Doing Theology.* The Promise of Homiletical Theology 1, edited by David Schnasa Jacobsen, 87–102. Eugene, OR: Cascade, 2015.

McLuhan, Marshall. *Understanding Media: The Extensions of Man.* New York: Signet, 1964.

Moltmann, Jürgen. "Session Two." Emergent Theological Conversations, Chicago, September 9–11, 2009. http://www.patheos.com/blogs/tonyjones/2013/12/02/jurgen-moltmann-audio.

Morse, Christopher. *The Logic of Promise in Moltmann's Theology.* Philadelphia: Fortress, 1979.

Moyd, Olin P. *The Sacred Art: Preaching and Theology in the African American Tradition.* Valley Forge, PA: Judson, 1995.

Niebuhr, Richard H. *The Kingdom of God in America.* New York: Harper, 1959. First published 1937.

Nieman, James, and Thomas Rogers. *Preaching to Every Pew: Cross-Cultural Strategies.* Minneapolis: Fortress, 2001.

Noort, Ed. "Vengeance is Mine: Some Remarks on the Concepts of Divine Vengeance and Wrath in the Hebrew Bible." In *God, Biblical Stories, and Psychoanalytic Understanding*, edited by Rainer Kessler and Patrick Vandermeersch, 155–69. Frankfurt am Main: P. Lang, 2001.

Nouwen, Henri J. M. *The Wounded Healer: Ministry in Contemporary Society.* Garden City, NY: Doubleday, 1972.

Olson, Karen. Preface to *Just Preaching: Prophetic Voices for Economic Justice*, edited by André Resner, xvii–xviii. St. Louis: Chalice, 2003.

Ong, Walter. *Orality and Literacy: The Technologizing of the Word.* New York: Methuen, 1982.

Osmer, Richard. *Practical Theology: An Introduction.* Grand Rapids: Eerdmans, 2008.

Peters, Ted A. "Where Are We Going?: Eschatology." In *Essentials of Christian Theology*, edited by William Placher, 347–65. Louisville: Westminster John Knox, 2003.

Pieterse, H. J. C. *Communicative Preaching.* Johannesburg: UNISA, 1987.

Bibliography

Plantinga, Cornelius. *Not the Way It's Supposed to Be: A Breviary of Sin*. Grand Rapids: Eerdmans, 1995.

Pomian, Krzysztof. "The Collection: Between the Visible and Invisible." In *Interpreting Objects and Collections*, edited by Susan M. Pearce, 160–74. London: Routledge, 1994.

Powery, Luke A. *Dem Dry Bones: Preaching, Death, and Hope*. Minneapolis: Fortress, 2012.

———. *Spirit Speech: Lament and Celebration in Preaching*. Nashville: Abingdon, 2009.

Resner, André. *Living In-Between: Lament, Justice, and the Persistence of the Gospel*. Eugene, OR: Wipf & Stock, 2015.

Roberts, Paul. *The Impulse Society: America in the Age of Instant Gratification*. New York: Bloomsbury, 2014.

Rutledge, Fleming. *The Undoing of Death: Sermons for Holy Week and Easter*. Grand Rapids: Eerdmans, 2002.

Sahlins, Marshall. *Historical Metaphors and Mythical Realities: Structure in the Early History Sandwich Islands Kingdom*. Ann Arbor, MI: University of Michigan Press, 1981.

Sauter, Gerhard. *What Dare We Hope?: Reconsidering Eschatology*. Harrisburg, PA: Trinity, 1999.

Searle, John. *Speech Acts: An Essay in the Philosophy of Language*. Cambridge: Cambridge University Press, 1970.

Simmons, Martha. Introduction to *9.11.01: African-American Leaders Respond to an American Tragedy*, edited by Martha J. Simmons and Frank A. Thomas, ix–xii. Harrisburg, PA: Judson, 2001.

Smith, Christine Marie. *Preaching Justice: Ethnic and Cultural Perspectives*. Eugene, OR: Wipf and Stock, 2008.

———. *Risking the Terror: Resurrection in This Life*. Cleveland: Pilgrim, 2001.

Smith, Ted A. "Eschatological Memories of Everyday Life." Keynote at Lived Theology Project, University of Virginia, May 23, 2013. https://youtu.be/5tpyWCHerio.

———. *The New Measures: A Theological History of Democratic Practice*. Cambridge: Cambridge University Press, 2007.

Songs of Zion. Supplemental worship resources 12. Nashville: Abingdon, 1981.

Stricklen, Teresa Lockhart. "The Way and The Way of Homiletic Theology." In *Homiletical Theology: Preaching as Doing Theology*. The Promise of Homiletical Theology 1, edited by David Schnasa Jacobsen, 153–76. Eugene, OR: Cascade, 2015.

Theissen, Gerd. *The Gospels in Context: Social and Political History in the Synoptic Tradition*. Translated by Linda M. Maloney. Minneapolis: Fortress, 1991.

Thurman, Howard. *Deep River and the Negro Speaks of Life and Death*. Richmond, IN: Friends United, 1975.

———. *Jesus and the Disinherited*. Nashville: Abingdon, 1949.

Tilley, Terrence. "Practicing the Faith: Tradition in Practical Theology." In *Invitation to Practical Theology: Catholic Voices and Visions*, edited by Claire Wolfteich, 89–106. New York: Paulist, 2014.

Tisdale, Leonora Tubbs. *Preaching as Local Theology and Folk Art*. Minneapolis: Fortress, 1997.

———. *Prophetic Preaching: A Pastoral Approach*. Louisville: Westminster John Knox, 2010.

Troeger, Tom. *Wonder Reborn: Creating Sermons on Hymns, Music, and Poetry*. New York: Oxford University Press, 2010.

Bibliography

Tutu, Desmond. Foreword to *Truth and Reconciliation Commission of South Africa Report*. Cape Town: Truth and Reconciliation Commission, 1999.

US Department of Health and Human Services. *Child Maltreatment 2012*. www.acf.hhs.gov/programs/cb/research-data-technology/statistics-research/child-maltreatment.

von Rad, Gerhard. *Old Testament Theology*. 2 vols. Louisville: Westminster John Knox, 2001.

Vos, Cas J. A. *Theopoetry of the Psalms*. London: T & T Clark, 2005.

Wainwright, Elaine. "The Gospel of Matthew." In *Searching the Scriptures: A Feminist Commentary* vol. 2, edited by Elisabeth Schüssler Fiorenza, 635–77. New York: Crossroad, 1994.

Walker, Wyatt Tee. *"Somebody's Calling My Name": Black Sacred Music and Social Change*. Valley Forge, PA: Judson, 1979.

Wallace, Mark I. "The Rule of Love and the Testimony of the Spirit in Contemporary Biblical Hermeneutics." In *But Is It All True? The Bible and the Question of Truth*, edited by Alan G. Padgett and Patrick R. Keifert, 66–85. Grand Rapids: Eerdmans, 2006.

Walter, Dietrich, and Christian Link. *Die Dunklen Seiten Gottes*. 2 vols. Neukirchen-Vluyn: Neukirchener, 2000.

West, Cornel. *Democracy Matters: Winning the Fight Against Imperialism*. New York: Penguin, 2004.

Westermann, Claus. *Elements of Old Testament Theology*. Atlanta: John Knox, 1982.

White, Ronald C. *A. Lincoln: A Biography*. New York: Random House, 2009.

Wilhelm, Dawn Ottoni. "God's Word in the World: Prophetic Preaching and the Gospel of Jesus Christ." In *Anabaptist Preaching: A Conversation Between Pulpit, Pew and Bible*, edited by D. Greiser and M. King, 76–93. Telford, PA: Cascadia, 2003.

Williamson, Clark M., and Ronald J. Allen. *A Credible and Timely Word: Process Theology and Preaching*. St. Louis: Chalice, 1991.

Willimon, William H., and Richard Lischer. *Concise Encyclopedia of Preaching*. Louisville: Westminster John Knox, 1995.

Wilson, Paul Scott. *The New Interpreter's Handbook of Preaching*. Nashville: Abingdon, 2008.

Wimbush, Vincent L. "The Bible and African Americans: An Outline of an Interpretive History." In *Stony the Road We Trod: African American Biblical Interpretation*, edited by Cain Hope Felder, 81–97. Minneapolis: Fortress, 1991.

Witherington, Ben. *Grace in Galatia: A Commentary on St. Paul's Letter to the Galatians*. Edinburgh: T & T Clark, 1998.

Wolterstorff, Nicholas. *Divine Discourse: Philosophical Reflections on the Claim that God Speaks*. Cambridge: Cambridge University Press, 1995.

Wood, Charles M. *Vision and Discernment: An Orientation to Theological Study*. Atlanta: Scholars, 1985.

Work, John W. *American Negro Songs: 230 Folk Songs and Spirituals, Religious and Secular*. Mineola, NY: Dover, 1998. First published 1940.

Zimmerli, Walther. *Old Testament Theology in Outline*. Atlanta: John Knox, 1978.